KATHARINE DREXEL
and the Sisters Who
Shared Her Vision

KATHARINE DREXEL
and the Sisters Who
Shared Her Vision

THE SISTERS OF THE BLESSED SACRAMENT

Margaret M. McGuinness

Paulist Press
New York / Mahwah, NJ

Photos used with permission, courtesy of Marquette University Archives, Bureau of Catholic Indian Missions Records; Sisters of the Blessed Sacrament Archives, Catholic Historical Research Center, Archdiocese of Philadelphia; Xavier University of Louisiana, Archives and Special Collections.

Cover photo of the 1940 Council, used with permission of the Catholic Historical Research Center of the Archdiocese of Philadelphia. Pictured *left to right*, Mother M. Agatha, Mother M. Philip Neri, Reverend Mother M. Katharine, Mother M. Jerome, Mother Mary of the Visitation.

Cover design by Sharyn Banks
Book design by Lynn Else

Library of Congress Cataloging-in-Publication Data
Names: McGuinness, Margaret M., author.
Title: Katharine Drexel and the sisters who shared her vision / Margaret M McGuinness.
Description: New York / Mahwah, NJ : Paulist Press, [2023] | Includes bibliographical references and index. | Summary: "As a critical biography, Katherine Drexel and Her Sisters looks frankly at the second U.S.-born saint from within the context of the religious order she founded and ties her sainthood to the Sisters' ministries to Blacks and Native Americans, not in the first place to Katharine Drexel's rejection of wealthy and white privilege for herself"—Provided by publisher.
Identifiers: LCCN 2022029950 (print) | LCCN 2022029951 (ebook) | ISBN 9780809156580 (paperback) | ISBN 9781587686962 (ebook)
Subjects: LCSH: Drexel, Katharine Mary, Saint, 1858-1955. | Christian women saints—United States—Biography. | Sisters of the Blessed Sacrament—Biography. | Heiresses—Pennsylvania—Philadelphia—Biography.
Classification: LCC BX4700.D77 M34 2023 (print) | LCC BX4700.D77 (ebook) | DDC 271/.97092 [B]—dc23/eng/20221014
LC record available at https://lccn.loc.gov/2022029950
LC ebook record available at https://lccn.loc.gov/2022029951

ISBN 978-0-8091-5658-0 (paperback)
ISBN 978-1-58768-696-2 (e-book)

Published by Paulist Press
997 Macarthur Boulevard
Mahwah, New Jersey 07430
www.paulistpress.com

Printed and bound in the
United States of America

To Liam, Benny, Addie, Cora, and Emi
Best. Grandchildren. Ever.

CONTENTS

Acknowledgments ix

Introduction. Katharine Drexel and Her Sisters 1

Chapter One. A Life of Wealth and Privilege 17

Chapter Two. The Richest Nun in America 41

Chapter Three. The Philadelphia Story 67

Chapter Four. Heading West: Founding and Funding
    Ministries to Indigenous People 87

Chapter Five. From Rural South to Urban North: SBS
    Ministries to Black Americans 119

Chapter Six. An Enduring Legacy: Xavier University
    of Louisiana 149

Chapter Seven. Walking in the Footsteps of a Saint:
    The Sisters after Drexel 171

Epilogue. The Journey Continues 195

Notes 201

Bibliography 237

Index 257

ACKNOWLEDGMENTS

*A*s anyone who has written a book knows, an author has many people to thank by the time the manuscript is ready for the publisher. This is especially true for those of us who have written books during a pandemic. Libraries and archives closed; travel became difficult, if not impossible; and everything just seemed to take longer than expected. I am happy that I can publicly recognize and thank those who have helped me during the years I have been living and working with Katharine Drexel and the Sisters of the Blessed Sacrament.

I am profoundly grateful to the archivists who have helped me over the last several years. Most of my research was conducted in the archival collections of the Sisters of the Blessed Sacrament, which are now at the Catholic Historical Research Center of the Archdiocese of Philadelphia. Shawn Weldon and Patrick Shank are extraordinary archivists and possess a tremendous amount of knowledge about the collections they curate, as well as the history of Catholic Philadelphia. They answered every email, welcomed me to the archives, and offered valuable suggestions about other sources I might consult. I join the long list of historians who are eternally grateful for Shawn and Patrick and their commitment to historical research. Stephanie Morris, former archivist for the Sisters of the Blessed Sacrament, was extremely helpful when the SBS archives were located at St. Elizabeth's. Her vast knowledge of both Mother Katharine Drexel and the congregation's archives made life much easier for me during the early stages of this project. Other archivists and librarians, including Sister Helen Jacobson, OSF (Sisters of St. Francis of Philadelphia), Maria Mazzenga and Shane MacDonald (the Catholic University of America), Irwin Lachoff (Xavier University of Louisiana), and the late John Carven, CM (Eastern Province of the Congregation of Mission), welcomed me to their archives and shared their knowledge of Katharine Drexel and the SBS. Thomas Lester (Archdiocese of Boston), Barbara De Jean (Diocese of Lafayette), Vincent Barraza (Xavier University of Louisiana), Catherine Lundeen (Evangelical Lutheran Church in America), Carolyn Osiek, RSCJ (Society of the Sacred Heart), Geoffrey Hetherington (Archdiocese of Atlanta), Carla Canady (Josephite Archives), and Stephanie Baddy and Katy Pereira (Diocese of Savannah) answered email queries and, when appropriate, emailed me copies of documents when COVID-19 made travel difficult. Jean McManus, Catholic Studies Librarian at the Hesburgh Library, University of Notre Dame, came to my rescue a couple of times when I was struggling to locate a source. Her willingness to help and her hospitality and friendship during the time I spent in South Bend made research trips to the Midwest productive and enjoyable.

Colleagues and friends at La Salle University were an invaluable help. Brother Joseph Grabenstein, FSC, answered a series of emails related to the work of the Christian Brothers in various schools administered or founded by either Katharine Drexel or Louise Drexel Morrell. Reference librarian Eithne Bearden helped with electronic searches and some tricky research queries. Librarians Sheryl Panka-Bryman and Maya Novák-Codgell helped with some sources I needed as the manuscript was nearing completion. Maureen O'Connell and I spent many hours talking about issues related to Katharine Drexel, race, and Philadelphia. I am grateful for our conversations and for her support during her tenure as chair of the Religion and Theology department. Department members Brother John Crawford, FSC, Father Frank Berna, Anthony Paul Smith, Jordan Copeland, Julie Regan, and Vivienne Angeles (now retired) were collegial and supportive and never failed to ask about the project. Jack Downey, now at the University of Rochester, served as a sounding board on topics related to Drexel and Indigenous People and helped me to think outside of the box.

I was fortunate to receive both a research leave from La Salle University and a Mother Guerin Research Travel Grant from the University of Notre Dame for the fall semester of 2018. I am grateful to the Cushwa Center for the Study of American Catholicism for the privilege of spending time at the University of Notre Dame. Cushwa Director Kathleen Sprows Cummings, a valued colleague and a good friend, encouraged this project from the beginning, read the manuscript, offered perceptive comments and suggestions, and saved me from some embarrassing errors. The book is better for her thoughtful critique.

Acknowledgments

This book was greatly improved by comments offered by James O'Toole, Peter Wosh, Carol Coburn, and Margaret Mary Reher, who also read all of part of the manuscript, and I thank them for their willingness to take the time to think about Katharine Drexel and the Sisters of the Blessed Sacrament with me. Marge Reher, along with Mary Ann Biller, good friends and mentors, took a chance on a brand-new PhD and hired me as an assistant professor at Cabrini University many years ago, so I guess they are at least partially responsible for this book!

Although many people listened to me talk about Drexel (not always willingly, I suspect), some deserve special mention because they shared their own knowledge and thoughts with me on this topic. Cecilia Moore, James Carroll, Patrick Hayes, Thomas Rzeznik, and Nick Rademacher, all fine historians in their own right, helped me understand some of the subtleties involved in this project. Sharon A. Murphy and Susie Pak patiently shared their expertise in business and economic history as I attempted to understand the ways in which the Drexel family accumulated wealth. Thomas Bonner graciously spent time discussing Xavier University of Louisiana with me. Barbara Miles met me in Carlisle, Pennsylvania, in a time before COVID-19, and showed me where Drexel and the SBS had walked and taught. Her tour did not leave out the cemetery where Indigenous children were buried rather than being returned to their ancestral lands. Sister Mary Dunning, OP, recently completed a major work on the history of the Sparkill Dominicans, but voluntarily sent me anything she found related to the SBS during the course of her own research. Cordelia Frances Biddle, a descendent of Anthony Drexel, met me for coffee one day and shared some stories about the woman who gave away her share of the family fortune. Catherine Osborne cheerfully answered technical queries about footnotes. Local historian Gene Thibodeaux, who I doubt will ever see this acknowledgement, returned my phone call and happily answered my questions about Church Point, Louisiana.

Sister Donna Gould, SBS, has been supportive of this project from the beginning. I am sorry we've not been able to connect much in person because the pandemic got in the way, but I'm hopeful there are some visits over coffee or meals in our future.

Christopher Bellitto has been an outstanding editor. He encouraged, commented, and sometimes nudged, all while recognizing that the pandemic had temporarily ground to a halt a good amount of historical research.

Finally, I thank my family. William Shipley, my spouse and best friend, Will and Sarah Shipley, and Erin and Travis Carson are my main cheerleaders and I'm glad they are in my corner! When I began this project, I had one very young grandson. Liam, now age six, has since been joined by his siblings Benny and Emily, and cousins, Addie and Cora. These five have enriched my life more than I can say, and I can't wait to see what they do to change the world! This book is dedicated to them.

Introduction

KATHARINE DREXEL AND HER SISTERS

"The dark skies brightened yesterday morning as Pope John Paul II declared Philadelphia's Katharine Drexel, two other nuns, and 120 martyrs saints of the Roman Catholic Church," *Philadelphia Inquirer* reporter David O'Reilly wrote on October 2, 2000. "Torrential rain, dazzling sunlight, a rumble of thunder, and even a rainbow came and went as church leaders, nuns, priests and laypeople joined in a canonization Mass both solemn and jubilant." When the pontiff officially declared Drexel a saint at 10:32 a.m.—the others elevated to sainthood that day were not particularly important to the paper's Philadelphia readers—"the rains that had been pelting Vatican City for more than an hour stopped." The crowd gathered in St. Peter's Square that day included members of the Sisters of the Blessed Sacrament, the congregation Drexel founded in 1891, the state representative from the district where the community's motherhouse was located, people who had grown up attending parishes and schools funded by the Drexel fortune, and Cordelia Biddle, great-great-granddaughter of Anthony Drexel, the uncle of the newly canonized saint. Some of those attending the canonization told reporters they had met St. Katharine before her death in 1955. Lois Harr, a resident of North Philadelphia, for instance, remembered meeting her at the motherhouse in Bensalem, Pennsylvania, just outside of Philadelphia.[1]

Katharine Drexel was not the first American elevated to sainthood in the Catholic Church; Frances Cabrini, Elizabeth Seton, Rose Philippine Duchesne, and John Neumann preceded her. She was not even the first American saint with ties to Philadelphia; John Neumann was the fourth bishop of the then Diocese of Philadelphia from 1852 to 1860 and his shrine is located at St. Peter's Church in the city's Northern Liberties section. Drexel, however, was the first saint born in the City of Brotherly Love (and Sisterly Affection) and spent most of her life in Philadelphia and its environs. Despite the city's celebration as "one of their own" was canonized, Drexel's legacy extended far beyond Philadelphia. Shortly after their father's death in 1885 left Katharine Drexel and her two biological sisters, Elizabeth Drexel Smith and Louise Drexel Morrell, in control of one of the largest fortunes in America, the women began to distribute their wealth by founding and funding Catholic churches and schools dedicated to the service of Black and Indigenous People. As a result, her name was familiar to Black Catholics throughout the country, including the Diocese of Lafayette, Louisiana, home to the largest Black Catholic church in the United States, and Indigenous People living on reservations throughout the Midwest and West. Both groups were represented at her canonization ceremony in 2000.[2]

The Making of a Saint

Katharine Drexel's life is often described as one that went from "riches to rags." Born in 1858 to Francis and Hannah (Langstroth) Drexel, it was expected that she would grow up to be a prominent member of Philadelphia's upper class. A successful banking firm established by her grandfather and continued by her father and uncles meant that the young woman and her two sisters would never want for anything. Drexel's biological mother died shortly after she was born and her father married Emma Bouvier, a devout Catholic with a deep concern for the poor, who taught Katharine the importance of philanthropy and service. Emma died in 1883 and Francis passed away two years later, leaving his three daughters, Elizabeth, Katharine, and Louise, among the wealthiest women in the United States.[3]

The Drexel women were determined to use their financial resources to help Black and Indigenous People, many of whom had little or no access to education. Elizabeth Drexel Smith died in 1890, and Katharine and Louise continued to found and fund schools and support priests and parishes dedicated to ministering to Indigenous and Black communities for the remainder of their lives. In 1891, Katharine founded the Sisters of the Blessed Sacrament for Indians and colored people—today known as the Sisters of the Blessed Sacrament—to further the work of meeting the educational and spiritual needs of the two groups she and her sister believed needed their financial help more than others. Katharine Drexel became known as the woman who renounced a life of wealth and privilege and used the money to serve Black and Indigenous People in the United States. For this reason, many came to believe she was worthy of canonization.

The movement to canonize Drexel began shortly after her death in 1955, when Mother Mary Anselm McCann, the superior general of the Sisters of the Blessed Sacrament, decided there was enough support from outside of the congregation to begin the process that would eventually lead to sainthood. Of particular importance in this decision was Katherine Burton's laudatory biography of Drexel entitled *The Golden Door*. According to Burton, the story was rather straightforward. A very rich young woman, who had been taught to practice charity by her very devout parents, chose to give her fortune to those living on the margins of society. She not only founded and sponsored schools and churches to educate—and evangelize—Black and Indigenous People, but she established a religious congregation dedicated to that very same work. In addition, Burton portrayed Drexel as "a patriotic as well as a pious hero." In other words, she was more than a good Catholic; she was a good American, and therefore her canonization would be especially meaningful for the United States. In 1959, Mother Anselm asked Philadelphia Cardinal John O'Hara to help begin the process that would lead to Drexel's canonization. O'Hara agreed but died shortly after the conversation took place. Cardinal John Krol, O'Hara's successor as Archbishop of Philadelphia, also supported efforts to canonize Drexel, however, and authorized opening the process in 1964.[4]

Saint making is expensive, but the Sisters of the Blessed Sacrament were able to use money from a fund established by Louise Drexel Morrell, Katharine's biological sister, designated for any "extraordinary work."[5] Mother Anselm believed that promoting Drexel's canonization fit the guidelines established by Morrell and drew from that fund for expenses related to this project. In 1964, the first issue of the *Peacemaker*, a quarterly publication dedicated to promoting Drexel's canonization, appeared. Although Drexel was not known as a "peacemaker" during her lifetime, the name was taken from a letter written by her spiritual advisor, Omaha Bishop James O'Connor, on the occasion of the feast day of her patron saint, St. Catherine of Siena. "May your patron-ess obtain for you the grace to be a peacemaker among the races, as she [Catherine of Siena] was among the nationalities," he wrote.[6]

Katharine Drexel's cause for canonization moved slowly but steadily through the process designed by the Catholic Church to assure the faithful that those elevated to sainthood are deserving of the honor. Evidence was gathered; interviews were conducted; and documents were prepared to present the founder of the Sisters of the Blessed Sac-rament as one who had done more than simply give away her vast for-tune to assist Black and Indigenous People. It was equally important to demonstrate that she had lived a life of holiness. Drexel, in other words, was more than simply an exemplary woman; she was a holy woman worthy of being named a saint. In 1981, Pope John Paul II—who can-onized more men and women than any previous pope to that point—authorized "the Roman review of the ordinary process," which was conducted in 1980–1981.[7]

Historian Kathleen Sprows Cummings notes that Drexel was one of the last saints who went through a review of this sort because in 1983 John Paul II promulgated *Divinus Perfectionis Magister*, a "comprehen-sive revision" of the canonization process. Because Drexel's cause was already under review at this time, Krol himself traveled to Rome to determine what impact the new guidelines would have on her cause. After being assured that Drexel's cause could go forward, Krol appointed Rev. Joseph Martino—later bishop of Scranton, Pennsylvania—to write her *positio*, a document that presents evidence proving a candidate is worthy of canonization. Martino completed the task in 1986, and John Paul II declared Mother Katharine Drexel venerable—the first step in the canonization process—that same year.[8]

Under the guidelines set forth in *Divinus Perfectionis Magister*, Drexel required only one miracle to reach the next stage of the pro-cess, known as beatification. The miracle attributed to Drexel took place in 1974 when a young boy named Robert Gutherman was cured of an ear infection that was expected to lead to a loss of hearing and perhaps even death. The parents of the fourteen-year-old followed a Sister of the Blessed Sacrament's advice "to pray directly to Mother Katharine and Mother Katharine alone."[9] When their son was pronounced cured, the Guthermans believed their prayers asking for Drexel's intercession had been answered, and that a miracle had taken place. Vatican officials agreed and Mother Katharine became Blessed Katharine Drexel in 1987.

During the ceremony, which Robert Gutherman was able to attend, John Paul II spoke of Drexel's dedication to and support for education. "What better way could be found to conquer the devastating effects of racism and to provide effective help for these disadvantaged brothers and sisters?" the pontiff asked.[10] Philadelphia Cardinal Anthony Bevilacqua expressed a similar sentiment in the form of a statement. "Mother Katharine established the Sisters of the Blessed Sacrament to give service to…the Blacks and Indians of this nation. The work she had done is now recognized in a special way by the Church itself through this beatification." A tapestry that depicted Drexel holding the hands of Black and Native children was prominently displayed during the ceremonies.[11]

In order for Katharine Drexel's cause to progress to the next level—which was canonization—an additional miracle needed to be reported and verified. The second miracle also involved a child suffering from hearing loss. Amy Wall was born in 1993 with the ability to hear very little. At the age of one, doctors stated that her hearing threshold tested at ninety decibels; normal hearing is considered to be between zero and twenty-five decibels. Wall's hearing loss was so severe that she "could barely hear shouting." After obtaining a second-class relic (which would have been an item frequently used or owned by her) of Blessed Katharine Drexel, Wall's family began praying to her for a miracle. In March of 1994—about five months after the family began to ask for Drexel's intercession—a preschool teacher at the Katzenbach School for the Deaf in Trenton, New Jersey, noticed that Wall was responding to sound. After a thorough investigation, authorities at the Vatican determined in 2000 that the restoration of Wall's hearing constituted a second miracle for Katharine Drexel. She was elevated to sainthood later that year.[12]

The fact that both miracles attributed to Katharine Drexel were hearing related was not lost on a number of scholarly observers. Writing in the *Josephinum Journal of Theology*, James Garneau noted that canonizing Drexel was not about wealth, but evangelization. "Tokens of charity, or even great acts of philanthropy, alone, will not convert hearts or unite people within the Church," he wrote. "Sacrificial love, however, inspired and nourished by a Eucharistic spirituality, combined with service to the poorest among us, will always bring men and women to Jesus Christ." Garneau then offered an explanation for why the new saint's two miracles were connected to hearing. "Are we listening to the voice of God in the midst of our prosperity? Do we hear the cry of the poor and the marginalized? Do we attend to the call of Jesus in his Eucharistic Presence to bring souls to Him?" The implication, of course, is that Katharine Drexel had indeed listened to the voice of God and heard the cries of the oppressed and made every effort to evangelize the people she and the Sisters of the Blessed Sacrament had come to serve.[13]

Drexel and Race: It's Complicated

Writing about Katharine Drexel and the Sisters of the Blessed Sacrament from the perspective of the third decade of the twentieth century is somewhat more complicated than it was when Burton published her 1957 biography. One cannot study a figure like Katharine Drexel in the twenty-first century without confronting the issue of race, which in the case of this particular person—even though she has been canonized a saint in the Catholic Church—is a very complex story. There is no doubt that Drexel devoted her adult life to helping Black and Indigenous communities in the United States. Lou Baldwin, a more recent biographer of Drexel, reports that Sisters of the Blessed Sacrament were ministering in sixty-one institutions at the time of her death; these included forty-eight elementary schools, twelve high schools, and one institution of higher education, Xavier University of Louisiana, the first and only Catholic historically Black college or university. In addition, Drexel had supported or subsidized hundreds of other churches and schools that were not staffed by the Sisters of the Blessed Sacrament.[14]

Katharine Drexel believed that Black and Indigenous People were entitled to the same rights and opportunities as white Americans. Her belief that all people should receive equal treatment—which was shared by Louise Morrell, her biological sister—clearly emerged in a proposal the two women sent to the board of managers of Philadelphia's St. Joseph's Hospital in 1927. Because "our Lord died on the Cross for the salvation of every human creature," the two sisters offered a plea "for one hundred thirty-five thousand (135,000) human beings in the city of Philadelphia of the Negro Race." Since their father, Francis A. Drexel, had designated the hospital as one of the twenty-seven charities named in his will, Drexel and her sister thought it was appropriate to ask that the money St. Joseph's received "be spent partially in opening its arms, even as were those of Jesus Christ on the Cross to the aforementioned race—extending its buildings in such a way, that this race may be cared for, even as our own." Drexel and Morrell specifically requested that the hospital use some of their father's money to provide "at least an endowment of twenty-five beds for the Colored of this diocese and that preference be given to patients recommended by the Sisters of the Blessed Sacrament."[15]

The women seemed to think such a gesture would help the Sisters of the Blessed Sacrament in their quest to provide educational opportunities and spiritual nourishment for Black and Indigenous People. Designating a number of beds in a Catholic hospital for Philadelphia's Black residents would only be one small step in any struggle to achieve racial equality, they reasoned, but it would at least be a step in the right direction and begin to provide resources related to health care to those who had been systemically denied them on the basis of race. The hospital's board of directors, however, rejected the women's proposal. Claiming St. Joseph's Hospital did not discriminate, the board noted they were "fully sympathetic" to the sentiments expressed in the petition and were happy to "cooperate with them in anything within their power on behalf of the colored race." But it was just not possible, they explained, to build an extension that would contain twenty-five beds reserved for Black patients. In addition to the cost involved, they were concerned that some Black Philadelphians, especially those "who repudiate such favors done them on the score that they are along the line of Southern discrimination, according to which separate provision is made for colored people to keep them apart from whites" would be unhappy with the proposed arrangement. "Even white people, to some extent," the letter continued, "might not like the idea of patronizing a hospital partly destined for colored people." The board of directors concluded that they could neither support this proposal nor recommend that the Sisters of Charity, who administered St. Joseph's, agree to implement the idea.[16]

This incident serves as a reminder that Drexel was not content for her own congregation to minister to Black and Indigenous People; she sometimes tried to encourage other Catholic institutions to serve those marginalized by the Catholic Church and U.S. society even if her efforts were ultimately unsuccessful. In addition to allocating millions of dollars to schools dedicated to the education of Black and Indigenous People, she attempted to use the power given to her by her wealth to call on church leaders (clerical and lay) to change the system of segregation as it existed in the United States at that time. Although women religious had very little power in either the Catholic Church or the larger society,

Drexel challenged the system when she believed it was feasible while staying within the boundaries set by the church's hierarchical structure.

The story of St. Joseph's Hospital also demonstrates, however, that although this request on the part of the Drexel sisters was certainly admirable, Black Philadelphians did not have a say in this discussion. The Drexel sisters did not consult with representatives from the Black medical community, for instance, concerning what changes needed to be made to the health care systems administered by either the city or the archdiocese in order to meet the needs of the community. And they neither asked nor expected Black civic leaders to offer an opinion about whether the plan proposed by the Drexel's was beneficial. Although many American Catholics would not have even written such a letter to the hospital's board of directors, the Drexel women did not bring Black voices into their conversation with St. Joseph's.

Despite a long history of philanthropy and service, questions remain related to Katharine Drexel, race, and the Sisters of the Blessed Sacrament. Historians are correctly challenging her reputation as an early civil rights activist. Some have even suggested that the schools for Black children staffed and administered by the Sisters of the Blessed Sacrament contributed to perpetuating segregation rather than simply enabling Black Americans to improve their socioeconomic status (see chapter 5).[17] Perhaps the most obvious concern when discussing the issue of race as it relates to Katharine Drexel and the Sisters of the Blessed Sacrament is the congregation's decision to refuse admittance to women of color. Although this is discussed in some detail in chapter 2, it is worth mentioning here that Drexel and the Sisters of the Blessed Sacrament (SBS) believed there were valid reasons for their decision. First, the sisters claimed that accepting Black women into the community would mean that the two (later three) existing Black congregations of women religious in the United States would lose members. Second, admitting women of color to the SBS, members of the congregation suggested, would draw attention away from the work of the community and its ministry to the marginalized. People—including potential financial supporters—would focus on the fact that the congregation was integrated rather than on the work the sisters were doing to assist Black and Indigenous People. Third, Drexel and future congregational leaders would be unable to send Black and white sisters to the same mission anywhere in the southern United States. Not only was it against the law for Black and white people to live in the same residence as equals, but the safety of the sisters would be compromised.

The reasons for prohibiting Black women from entering the Sisters of the Blessed Sacrament are weak by today's views on issues related to racism, justice, and equity. At the same time, other components of the history and work of the SBS must be taken into account when addressing this issue. People who engage with Drexel's life and legacy, for instance, must weigh the congregation's refusal to admit Black women with the establishment and sponsoring of Xavier University of Louisiana. Firmly believing that Black people could only succeed in the United States if they had access to a proper education and realizing that American Catholic institutions of higher education usually refused to admit nonwhite students, Drexel's solution was to found a university. Located in the state with the greatest concentration of Black Catholics in the country at the time, Xavier offered—and continues to offer—Black people the opportunity to prepare for careers in medicine, law, pharmacy, and business.

Speaking at a banquet celebrating the Diamond Jubilee of the Sisters of the Blessed Sacrament in 1966, Judge Raymond Pace Alexander forcefully reminded those present of Katharine Drexel's contributions to Black Americans. Drexel "became the first person in recorded history at that time...to have left so vast a fortune for the religious, intermediate, and higher education of the colored people and the Indians of America," the prominent Black Philadelphian argued. Had other Americans of wealth and power—and Alexander was referring specifically to the Protestant establishment—done what Katharine Drexel had, he continued, "the poverty, illiteracy, the homeless and jobless Negro after emancipation would have been solved and within twenty to thirty years they would have been integrated in the total community as useful productive, highly regarded and well-established American citizens." Drexel was the only one willing to devote her time and money to the education of Black Americans (and Indigenous People) during the late nineteenth and the first half of the twentieth centuries, Alexander maintained; had others followed her lead the issues related to race and racism in the United States during the mid-1960s might have been very different.[18]

When Bishop Joseph Martino submitted the *positio* advocating for Katharine Drexel's canonization, he addressed the question of race by placing the future saint within the context of the history of "race relations in North America and portrayed Drexel as a woman constrained by the limits of her time." Kathleen Sprows Cummings notes that Martino argued "Drexel had accepted the laws of segregation and admitted Black sisters as soon as she was able." The case laid out in the *positio* was supported by the fact that at the time it was written, Sister Juliana Haynes, the first Black woman professed as a Sister of the Blessed Sacrament, was serving as president of the congregation. Although Katharine Drexel was very ill by the time Haynes entered the SBS, she and a novice from the Navajo tribe "presented Mother Katharine with 'spiritual bouquets' on her birthday and on Christmas [to make sure she] 'knew she had a black novice and an Indian novice.'" The framework developed by Martino situated Katharine Drexel within the dynamics of U.S. society in the late nineteenth and early twentieth centuries, as well as those within the Catholic Church at that time, and concluded she had done all she could to eliminate racial injustice in the United States.[19]

Engaging in a ministry to Black and Indigenous People does not necessarily mean one is anti-racist or an activist advocating for racial justice. In the parlance of the third decade of the twenty-first century, Katharine Drexel was not anti-racist, as historian and author Ibram X. Kendi and others have used the term. Offering a definition of an anti-racist as "one who is supporting an antiracist policy through their actions or expressing an antiracist idea," Kendi goes on to explain that "anti-racism is a powerful collection of antiracist policies that lead to racial equity and are substantiated by antiracist ideas."[20] Katharine Drexel was a wealthy white woman who lived her entire life in Philadelphia and its immediate environs. Her travels to the western and southern United States certainly gave her the opportunity to see the conditions under which Black and Indigenous People were forced to live because of national and local policies, but she devoted only a small part of her time to attempt to change those policies or to undertake any sort of study that would result in an understanding of the racist ideas that led to their implementation. Within a decade after her death, at least some members of the congregation would be part of larger movements seeking equality and justice for marginalized groups in U.S. society and the American Catholic Church (see chapter 7). The fact is that Katharine Drexel was a wealthy woman of the late nineteenth and early twentieth centuries, and she reflects the positive and negative components of those decades. Many American Catholics consider her the patron saint of racial justice and philanthropy, but it is because Drexel is considered a holy woman who chose to distribute her fortune in ways that would assist Black and Indigenous People and tried to promote equity within Catholicism, not because she was a social activist advocating for racial justice as we understand this concept in the third decade of the twenty-first century.[21]

Exceptional, Not Unique

Many biographies and histories of saints, regardless of the century in which they lived, are hagiographical rather than critical, and those that have been written about Katharine Drexel are no exception. Previous biographers of Katharine Drexel have taken her sanctity for granted, and there is good reason for this because by the time she died in 1955 at the age of ninety-six, many leaders in the U.S. Catholic Church believed it was a foregone conclusion that she would eventually be canonized. The emphasis that has been placed on her sanctity means that the story of her life has been sanitized; it is often hard to find the "real" Katharine Drexel, even when examining the thousands of documents that detail the story of her life and work in the SBS congregational archives.

There is no doubt that Drexel accomplished a great deal of good during her life, but in order to focus on what she *did* this study does not aim to be a biography, but an examination of her in light of the congregation she founded and the era in which she lived. Drexel is unique among American women religious because she continued—with the help of her congregational council—to distribute funds to those seeking help to build churches and schools to serve Black and Indigenous People after she entered religious life. At the same time, she used some of her fortune to build schools that would be staffed by the Sisters of the Blessed Sacrament for Indians and Colored People. This meant that she headed both a community of women religious and what was, in effect, a philanthropic foundation. But her money was only as helpful as the people to whom it was entrusted. She could not have done the work she did without a cadre of men and women religious willing to accept her terms for living and working on reservations and in Black communities. Because the founding of the Sisters of the Blessed Sacrament meant that Drexel was able to ensure that she could fund *and* staff schools, it is important that the congregation be an integral part of the story of the woman who gave up her fortune to serve God and others. Although the money Drexel donated was obviously a tremendous help in serving

Black and Indigenous People, the presence of a community of women religious prepared to spend their lives ministering to these populations provided a critical mass of people to ensure that the work was carried out.

Although Katharine Drexel's great wealth differentiated her from other women religious, as a congregation the Sisters of the Blessed Sacrament are not unique. Like many other communities, including the Sisters of Mercy, Sisters of St. Joseph, and Sisters, Servants of the Immaculate Heart of Mary, the SBS were primarily teachers. In addition, other congregations—the Sisters of Loretto, the Sisters of St. Francis of Philadelphia, and the Grey Nuns—dedicated some personnel and resources to Black and Indigenous ministries. In 1892, one year after the SBS was founded, Margaret Mary Healy Murphy established the Sisters of the Holy Ghost and Mary Immaculate to work with Black and Latinx people. In addition, the Sisters of the Blessed Sacrament lived under the same hierarchical structure and governance as other U.S. sisters and did not begin to develop new ways of interacting with the Catholic Church and American society until the aftermath of the Second Vatican Council (1962–1965). What makes the Sisters of the Blessed Sacrament exceptional was their ability to distribute money for projects that would not be built or staffed by the congregation because the majority of American Catholics clergy and laypeople were not willing to provide the necessary resources to assist Black and Indigenous People.

Chapter 1, "A Life of Wealth and Privilege," situates the future saint within the context of her family. When Katharine was born in 1855, the Drexel family was still relatively new to Philadelphia. Francis Martin Drexel, her grandfather, did not arrive in the United States until 1817, but was well on the way to becoming a man of wealth by 1837. Unlike many other elite Philadelphians who were members of the Protestant Episcopal Church, Francis Martin Drexel and his wife were Catholic. Their children were raised in the Catholic Church and, with the exception of Anthony (founder of Drexel University), were married in the Catholic Church. Although Katharine's parents were married in a Catholic ceremony, her mother, Hannah Langstroth Drexel, was not a Catholic. Hannah died shortly after Katharine's birth and her father remarried in 1860. Emma Bouvier Drexel was a devout Catholic and transmitted both her faith and the belief that she had a responsibility to assist those in need to the three Drexel daughters, Elizabeth, Katharine, and Louise.

Emma Drexel died in 1883. When Francis died two years later, the Drexel sisters found themselves the recipients of a tremendous fortune. As they began to use their money to build schools and churches for Black and Indigenous People, Katharine was discerning whether she was being called to religious life. She entered the Sisters of Mercy novitiate in Pittsburgh in order to found her own congregation, the Sisters of the Blessed Sacrament for Indians and Colored People.

The second chapter, "The Richest Nun in America," details Drexel's work as the leader of a religious congregation and what was essentially a one-woman philanthropic foundation. As the superior of the Sisters of the Blessed Sacrament, she was responsible for ensuring the congregation's Rule was approved by Rome, as well as supervising the formation of novices, recruiting future members of the congregation, and assigning sisters to a ministry. Although the Great Depression and the implementation of a federal income tax hindered their ability to assist everyone who asked, Mother Katharine still tried to support those working with Black and Indigenous People.

The work of Katharine Drexel and the Sisters of the Blessed Sacrament in Philadelphia is the subject of the third chapter. Although Drexel funded and visited churches and schools throughout the United States, she spent her entire life either in Philadelphia or at the SBS motherhouse in Bensalem, just outside of the city. Her commitment to the city's Black Catholic community began before she entered religious life when she contributed to St. Peter Claver parish, founded in 1886. Drexel and the SBS would be heavily invested in four Black parishes located throughout the city.

"Heading West: Founding and Funding Ministries to Indigenous People" is the subject of chapter 4. Drexel's financial contributions to Catholic schools and churches located on reservations began before she founded a religious congregation, but the establishment of the SBS allowed her to staff and administer schools dedicated to evangelizing and educating Indigenous People. The SBS were involved in several residential schools, three of which—St. Catherine's in Santa Fe, New Mexico; St. Michael Indian School in Arizona; and St. Paul's in Yankton, South Dakota (now the Marty Indian School)—are profiled in the chapter.

Drexel and the congregation's work with Black Americans is the focus of chapter 5. The Sisters of the Blessed Sacrament, under Drexel's leadership, agreed to staff a number of parochial schools throughout the south connected to Black parishes. In addition to providing teachers for schools in urban and rural areas, including New Orleans, they also established a number of small rural schools throughout southwestern Louisiana, in what are now the Dioceses of Lafayette and Lake Charles. Since there were not enough SBS to serve as teachers, laywomen, usually graduates of Xavier University of Louisiana, were hired to teach in these schools. Drexel usually paid the salaries for these young women. In addition, the congregation accepted responsibility for schools in northern cities, including New York and Chicago.

The most enduring ministry of Drexel and the SBS is Xavier University in New Orleans, Louisiana, and chapter 6 is devoted to this topic. Drexel believed that Black people would not achieve equality in the United States until they had received an education that would allow them to enter the business and professional classes. In 1915, Xavier University Preparatory School was opened under SBS auspices, and ten years later Xavier University was officially established. Xavier University is the only Black Catholic university in the United States and the only Catholic institution among the Historic Black Colleges and Universities. It was designed to offer a classical education rather than the sort of industrial-vocational training offered at schools such as Tuskegee University in Alabama. When the university was founded, it included a liberal arts college as well as a college devoted to teacher education. The story of the university is part of the larger story of race and racism in the United States, including the struggles of the Civil Rights era and the Black Lives Matter movement.

The final chapter is entitled, "Walking in the Footsteps of a Saint: The Sisters after Drexel." Katharine Drexel died in 1955, but she stepped down from the position of mother superior in 1935. Although she continued to take an active interest in congregational matters, her voice was slowly silenced as her health—physical and mental—deteriorated. After Drexel's death, the Sisters of the Blessed Sacrament continued their ministries while responding to changes taking place in the Catholic Church and U.S. society. The Second Vatican Council (1962–1965) led to changes in religious life throughout the world. Some SBS participated in experiments related to small group living (as opposed to large convents) and proposed new ways of ministering to Black and Indigenous People. In addition, some were actively engaged in the Civil Rights Movement, and the integration of parochial schools in the South.

Like many religious communities in the United States, declining numbers and an aging population meant that Sisters of the Blessed Sacrament were forced to make difficult decisions related to closing ministries, including some that had been a vital part of the community's work for many years, such as St. Catherine Indian School in Santa Fe. In the third decade of the twenty-first century, St. Michael Indian School and Xavier University of Louisiana remain key ministries of the SBS, but members of the congregation are ministering in Massachusetts, Pennsylvania, Florida, Georgia, Tennessee, Louisiana, Virginia, Arizona, and New Mexico.[22] In their ministries—whether they are actively engaged in working with the marginalized or praying for those in need of assistance—they continue to honor the legacy of Mother Katharine Drexel through their work with underserved populations throughout the United States.

Chapter One

A LIFE OF WEALTH AND PRIVILEGE

*A*braham Lincoln's assassination on April 15, 1865, dominated the news in Philadelphia and throughout the nation. The funeral for the fallen president was held on April 19 in the East Room of the White House, but attendance was restricted to "dignitaries only: President Johnson, cabinet members, generals, governors, senators, and representatives." The following day, however, forty thousand people paid their respects to the fallen president as he lay in state in the Capitol Rotunda before his body was placed on a train and taken to his final resting place in Springfield, Illinois. Despite the objections of Mary Todd Lincoln, the funeral train stopped at ten cities, including Philadelphia, before it arrived at its destination in order to allow people to "bid [Lincoln] a formal good-bye."[1]

Eight-year-old Katharine Drexel was certainly too young to understand the implications of a presidential assassination, but she and her family could hardly help but be drawn into the excitement that gripped Philadelphia over the planned arrival of Lincoln's funeral train on April 22. The funeral procession was to pass right by her family's home at 1503 Walnut Street, but Katharine's parents disagreed over whether their three young daughters should be able to watch as it made its way from the train station to its final stop. Emma Drexel believed the girls, whose ages ranged from nine to one, were too young, but her husband, Francis Drexel, argued that this was a day that would live forever in the city's history and the girls should join their fellow Philadelphians in paying homage to the slain president. Francis's views prevailed, and

17

the entire family watched the procession pass by from the upper windows of their home. "For the children," Cordelia Biddle wrote, "it was a nightmare vision: the tear-drenched faces contorted with emotion, the cortege noiseless save for the rolling wagons and tramping feet."[2]

Although she was a young girl when Lincoln's funeral train passed through Philadelphia, her experience of this event reminds us that any examination of Katharine Drexel must take into account the world in which she and her sisters—Elizabeth and Louise—were raised. It was a world shaped at least in part by the Civil War and the events that followed Lee's surrender at Appomattox, including Lincoln's assassination, but the Drexel family would also be influenced by the years defined as the Gilded Age, including great wealth and financial panics, as well as government policies related to Black and Indigenous People.

The Making of Millionaires

Katharine Drexel was born on November 26, 1858, into a family of wealth and privilege. Her grandfather, Francis Martin Drexel (1792–1863) was born in Dornbirn, Austria, and as a young man spent some time working as an itinerant portrait painter. Working in Basel, Switzerland, in 1817, Drexel decided to board one of the many boats sailing down the Rhine River to Amsterdam in order to book passage on a ship to the United States. Seventy-two days after the *John of Baltimore* set sail from Texel, Francis Drexel found himself in Philadelphia. He "promised himself that if he fared poorly in America he would return to Europe after six months; if he did well, he would stay for six years; but by no means would he settle permanently."[3] He did not keep that promise.

When Francis Drexel arrived in the city, he found lodging with a family on Broad Street. During his first month in Philadelphia, Drexel painted portraits of the women of the family with whom he was staying and began to develop a reputation as a portraitist throughout the city. Philadelphians attending the 1818 Exhibition at the Pennsylvania Academy of Fine Arts could view nine oil paintings and two drawings completed by Francis Drexel. Although he did not amass a great fortune as a painter, Drexel made enough money to live comfortably. "For more than eight years he worked industriously in Philadelphia at his chosen field, in which he neither starved in a garret like Van Gogh nor made a fortune like Sir Joshua Reynolds, but in his own words 'continued to do middle well.'"[4]

In 1821, three years after his arrival in Philadelphia, Drexel married Catherine Hookey at Holy Trinity Church, a German parish. They would eventually have six children: Mary Johanna, Francis (Katharine's father), Anthony (founder of Drexel University), Joseph, Heloise, and Caroline.[5] Drexel continued to develop his career as a painter while he and his family took up residence at 40 S. 6th Street. His ability to earn a living from this work faltered when his brother-in-law, Bernard Gallagher, spread rumors intended to damage his reputation and he lost a number of commissions. It is unclear what drove Gallagher to spread these rumors—the specific charges are shrouded in mystery—but they pushed Drexel to leave his wife and children for about five years in order to travel to South America to make enough money to support his family. He arrived home in 1830 and remained in Philadelphia for approximately five years, leaving for Central America again in 1835. Francis did not stay long in that area, however, and was back with his family by early 1837.[6]

During the Financial Panic of 1837, Francis M. Drexel began operating a business trading currency in Louisville, Kentucky. At the time he began getting involved in currency trading, it was often referred to as "money shaving." Paper currency was issued by individual chartered banks rather than the federal government, and these banks, all but one of which were chartered by individual states, were allowed to issue their own notes, "a privilege that required the issuing bank to redeem those notes in specie (gold or silver or some equivalent) on demand."[7] The only national bank at the time, the Second Bank of the United States (1816–1836) was neither liked nor trusted by President Andrew Jackson, who believed it had an unfair advantage over banks chartered by the states. Jackson vetoed the bank's national charter, and as a result, it expired in 1836.

Drexel and his sons did not exclusively focus on banking. Each year merchants from other parts of the United States converged on Philadelphia to order goods for the coming year. The paper notes they brought with them could not usually be redeemed more than one hundred miles from the issuing bank; they sold their notes to currency traders like Francis M. Drexel, who tried to buy them for the lowest price possible. According to Dan Rottenberg, Drexel could be "as petty and grasping" as any other currency trader in Philadelphia, doing whatever he could to buy low and sell high.[8]

After the Panic of 1837 subsided and the economy was once again stable, Drexel began to expand his business by buying and selling foreign bills of exchange. These were essentially nineteenth-century IOUs: a bill of exchange promised to pay a specific sum at a future date. Buyers would often issue a bill of exchange to tide them over until they could return home and begin to sell their recently purchased goods. By 1847, the business operated by Francis Martin, Anthony, and Francis A. Drexel was well on its way to becoming a private bank. They continued to make money by buying government bonds—when the U.S. government needed money to finance the Mexican War, for instance, the Drexels sold $49.2 million worth of 6 percent ten- and twenty-year bonds. But like other private banks, Francis Drexel and his sons had to expand their business outside of Philadelphia. In order for this to happen, banks often built "branch" organizations, which functioned as mostly independent enterprises, although some partners of the original firm were often owners or managers. The first branch in which the Drexel's were involved—Drexel & Smith—was founded in Chicago in the 1840s. The firm was able to begin doing business in New York City in 1855 when the Drexel name was added to J. T. Van Vleck, Read, & Co.[9]

The family had made enough money during the 1840s and 1850s that by the outbreak of the Civil War, Francis M. Drexel was one of at least twenty-five millionaires residing in Philadelphia, and the bank was one of the largest and most influential in the United States and well positioned to assist in financing the war. Despite its reputation as a city with a strong Quaker abolitionist presence, most Philadelphians were rather apathetic, and even divided, about the institution of slavery; after all, Southern merchants were some the city's best customers. When the Civil War began, however, the city identified as staunchly pro-Union. Although there is no evidence that the Drexels were involved in the abolitionist movement, there is also nothing to indicate that the family either supported or directly benefited from the enslavement of human beings. Along with their Philadelphian friends and neighbors, they supported the Union cause.

The firm's war involvement stemmed from a partnership that Anthony Drexel forged with financier Jay Cooke. Cooke's marketing skills, which included advertising in newspapers and appealing to patriotism in order to sell bonds, helped resolve about "$360 million, or nearly 75 percent of the Union's bond issues, sometimes raising as much as $2 million in a single day."[10] Although Anthony Drexel served primarily as a silent partner in this venture, offering advice as needed, the firm made a considerable amount of money during these years. When hostilities ceased after Lee's surrender at Appomattox, the government floated "offerings to refund its Civil War loans at lower interest rates, which Drexel & Co. helped sell."[11]

A Life of Privilege

When Francis M. Drexel died in 1863, "Drexel & Co. was firmly established as one of the nation's leading investment houses."[12] Although she was too young to understand how her grandfather, father, and uncle accumulated their fortune, Katharine Drexel clearly benefited from the family's wealth and position in society. Anthony and Francis A. Drexel, along with their brother Joseph, would continue the work her grandfather had started, which ensured that the adult Drexel sisters had access to more disposable income than any other American Catholic women.

Francis Drexel's oldest son—Francis Anthony—married Hannah Jane Langstroth on September 28, 1854. His wife, a non-Catholic, was a member of the Dunkards or Dunkers, whose members baptized believers by "dunking them." (Today the denomination is known as the Church of the Brethren.) Their first daughter, Elizabeth, was born on August 27, 1855. Their second daughter, Katharine, who was named Catherine Mary after her paternal grandmother (Catherine Hookey Drexel), was born on November 26, 1858.[13] Francis Drexel baptized his daughter on the day she was born, but a formal ceremony took place on December 29 in Philadelphia's Church of the Assumption. Katharine's godparents were her father's siblings, Joseph Drexel and Mary Drexel Lankenau.[14]

Hannah Drexel never recovered from childbirth and died the day after her daughter was baptized. She was buried in the Germantown Church of the Brethren Cemetery. In 1946, however, the Sisters of the Blessed Sacrament (the congregation founded by Katharine Drexel) asked Philadelphia Cardinal Dennis Dougherty to transfer Hannah Drexel's body to the Shrine of the True Cross in Philadelphia. Drexel's other immediate family members were interred there, and it made sense that her biological mother should be buried with her husband and other family members. Although Hannah was not a Catholic, which meant that according to canon law she could not be buried in a Catholic cemetery, members of the congregation argued that the family believed Hannah was in the process of converting to Catholicism at the time of her death and was therefore eligible for interment in consecrated ground.

Formal portrait of the Drexel children; left to right, Mother Katharine Drexel, Louise Drexel Morrell, Elizabeth Drexel Smith. Courtesy of SBS Archives, CHRC, Archdiocese of Philadelphia.

The account of Hannah Drexel's reburial in ground consecrated by the Catholic Church clearly has some gaps that cannot be filled. As Lou Baldwin notes, these gaps are both theological and historical. The theological problem can be stated rather simply. Hannah's death was not sudden; she lived just over a month after giving birth to Katharine. If she was indeed taking instructions in order to enter the Catholic Church, Baldwin asks, why wasn't she baptized conditionally and buried in a Catholic cemetery? The historical question is a bit more complicated. Katharine Drexel apparently believed the story that Johanna Ryan, her childhood nurse, recounted. Ryan contended that Hannah had once said that if she "knew more about the teachings of the Catholic Church she might come into it." The problem with this account, Baldwin explains, is that Ryan was not employed by the Drexel family until after Hannah's death. Hence, "One suspects Katharine, to whom the Catholic faith was of paramount importance," Baldwin writes, "was willing to accept a pious story that would make her mother a Catholic by desire. Cardinal Dougherty, who had great respect and affection for Katharine Drexel, acceded to her congregation's request and permitted the transfer of Hannah's remains in the family crypt at the Shrine of the True Cross."[15] The potential myth of Hannah Drexel's desire to convert to Catholicism exemplifies the ways that history may be slightly changed when examining the life of someone proposed for canonization in the Catholic Church.

Katharine and Elizabeth were sent to live with Anthony and Ellen Drexel after Hannah's death. They joined the couple and their three young daughters in the developing area of West Philadelphia, where Anthony Drexel had built a house that covered most of a city block. Anthony joined the Episcopal Church when he married his wife, and he and his family were members of the Church of the Savior.[16] Although he left the church in which he had been raised, there is no indication that Katharine Drexel's uncle and her father were estranged over the issue of religion. Anthony Drexel and his niece also maintained a friendly relationship and she often sought his financial advice as she began to use her vast fortune to assist Black and Indigenous People.

The Drexel children returned to their home shortly after Francis married Emma Bouvier (great-great-aunt of Jacqueline Bouvier Kennedy Onassis) on April 10, 1860. Although Francis M. and Catherine Hookey Drexel were active in the work of Philadelphia's Catholic community—Francis, for instance, had briefly served as a trustee at Holy Trinity Church and his father-in-law, Anthony Hookey, was one of the founding trustees—they and other prominent Philadelphian Catholic families tended to deemphasize their religion. "Frequently they married

Protestants as a way of melting into the landscape without incurring disapproval from their families of fellow Catholics. And as they succeeded in business or civic affairs, they became less inclined to blindly accept the word of bishops, cardinals, or the pope."[17] Many wealthy Philadelphian Catholics—including Anthony Drexel—became practicing Episcopalians. Katharine Drexel's aunt, Mary Johanna Drexel, also married a Protestant, a wealthy businessman named John Lankenau. Unlike her brother, however, Mary Lankenau remained a Catholic for the rest of her life.

Emma Bouvier, however, was a very devout Catholic and there was never any question that she and her husband would leave the church in which they were raised in order to blend into Philadelphia society. This fact should have made her mother-in-law, Catherine Hookey Drexel, happy, but Emma's puritanical and reclusive personality—she sometimes did not even attend family gatherings—meant that the two women did not enjoy an easy relationship. In fact, when Catherine Hookey Drexel died in 1870, she may have expressed her displeasure with her daughter-in-law by not including Louise, the daughter of Francis and Emma Drexel, in her will.[18]

Emma Bouvier Drexel raised Katharine and Elizabeth as if they were her biological daughters and continued to do so after Louise was born in 1863. According to Drexel's biographers, Katharine did not realize Emma was not her biological mother until she was thirteen years old. If Elizabeth knew, she apparently never said anything to Katharine. "It began," according to Sister Consuela Duffy, "with her wonderment about the fact that she and Lizzie had three grandmothers while all the rest of her cousins had two."[19]

Emma's devotion to Catholicism had a great impact on her husband and three daughters. Herself a graduate of the Academy of the Sacred Heart (renamed Eden Hall), a school operated by the Society of the Sacred Heart in the Torresdale section of Philadelphia, Emma enrolled Elizabeth there when she was old enough to start school. Before Katharine was ready for school, however, Emma decided to have her children educated at home. She supervised their intellectual and spiritual development and at the same time saw that they assisted in her charitable endeavors.

Emma Drexel personally supervised her daughters' religious education and faith formation, and made sure they were prepared for first communion and confirmation. Katharine received both sacraments on the same day, June 3, 1870. There is, however, no formal sacramental record of her confirmation. The Sacred Heart sisters suspect that her record—along with others—was lost when the congregation moved their school from Center City Philadelphia to the Torresdale section of the city. Katharine's own letters from that era focus on her first communion and do not mention confirmation. Writing to her aunt, Madame Louise Bouvier, for instance, she happily described the festivities following Mass; her parents had paid for a breakfast for the entire class of communicants. Her aunt, however, was unimpressed with the letter and chastised Katharine, writing she was "disappointed. I did not want or care to know about the breakfast, but I did want to know your thoughts and feelings as you received our dear Lord."[20]

Francis Drexel exemplifies the wealthy Catholic laymen of the 1860s and 1870s, who believed they had a responsibility to help those in need. In addition to financial support, many of them volunteered their time to serve on boards of charitable institutions—such as hospitals and orphanages—and helped religious leaders, including bishops and superiors of religious congregations, navigate the worlds of business and finance. Drexel "sat on virtually every charitable board connected with the Philadelphia Archdiocese, and of course, was a major contributor as well." His financial and voluntary contributions to archdiocesan institutions allowed the family to sometimes use their influence in order to ensure that a child without a stable home life could be admitted to a Catholic childcare facility.[21]

Emma Drexel developed her own methods for practicing charity common for a woman of her socioeconomic status, and she instilled in her daughters the idea that they also had a responsibility to help those in need. In the 1870s, middle-class Catholic laywomen often participated in charitable activities by joining benevolent societies that allowed them to donate time and money to various institutions and causes. Emma Drexel and other upper-class women, however, also tended to perform charitable work apart from any organizational structure. Rather than donating to and raising money for a number of causes, Emma essentially practiced charity from her home. "She conducted an extensive social service project from her home, distributing money to the poor three times weekly for necessities like rent, food, fuel, and clothing." In order to ensure that the recipients of her largesse were being honest about their needs, she recorded the names of those to whom she provided assistance and noted the reasons for the donation. Historian Mary

Oates described Emma as managing her work "scientifically, insisting that reform was a 'higher charity' than simple almsgiving."[22] Katharine Drexel later remembered her mother's approach to helping those in need and for holding people accountable according to careful records:

> She employed someone to go around and visit the poor and she (the woman employed) made a report to my mother. If the report were favorable and the woman had given the person a ticket, the ticket could be presented to my mother in person....My mother would try to devise means of giving the needed help right then and there....Everything given out was noted down in a book, so that Mama knew if the same need was brought to her again very soon it was because the right use had not been made of the thing given before.[23]

Three days a week those who had received tickets arrived at the Drexel home hoping to benefit from the philanthropist's largesse. Emma Drexel and her assistant often disagreed on those who "deserved" help; she was more inclined to accept someone's story of need than the woman hired to help document and distribute the money.[24]

Emma Drexel instilled in her daughters the idea that philanthropy was not only a responsibility; it was in fact, a privilege. The family's vast wealth gave the Drexel women the opportunity to serve those in need. To ensure that Elizabeth, Katharine, and Louise understood her position, she would only allow them to be part of her work "on [the] condition that any alms they might give, or anything they might do should be done only at the cost of personal sacrifice from their own funds."[25] In addition, if they joined their mother as she visited the poor, they were expected to dress simply. Emma did not want her daughters to give those they were visiting the idea that they considered themselves superior to others.

In 1870, Francis Drexel purchased a seventy-acre farm in the Torresdale section of Philadelphia and built a residence that became the family's summer home. The area was originally developed by Charles Mcalester, a "banker, broker, and diplomat," who purchased the land and divided it into estate size lots, naming the area Torresdale after his family's estate in Scotland. By the end of the nineteenth century, the area had become something of a resort community for the wealthy, and Francis Drexel joined other privileged Philadelphians using the land to develop a vacation estate.[26] The family named their summer home St. Michel.

When the Drexel family first began to vacation at St. Michel, St. Dominic's, the local parish church, was about three miles away. The intensely devout Emma Drexel worried that the area children were not receiving an appropriate religious education, and as a result, decided to start a Sunday school. Although her original plan was for the school to serve the children of St. Michel's employees, at one time there were as many as fifty children receiving religious instruction from Katharine and her older sister. The school was only open during the summer months, but the children were gathered together at Christmas to receive gifts from the Drexel family. Louise Morrell remembered that "just before St. Michael's [sic] was closed for the winter, prizes were given out for the best lessons and best attendance, and on Christmas Day the children assembled for a celebration when they received useful gifts (such as dresses, knitted jackets, etc.) also cake, candy, etc."[27]

The Sunday school funded by Emma Drexel and staffed by her daughters combined philanthropy and faith formation. In addition to offering religious education and sacramental preparation to children who would not otherwise have access to Sunday school, the family clearly provided material assistance to the students in the form of "useful gifts." Perhaps most significant for this study of Drexel, the Sunday school served as a model for the work that would be undertaken by Katharine and her sisters. Just as Emma Drexel practiced philanthropy as an individual rather than through an organization or foundation, the Drexel sisters would follow their mother's model of charity and philanthropy, making decisions on their own without benefit of boards of trustees.

Faith and Privilege

The Drexel fortune continued to increase after the death of Francis M. Drexel. In 1871, Anthony and Francis A. Drexel entered into a partnership with J. Pierpont Morgan and formed Drexel, Morgan & Co., which the *Commercial and Financial Chronicle* described as "one of the most important changes in banking circles announced at this time." The family fortune allowed Katharine, Louise, and Elizabeth to enjoy all of the privileges of the American upper classes during the latter decades of the nineteenth century. In addition, to their luxurious home in Center City Philadelphia and their summer home in Torresdale, they often spent time away from Philadelphia in the fall. On one occasion, the family journeyed to Colorado, and they also spent time in New Hampshire's White Mountains. In 1874, the entire family embarked on a nine-month grand tour of Europe, visiting England, France, Italy, Germany, Austria, and Switzerland. Although they toured palaces, museums, and gardens, the sisters also spent time at shrines and other religious sites. In Siena, for instance, Elizabeth and Katharine were able to look at the body of what they thought was St. Catherine of Siena sitting up in a chair. The body, the guide told them, was "just as limber as it had been when placed in the chapel 450 years ago." When told it was customary to kiss the feet of the saint, the girls reluctantly complied. Although Katharine professed a special devotion to this saint, she wrote in a letter home that the "whole effect of the shrine was awful."[28] The sisters later discovered that they had kissed the feet of a saint they knew nothing about, Catherine of Bologna.

Katharine's formal education—such as it was—ended in 1878. She continued to live the life of a wealthy socialite, spending time in Cape May, New Jersey, and attending parties and balls with other young men and women of her social class. There is one mention of a "gentleman caller," but she was only seventeen years old when this purported visit took place. There are no other indications that she was ever seriously involved with anyone or considered marriage.[29]

In 1879, the year Katharine made her debut, Emma Drexel was facing serious health issues. Although she knew that she was most likely very ill, Emma chose to keep that fact hidden from her husband and daughters. When she finally sought medical help, the diagnosis was breast cancer, and there was little that could be done to improve her condition. Hoping that a change of scenery would help his wife, Francis Drexel took the family to Sharon Springs, New York, in 1882. Emma's condition worsened, however, and by the time the family returned to Philadelphia she was bedridden. She died on January 29, 1883.[30]

The family was devastated by Emma's death. Francis Drexel spent hours alone in his room, and Katharine, Louise, and Elizabeth wondered if they had done enough to help her. Hoping that a change of scenery would help mitigate the grief they were experiencing, the four Drexels left Philadelphia for Europe in October of 1883, and remained away until April 1884. When they returned to Philadelphia, Francis—

who had temporarily left his job at Drexel & Co. to focus his attention on Emma—took his daughters with him on a business trip to the western part of the country to determine if the bonds being issued for the Northern Pacific Railroad constituted a sound investment. The family's final destination was Portland, Oregon, with several stops along the way, including Yellowstone National Park; altogether they traveled about seven thousand miles.[31]

This trip was especially significant for the future ministry of Katharine Drexel. In addition to gaining "insight into the world of finance," she became aware of the physical and spiritual difficulties faced by those ministering to Indigenous People.[32] When the family arrived in Tacoma, Washington, for instance, they discovered that Rev. Peter Hylebos, a Belgian missionary whom they had met on their recent European trip, was serving the area's native community at a mission chapel. When Katharine discovered the chapel contained no artwork portraying Our Lady of Grace—for whom the chapel was named—she purchased a statue for the building, which had to be transported to the reservation by canoe after its arrival in Tacoma. It was the first financial contribution Katharine Drexel would make designated for the evangelization of Indigenous People.[33]

The lives of the Drexel sisters would change in a dramatic way yet again when their father died on February 15, 1885. It was clear that the three young women were about to become very wealthy in their own right; Francis Drexel's estate was one of the largest ever recorded in the United States. As might be expected, he left the bulk of his $15.5 million estate in trust to his three heirs in order to provide each of them with a substantial annual income. Hoping to protect his daughters from men seeking to marry them for their money, Francis included a "spendthrift clause," a provision often included in wills that involved large amounts of money, which prohibited any future husband from being involved with his wife's property. The principal of the trust was to be inherited by any future grandchildren. If his daughters did not have children—and this turned out to be the case because although Louise and Elizabeth both married, there were no surviving grandchildren—the money was to be distributed among the twenty-seven charities that had been the beneficiaries of about 10 percent (about $500,000) of the vast fortune in Francis's will, including Philadelphia's St. John's Orphan Asylum, St. Mary's Hospital, and the House of the Good Shepherd. "By assuring the daughters a regular income, and by stipulating that if they died childless the trust principal would go to charity," Dan Rottenberg wrote, "the will effectively discouraged suitors and encouraged the daughters' charitable instincts."[34]

Katharine Drexel struggled with health issues after the death of her father. Although it is impossible to diagnose her illnesses in twenty-first century terms, her biographers have described her health crisis in several ways; all attribute her problems to losing both of her parents within a couple of years of each other. Sister Consuela Duffy notes that she experienced an "attack of jaundice" followed by "severe internal trouble [that] caused a loss of weight and a general weakening of her whole system." In a 2014 biography of Drexel, Cheryl Hughes suggests, "Her condition would have been recognized today as clinical depression and treated accordingly." In the same year, Cordelia Biddle simply noted that Francis's death "dealt a critical blow to [her] physical and mental health....Everything lost meaning for her, everything seemed hopeless; there were days when it was difficult to clamber out of bed. When she spoke, her words were few and perfunctory. Mostly she cried or stared into space, inconsolable and mute."[35] Whether her illness was primarily physical or could be attributed to depression, her sisters were clearly worried about her and proposed another European tour to perhaps ease Katharine's pain. She agreed, and in July of 1886, the Drexels sailed for Europe.

Perhaps the most significant event on this extended tour occurred when the three women received an audience with Pope Leo XIII. During the course of their conversation, thirty-one-year-old Katharine—who by this time was already providing financial support for a number of Native missions—asked the pope to send missionaries to work on reservations. In response to her request, Leo supposedly said, "Why not, my child, yourself become a missionary?" Katharine later told Sister Consuela Duffy that after Leo's response, she felt very ill and had to leave the audience. "Once outside, she sobbed and sobbed much to her sisters' dismay. She did not know, she said, what Pope Leo meant, and she was very frightened and sick."[36]

There is very little information surrounding the women's audience with Leo XIII. Biddle refers to the event as a "myth," and reports that Katharine's journals do not mention the exchange she had with the pontiff. Duffy agrees that the story cannot be corroborated but claims the "effects of this interview were too deep in Katharine's soul for recording in a letter."[37] The story, however, parallels a supposed encounter between

St. Frances Cabrini and Leo XIII that took place in 1887, shortly after Katharine's purported encounter. When Cabrini traveled to Rome to ask Pope Leo XIII for permission to send members of her newly formed religious congregation to Asia, Leo responded, "Not to the east, but to the west....Go to the United States. There you will find the means which will enable you to undertake a great field of work."[38]

Historian Kathleen Sprows Cummings has demonstrated that there is "considerable evidence that by the time Cabrini had met with Pope Leo she had already made a firm decision" to work in the United States. In fact, Cabrini herself later explained that she made her decision during a moment of private prayer. It appears, Cummings concludes, that Cabrini "had sought Leo's blessing, not his instruction." The two stories involving Pope Leo XIII and two future saints—Cabrini and Drexel—gave both women a papal source of authority for the work they planned to undertake. Whether or not the stories are true is another matter. Although the story of Katharine Drexel's meeting with Leo XIII is helpful when looking back on a person's life in order to understand why he or she chose a particular path, as well as evidence of sanctity, in the end it may or may not be accurate. What is clear is the fact that Drexel had been considering entering religious life for several years prior to her audience with the pope, and this interview, if it occurred, did not lessen her desire to serve God and the underserved.[39]

The Making of a Family Philanthropic Tradition

After the death of their father, the Drexel sisters suddenly found themselves able to assume the roles of philanthropists that their parents had modeled. Francis Drexel had willingly contributed to a number of Philadelphia Catholic institutions, but the Drexel women were now free to develop their own ideas on how their money should be spent. One of the first decisions made by the three women concerned a memorial for their father. They decided to establish the Francis A. Drexel Chair of Moral Theology at the Catholic University of America in 1888.[40] In addition to the establishment of an endowed chair, the women also continued their father's practice of assisting various Catholic churches and religious congregations in financial need. This led, for instance, to a

$30,000 donation to the Sisters of St. Francis of Philadelphia so that they could build St. Agnes Hospital.[41]

Each of the Drexel sisters tried to determine ways in which she could use her inheritance to help those in need of physical or spiritual assistance. Elizabeth, for instance, suggested building a residential school for boys with nowhere else to go; she aimed to provide housing as well as the necessary skills for them to become self-sufficient adults. To implement this idea, Elizabeth purchased property in the Eddington section of Philadelphia—about three miles from the family's summer estate—and built St. Francis de Sales Industrial School, which opened in July 1888. When Elizabeth died in 1890, Louise, with Katharine's help and support, took over as the school's chief supporter and benefactor. In addition, the sisters agreed to jointly contribute $120,000 a year for eight years to ensure that the school would remain on a firm financial footing.[42]

Shortly after her father's death, Katharine began to donate a portion of the income derived from her inheritance to Native missions, and—applying the methods and practices she had learned from her mother—began visiting reservations in order to evaluate needs and assess how contributions had been spent. In 1887, for instance, she and her sisters traveled throughout the American West to observe for themselves problems faced by Indigenous People. Their first stop was the Rosebud Reservation in what is now South Dakota. Katharine had contributed $15,000 for a building on the reservation that was to be named for Francis A. Drexel, but she and her sisters were anxious to find "additional ways to offset the enforced privations on reservations lands and encourage the spread of Catholicism."[43]

After leaving Rosebud, the women and those accompanying them—Father Joseph Stephan, director of the Bureau of Catholic Indian Missions, and Omaha Bishop James O'Connor—continued on their trip to observe Catholic missions throughout territory that had been allocated to Indigenous People. Historian Anne Butler writes that the women "evaluated and found wanting the Catholic institutions in place for Native Americans." In fact, "as the small troupe moved deeper into the hinterlands, it realized that the poverty of the Indians and the handful of missionaries worsened."[44] Katharine Drexel recognized early on that Native missions could clearly benefit from her generosity; she also realized there were many people hoping to be recipients of the sisters' largesse. As we will see in the following chapter, Katharine would have to function as a one-woman philanthropic foundation if she wanted to judiciously distribute funds to these missions and keep track of how her money was spent.

Answering a Call

Ordained a priest in 1845, James O'Connor began his ministry in Pittsburgh, where his brother, Michael O'Connor, had been named bishop. In 1862, he was appointed rector of Philadelphia's St. Charles Borromeo Seminary, a position he held for about ten years. O'Connor became acquainted with the Drexel family when he became pastor of St. Dominic Church, located near their Torresdale estate, in 1872. (He also served as chaplain of Eden Hall, which had moved from Center City to Torresdale in 1847.) He quickly became a valued friend of the family, even serving as confessor to the "Ladies on Walnut Street."[45] Although he left the parish four years later when he was appointed vicar apostolic of the Nebraska Territory, O'Connor remained in touch with the Drexels, especially Katharine. Surviving letters demonstrate that the new bishop encouraged the Drexel family's interest in missions for Indigenous People. Writing to Katharine in 1878, for instance, he described the problems he was facing related to evangelization of this marginalized group: "I cannot say that everything looks just 'lovely' out here, though I see much to encourage me. The missions [to Indigenous People] are far more numerous than I expected, harder to reach, and sadly in want of priests. To provide for them will be my chief difficulty."[46] His concern to support Native missions located within his jurisdiction perhaps led O'Connor to be especially interested in the money administered by the very wealthy Drexel women.

Katharine Drexel's relationship with O'Connor continued after he was named first bishop of Omaha, Nebraska, in 1885, and she confided in him her belief that she was being called to spend the remainder of her life as a Catholic sister or nun. Her immediate family had not been especially supportive of any of their children actualizing a religious vocation. Emma Drexel—despite her strong faith and commitment to serving the poor—did not encourage her children to enter religious life. Drexel once told O'Connor that her mother had told them, "I do hope God will not give you, my children, a religious vocation. If He does, I must submit; but I shall never permit you to enter a convent until you are at least 25 years of age."[47] Emma's reluctance to encourage religious vocations among her children may have been influenced by her own family's experience. An obituary for her sister, Mother Louise Bouvier, published by the *Baltimore Sun* reported that her parents vehemently opposed her entrance into the Society of the Sacred Heart. Despite her mother's entreaties, Mother Bouvier left her family's home in Philadelphia "and never looked back." "'It was God or my mother,' she reportedly declared. 'I loved my mother, but I loved my God better.'"[48] Emma never suggested that she would create a situation as dramatic as that described by the *Baltimore Sun*, but she certainly did not encourage her daughters to consider religious life.

Katharine and O'Connor entered into a five-year correspondence on the subject of her suitability for religious life. After her father's death in 1885, Drexel's focus on religious life intensified. In August 1885, she wrote to her spiritual advisor that she was sure God was calling her to the "convent." "But when is it prudent for me to obey the call? Next week? This Fall? This Winter? In what religious order?" She asked for O'Connor's help in answering these questions. "Please tell me, dear Father, what I should do to save my own soul, to save as many souls as possible, to devote myself and all that I have to God and to His church."[49] The bishop was not moved by her enthusiasm. O'Connor insisted for quite some time that he—as her spiritual advisor—did not believe she would make a "good" sister. In a letter to Drexel written in 1885, he told her, "The conclusion to which I have come in your case is that your vocation is not to enter a religious order." The only order he would recommend, O'Connor added, was the Society of the Sacred Heart and she did not have the "health necessary to enable you to discharge the duties that would devolve on you as a member of that society." But, O'Connor continued, God definitely had a plan for the young heiress. "He wishes you, in my opinion, to be in the world, but not of it, and to labor there for your own salvation, and the salvation of others, just as you are now doing." Drexel had the chance, O'Connor suggested, to save the rich as well as the poor; she might even influence some of her relatives (i.e., Anthony Drexel) to return to the Catholic Church. The bishop would continue to make this argument for the next several years.[50]

The correspondence between Drexel and her spiritual advisor did not solely focus on the idea of religious vocation. In addition to offering his opinion on her suitability for religious life, O'Connor often bemoaned the difficulty he was having finding sisters and priests willing or able to work with Indigenous People. He certainly recognized the importance of Drexel's financial support for Native missions, claiming in an 1887 letter that she was doing more for them "than any religious or even religious community has ever done." In the same letter he reiterated his conviction that she was not suited for religious life, telling her, "If nothing else, the state of your health is of itself sufficient to settle the matter for the present."[51]

In the same letter O'Connor proposed what he must have considered a solution to the seemingly unsolvable dilemma of Drexel's desire to enter religious life and his refusal to allow her to do so. He decided to request permission from Philadelphia Archbishop Patrick Ryan to invite the Sisters of Providence (Montreal, Canada) to open a novitiate in Philadelphia. The congregation had extensive experience ministering to Indigenous People in the West but struggled to communicate because their primary language was French. Katharine, he suggested, could fund the novitiate. This would solve several problems for the Bishop of Omaha. The novitiate would produce English-speaking sisters who would be assigned to work in his part of the country; the sisters in Philadelphia would be financially comfortable thanks to a benefactor; and Drexel would have something to occupy her time and a way to channel her religious energy. In the end, the project fizzled before it began; the Sisters of Providence were unable to spare any members of their congregation to be a part of the Philadelphia novitiate.[52]

O'Connor appeared unable to separate Drexel's desire to enter religious life from the reality that if it were not for Katharine and her sisters, Catholic missions to Indigenous People would be in a very sorry state. If Drexel were to enter a religious community, her share of the Drexel wealth would transfer to that congregation. As a mere postulant, novice, and then professed sister, she would have no say in how her money was distributed. Congregational leaders would make those decisions. O'Connor and his fellow bishops would have little say in how much of her money would be spent on Native missions, as opposed to building schools and hospitals for recent immigrants. As Anne Butler wrote, "Any life-changing decision of Katharine Drexel, the reluctant heiress, to relinquish control of her trust—either through marriage or membership in a religious community—threatened the mission enterprise in the West."[53] O'Connor was a male authority figure in a church to which the wealthy Katharine Drexel was devoted, and serving as her spiritual advisor and confidante in matters related to her vocation to religious life allowed him, in theory at least, to keep a close eye on her money. His reluctance to allow Katharine Drexel to enter religious life indicates that he was at least attempting to influence her decisions related to philanthropic projects perhaps at the expense of her vocation.

Despite O'Connor's arguments, Drexel refused to give up on her desire to enter a religious community. Although she was clear that if God called her to "remain in the world," she would do so, she continued to push back at O'Connor's objections. Noting that Louise was marrying Edward Morrell in 1889, she wrote, "You allowed Louise to take Mr. Morrell [her husband]," and

> What about *her* income to the poor!—Are you afraid to give me to Jesus Christ?...It appears to me, Reverend Father, that I am not obliged to *submit* my judgment to yours, as I have been doing for two years, for I feel so sad in doing it, because the world cannot give me peace, so restless because my heart is not rested in God.[54]

This argument worked and O'Connor relented, telling her, "This letter of yours, and your bearing under the long and severe tests to which I subjected you, as well as your entire restoration to health, and the many spiritual dangers that surround you, make me withdraw all opposition to your entering religion." In this letter, he also indicated his worry over "well-meant *plans* made by those of your own flesh and blood to *entangle* you and Lizzie [Elizabeth] in more worldly alliances."[55]

With the matter of Drexel's religious vocation settled, O'Connor turned his attention to determining what congregation she might enter. In the same letter in which he finally acquiesced, O'Connor suggested she consider "the Sacred Heart, the Sisters of Mercy, and the Ursulines of Brown County Ohio."[56] Drexel was seeking a congregation that ministered exclusively to Black and Indigenous People, allowed daily reception of the Eucharist, and was not too strict. He did not recommend a favorite of his spiritual advisee, the Sisters of St. Francis of Philadelphia. In a subsequent letter he explained that—in his rather harsh view— the Franciscans "are not ladies. There is perhaps not one of them that would have a much stronger claim to be considered such, than your maid Johanna." She should remember that "for a lady of your antecedents, position, and habits, to be able to pass her whole life in the most intimate, daily, and hourly intercourse with women of the peasant class, would require a fortitude that is vouchsafed to very few indeed."[57] In addition, if Drexel entered the Franciscan Sisters of Philadelphia, she would no longer have control of her money. Others would be involved in decisions related to how the funds would be allocated.

For her part, Drexel initially had no intention of establishing a new religious congregation. In 1889, she wrote to O'Connor and listed several reasons why she would only enter a congregation that was already in existence. First, she was attracted to the contemplative life. She did not want to be involved in issues related to administration and leadership of religious congregations but sought a life of prayer and meditation. Second, Drexel did not believe that she herself was suited for the life of a missionary. Third, it was, she reflected, more efficient to enter an order that already existed. Why should she spend a great deal of time developing a Rule and completing all of the other tasks related to a new religious community?[58] In the end, however, she told O'Connor that she would indeed found a new order "if it was God's will."[59]

O'Connor's response, despite his initial hesitation about her vocation, was now adamant: she must found a new community. He wrote that he was "never so sure of any vocation, not even my own, as I am of yours. If you do not establish the order in question, you will allow to pass an opportunity of doing immense service to the Church which may not occur again." After responding to each of her concerns, he issued what was tantamount to an order. "I regard it as settled that you are to establish a new order, and I shall go to Philadelphia merely to arrange the details. The Church has spoken to you, through me, her unworthy organ, and you must hear her or take the consequences." In this same letter, the bishop informed Drexel that she would enter the novitiate of the Sisters of Mercy in Pittsburgh. Drexel was willing to follow O'Connor's instructions and informed him that she would enter the novitiate on April 30; she also asked her spiritual advisor for a letter of introduction to the superior. Drexel made all of the necessary preparations and informed family members and friends— including Anthony Drexel—about her decision to enter religious life. After completing a novitiate with the Sisters of Mercy in Pittsburgh, where she would be formed to lead a new religious congregation, she would return to Philadelphia and begin the process of creating the Sisters of the Blessed Sacrament.[60]

Katharine Drexel's decision to enter religious life made the Philadelphia papers. The *Public Ledger* reported on her May 7 departure for Pittsburgh:

> On Monday morning, Miss Drexel attended Mass at St. John's Church in the city and chose that sacred place to take farewell of her relatives, excepting such as would accompany her and one or two very intimate friends. She was attired all in black and according to custom, knelt in front of the altar and dedicated (herself) to the Virgin Mary. The Mass over, her distant relatives, her old governess and maid and one or two faithful servants crossed from the other aisle and bade her farewell....Although evidently deeply and greatly affected, she did not shed tears and in the very severe ordeal showed remarkable fortitude.[61]

A Novice in the House of Mercy

Reporting as a novice to the Sisters of Mercy in Pittsburgh was the beginning of what would become Katharine Drexel's work for the remainder of her life. Sister Consuela Duffy, a biographer of Drexel's, claims O'Connor chose the community where Drexel would spend her years as a postulant and novice. O'Connor's brother, Michael, had translated the Mercy Rule into Latin during the early years of the congregation, and later brought the first sisters from Ireland to Pittsburgh to begin their work of ministering to the city's Catholics. Both brothers "had a high opinion of [the Sisters of Mercy's] spirituality and capabilities."[62]

Although the purpose of Drexel's novitiate was to be "formed" as a woman religious, she was not expected to adhere to all the rules of governing the eighteen-year-old novices with whom she entered. Religious life at the end of the nineteenth century, including the novitiate, involved a regimented lifestyle designed to keep one removed from the world. Novices were rarely allowed to receive visitors—except on special occasions or feast days—and almost never left the convent grounds except for reasons related to medical issues. Drexel, however, experienced a novitiate that was designed especially for her. She did not have to surrender control of her money and she was able to remain involved with the Indigenous missions she was funding. In addition, Drexel continued to consider requests for funding churches and schools devoted to Indigenous People, and sometimes even left the convent if a business matter required that she appear in person. In short, Drexel's novitiate involved more than prayer, spiritual reading, and training in self-discipline. She also "received intense instruction from the Sisters of Mercy in convent administration and spiritual oversight of nuns—not among the usual lessons for postulants and novices."[63]

James O'Connor died in 1890 while Drexel was still in the novitiate, and Philadelphia Archbishop Patrick Ryan took on the role of spiritual advisor and began providing input on financial decisions. Ryan was determined that the Sisters of the Blessed Sacrament for Indians and Colored People, the name chosen by Drexel and O'Connor for the new congregation, would be based in Philadelphia. Drexel acquiesced despite the entreaties of those who hoped she would settle in the West and moved her small nascent community into temporary quarters in what had been the family's summer home in Torresdale. One of Drexel's first tasks involved purchasing property in Bensalem—just outside of Philadelphia—where she could build a proper motherhouse for herself and the sisters who would join her in this work.

Louise married Edward Morrell in 1889, shortly before Drexel left for Pittsburgh, and in 1890, Elizabeth married George Smith, but Drexel remained in close contact with her biological sisters during her time in the novitiate. Both Louise and Elizabeth supported their sister's decision to spend the remainder of her life as a woman religious. Shortly after Katharine left for Pittsburgh, Elizabeth wrote to a friend, "Let me assure you that on Kate's account we feel nothing but tranquility and contentment. She went to the Convent with the ardor and joy of one, who at length after long delay, finds the desire, *nay* longing of years satisfied." If Katharine decided religious life was not for her, Elizabeth continued, the family would welcome her back.[64] When Elizabeth died in childbirth in September 1890, Drexel was able to leave the novitiate in order to attend her funeral. (Louise and Edward Morrell were on their way home from Europe and did not arrive in time.) Sister Mary Dolores Letterhouse described the impact of Elizabeth's death "as a calling of deep unto deep which only silence can eloquently express." Katharine Drexel chose to name the new motherhouse St. Elizabeth in honor of her sister, and Louise and Katharine committed to supporting St. Francis in Eddington, which their sister had founded. Elizabeth Drexel Smith's death meant that Katharine and Louise Drexel Morrell now controlled the fortune left by Francis A. Drexel.[65]

Mother Katharine Drexel, as she would be known for the rest of her life, took vows as a Sister of the Blessed Sacrament for Indians and Colored People in February 1891. She chose to identify the congregation with the Blessed Sacrament because of her devotion to the body and blood of Christ in the Eucharist. The second part of the name distinguished the congregation from an already existing community with the same title and also made clear that the women would work exclusively with Black and Indigenous People.[66] Along with Sister Mary Inez, a Mercy sister who would temporarily serve as novice director for the new community, Drexel left Pittsburgh to begin forming her new congregation and was soon joined by thirteen women interested in her vision. By choosing to enter the Sisters of the Blessed Sacrament, these thirteen women "bonded with the most powerful, and certainly the richest, woman in the American Catholic Church." Despite her wealth, Drexel needed these women if she were going to realize her plan to educate and catechize people belonging to two groups systemically marginalized by white America. As Anne Butler explained, Drexel was no idealist; she "concentrated on practical plans, devising a Catholic agenda for women reformers." She did not develop theories on systemic poverty or racism; rather she founded and funded institutions designed to improve the lives of those who had been pushed aside by those in positions of power. A woman of privilege, she would spend much of the remainder of her life focused on ways in which to distribute her great fortune to those she believed were most in need.[67]

Chapter Two

THE RICHEST NUN IN AMERICA

*M*other Katharine Drexel had been financially supporting St. Stephen's mission in Wyoming since 1885, about one year after it was founded to serve the Arapaho and Shoshone tribes. Despite her help, St. Stephen's had struggled to survive almost since its inception. Founded by Jesuit Father John Jutz and Brother Ursus Nunlitz in 1884, the mission had come under the authority of the Missouri Province of the Society of Jesus in 1886. The following year, Drexel built a school for the mission staffed by the Sisters of Charity of Leavenworth (Kansas). In 1888, F. X. Kuppens, SJ, arrived to take charge of the mission, but departed a year later, leaving St. Stephen's in debt. When the school ceased to operate in 1890, the Sisters of Charity returned to Kansas. The Sisters of St. Joseph briefly replaced them, but Drexel could not find a congregation willing to assume permanent responsibility for the school. Was it possible, she wondered, to send Sisters of the Blessed Sacrament to St. Stephen's? Shortly after her profession as a Sister of the Blessed Sacrament in 1891, Drexel asked Archbishop Patrick Ryan's permission to visit St. Stephen's herself and assess the situation.[1]

Accompanied by Sister Patrick and Cheyenne Bishop Maurice Burke, Drexel found that the school building was in good shape and fully furnished; the Sisters of the Blessed Sacrament could certainly start teaching at St. Stephen's at the beginning of the 1892–93 school year. Before heading back east, she promised parents that St. Stephen's would indeed reopen. Drexel was so sure that the SBS would be teaching at St. Stephen's that on the way home, she stopped in Chicago to order supplies the sisters and children would need for the upcoming academic year.

While Drexel was visiting St. Stephen's, Mother Sebastian, superior of the Sisters of Mercy in Pittsburgh, visited the community's temporary novitiate and motherhouse in Philadelphia. Unconvinced that members of the new congregation were ready to be sent to missions as far away as Wyoming, Mother Sebastian expressed her concerns to Ryan, who agreed with her argument. When Drexel and her companion stopped briefly in Pittsburgh on their way home, Mother Sebastian informed her that no Sisters of the Blessed Sacrament would be working at St. Stephen's anytime soon; both she and the archbishop believed the sisters needed more formation and training before they would be ready to leave the motherhouse. Drexel protested, noting that Ryan had implicitly approved of her idea by allowing her to travel to Wyoming to see if it was an appropriate place to mission sisters. When she returned to Philadelphia, however, she discovered that Mother Sebastian was correct; Ryan had no intention of allowing the SBS to staff a mission in Wyoming at that time.[2]

St. Stephen's did open because the Sisters of St. Francis of Philadelphia agreed to send sisters to staff the school for the 1892–93 academic year. Their Foundation Book notes, "With the consent of the proper Ordinary…and at the request of Mother Katharine Drexel, this Mission was accepted." Getting to St. Stephen's was not easy. Leaving Philadelphia on August 11, 1892, the sisters arrived in Wyoming three days later. After staying overnight in Rawlins, four sisters left by stage for Lander the following morning; the other two followed them the next day. From Lander, it was 175 miles to St. Stephen's. By September, the children had arrived, and St. Stephen's School was once again operating.[3]

This story has been told by Drexel biographers as a way of demonstrating her enthusiasm for the work to which her congregation was committed and her willingness to embrace the religious vow of obedience and follow the commands of those in authority. Sister Consuela Duffy, SBS, places the story within the context of Drexel's deep concern for Indigenous People. "All the pent-up zeal of her soul," Duffy writes, "all the impelling desires of her generous charity to help the American Indian longed for this opportunity dawning, she thought, for her young community." When she heard the news from Ryan himself, Duffy explains, "It was not easy for her to see her first missionary plan halted like this, but she accepted it as the will of God."[4] Writing over thirty years after Duffy's biography was published, Lou Baldwin framed the story of Drexel's meeting with Ryan around the idea of "obedience of the judgment"; she would submit to the will of the archbishop "no matter what his decision." Both Duffy and Baldwin are quick to point out that Drexel came to realize that Ryan's decision was correct. Drawing from the congregational annals, Duffy quotes Drexel: "Oh how audacious I was in those days [the years immediately following the congregation's founding]. Almighty God was certainly good to save us from such a mistake. I see now what a wild scheme it was. It would have been the ruination of our little Congregation."[5]

This story, however, also demonstrates the two parts of Drexel's work with Native and Black communities. On the one hand, she was an extremely wealthy woman dedicated to distributing her inheritance to working with people she believed most needed her support. In her position as a well-respected philanthropist, Drexel wielded a good deal of power. Acting as essentially a one-woman foundation, she decided who received funds, how much the recipient would receive, and how the money would be spent. She could demand to view architectural plans, ask for changes to the proposed church or school, and require that the money be returned if certain conditions were not met.

At the same time, she was the founder and superior general of a new religious community. Although her position as congregational leader certainly gave her the ability to set rules and regulations governing the Sisters of the Blessed Sacrament, she was not the final authority. That role belonged to the archbishop of Philadelphia and—to a lesser extent—the bishops of the dioceses in which the SBS worked. The story of St. Stephen's Mission and School is one example of an episode in which both strands of Drexel's work converge. She could decide to fund the mission and its school, and she could determine that a congregation needed to be convinced to staff the school. In the end, however, she was not allowed to send members of her own congregation to St. Stephen's. Women religious were expected to defer to the authority of clerical leaders and Katharine Drexel was no exception to this rule. It is this telling paradox of intent, power, authority, and obedience that will be explored in this chapter.

Sisters of the Blessed Sacrament for Indians and Colored People

When newly professed Mother Katharine Drexel arrived back in Philadelphia in 1891, she assumed the role of mother superior of the Sisters of the Blessed Sacrament for Indians and Colored People.[6] She did not arrive alone; the congregation's newest postulant, Katherine O'Connor—later Mother Mercedes—accompanied her. On May 20, Mother Inez, RSM—who was to serve temporarily as the mistress of novices—arrived with six SBS novices and Agnes Gillen, the first woman to become a postulant under Drexel's direction. Five days later, six additional novices and postulants joined the group, which meant the new community numbered sixteen, although Drexel was the only one who had taken vows. Ida Mae Coffey, the first child to be placed under the care of the Sisters of the Blessed Sacrament, completed the group. Mother Katharine, as she was now known, immediately began work as both the leader of a new religious congregation and the wealthiest female philanthropist in the United States. She was the richest nun in America.[7]

Of the first twenty-two women to enter the Sisters of the Blessed Sacrament, nineteen "persevered" or completed their time in formation, which took place in two phases known as the postulancy and novitiate. The median age for these early members of the congregation was twenty-two, and the majority of them were from Pennsylvania. Most of the women had at least an elementary school education; some had finished high school; at least one had completed some college courses. None of the women had any experience living among or working with Indigenous People, but some believed they were called to work with this population. Sister Mary Frances, who entered the SBS in 1905 (about fifteen years after the original group), remembered that she "had had a great love for the Indians" since childhood. "When she became certain that God was calling her to the religious life, she wanted to enter an order which worked among the Indians full time and not part time as the Ursulines did in a few schools." Others who entered the congregation during its early years had taught Sunday School at St. Peter Claver, a Black Catholic parish in Philadelphia (see chapter 3). Although the new sisters' living conditions were less than ideal and they were prohibited from beginning work at St. Stephen's in Wyoming, they eventually were able to move into St. Elizabeth's, which would be the permanent motherhouse, and begin work among Black and Indigenous People.[8]

As mother superior—and later superior general—Drexel joined a number of women, including Elizabeth Ann Bayley Seton, Frances Cabrini, Cornelia Connelly, and Rose Hawthorne Lathrop, who found themselves governing a community at the same time they were learning how to live and act as a woman religious. Drexel soon discovered that there were always a number of practical items that needed almost immediate attention. The first major issue she resolved concerned the location of a motherhouse for the community. When they first arrived in Philadelphia, Drexel and the sisters lived at St. Michel—her family's former summer estate—and used the building as a temporary novitiate until a new motherhouse in Bensalem was completed. Plans called for a school for Black children to be located on the grounds (see chapter 3), and some of the area's residents objected to Black children living and attending school in their neighborhood. On July 16, the day the cornerstone of the building was laid, rumors circulated that "critics intended to disrupt the scheduled events, and perhaps even blow up the grandstand." Fortunately, the day passed without incident, and Ryan was able to preside over the ceremony in which the sisters received the distinctive habit of the SBS, and to bless the cornerstone of the new motherhouse.[9]

Developing a Rule (or Constitutions) for the SBS consumed a good deal of Drexel's time during the early years. A congregation's rule governs every aspect of a religious community's life, including regulations and procedures related to governance, prayer and spiritual life, and mission. Because she had completed her novitiate under the Sisters of Mercy, Drexel and her sisters originally followed the rule of that community. After examining examples of rules from many congregations she decided that the one used by the Sisters of Mercy was still the most appropriate because "its combination of the spiritual and corporal works of mercy and deep interior prayer was best suited for the Sisters of the Blessed Sacrament."[10] The rule she chose had to be adapted to reflect the fact that the new congregation was a missionary community, and when that task was completed Drexel could begin the process of seeking approval of the Sisters of the Blessed Sacrament from Rome.

Before finalizing and seeking approval of the rule, the community had to secure a *decretum laudis*, or decree of praise from the pope, which would recognize the existence of the Sisters of the Blessed Sacrament and validate the "noble work" they were doing. When the *decretum laudis* was received in 1897, work on the rule could finally begin. Lou Baldwin describes the process of preparing a congregation's rule for approval as a "slow, painstaking process," and this was clearly the case in this instance because the SBS rule was not ready to send to Rome until 1905.[11]

Previous Drexel biographers indicate that she did not envision that there would be any problem in having the Rule and Constitutions approved by Propaganda Fide's Commission to Review the Rules of Religious Institutes. When Ryan congratulated the community on receiving the *decretum laudis*, he noted that Leo XIII had "proclaimed the Institute to be God's work for His most neglected children, and that all that remained to be done was to have the Rule translated…and sent to Rome."[12] The process was, of course, more complicated than Ryan implied. The Rule and Constitutions were drafted, edited, and revised multiple times before they were ready to be sent to Rome for approval. After review, the commission praised the Sisters of the Blessed Sacrament, but did not approve the Rule because "it did not conform to the Normae, the established norms for such congregations."[13] The Rule of the Sisters of Mercy that Drexel used as a model and guide had predated the current norms approved by Propaganda Fide and the SBS Rule and Constitutions would have to be revised in order to receive the Commission's approval.

Drexel and the members of her community were frustrated by this series of events and were unsure how to proceed. When Mother Frances Cabrini unexpectedly visited Drexel in May 1907, Drexel received some sage advice. Cabrini apparently stopped at the motherhouse to thank Drexel and the SBS for the hospitality they had shown to Mother M. St. Ignatius, who had been sent to Philadelphia to ask Ryan for permission to solicit money from the city's Italian population. While the two congregational leaders were conversing, Drexel took the opportunity to ask Cabrini for advice about seeking approval for the SBS Rule and Constitutions. Cabrini, who understood the way the Vatican worked, explained that mailing the documents to Propaganda Fide did not guarantee that anyone would look at or bring them to the attention of the appropriate Vatican bureaucrats. She reportedly told Drexel, "If you want to get your Holy Rule approved, take it there yourself and bring it back with you—approved."[14] Even though Drexel was not at all sure that Ryan would sanction such a trip, Cabrini advised her to ask the archbishop for permission. When Ryan voiced his approval, Drexel made plans to follow Cabrini's advice. She left for Rome on May 11, 1907, and the Rule was approved on July 9. In November of that year, the Sisters of the Blessed Sacrament were able to hold their first "official" General Chapter, and Drexel was elected superior general.

Drexel herself took her vow of poverty very seriously and stories about her refusal to spend money on herself are found throughout the congregational annals. Mother Mary Mercedes recounted one such narrative in a letter sent to SBS convents in 1915. While on a trip to visit a number of congregational missions, the two sisters were approached by a young man who offered them his private drawing room on the train so they would not have to spend the night sitting up in one of the cars. When Drexel declined because of the sisters' vow of poverty, he approached Mother Mercedes and asked her to convince her superior; he had two aunts that were nuns, he explained, and he knew the sisters would prefer to be out of the public eye if possible. After a long argument Drexel finally acquiesced, but informed Mother Mercedes she would never have agreed if they were younger and more attractive. She did not want, she explained, to put the sisters at any risk. The young man, who was employed by Standard Oil, arranged for the sisters to remain in a private drawing room until they arrived at their destination the following evening.[15]

Drexel took a personal interest in the ways in which the SBS interacted with each other as a community and did not hesitate to speak out when she wanted to discontinue or change a part of daily life. In 1916, for instance, she informed the congregation that the festivities surrounding St. Patrick's Day would be significantly scaled back. "We are an American institution," she reportedly said, "and we accept, most gladly, persons of French, German, Spanish, Polish, or any other nationality into our ranks. Therefore, it is not fitting that we should emphasize one State more than another, except in a spiritual way." Black was noticeably absent from the list.[16]

In addition to governing the congregation and interpreting the Rule, Drexel developed a plan to recruit women who felt called to devote their lives to ministering among Black and Indigenous People. By the time the SBS had moved into their motherhouse in Bensalem, forty-one young women had entered the congregation; twenty-two "persevered," which means they had remained faithful to their vocation throughout postulancy and the novitiate. If the SBS were to be educators, however, Drexel needed a steady stream of postulants, the first step toward becoming a vowed religious.[17] Bishops and priests constantly asked for SBS to work in schools within their parishes and dioceses, and there were simply not enough sisters to go around. Most young American women interested in religious life had attended either an elementary or secondary school where they came into contact with sisters from one or more established congregations. The sisters teaching in Catholic schools willingly answered questions, and in many cases, provided a model for interested young women to emulate. The Sisters of the Blessed Sacrament, however, did not teach in large parochial high schools; their elementary schools were located on reservations or designated specifically for Black children. As a result, they did not have a critical pipeline of women interested joining the congregation after graduating from high school. Drexel was not averse to recruiting among U.S. Catholic women, but in order to do so she needed the permission of the local bishop and that was not always forthcoming. In 1932, for instance, Albany Bishop Edmund F. Gibbons informed her that he was "obliged to report unfavorably" concerning her request to appeal for vocations to her congregation. "The local communities of Sisters are not able to secure vocations enough for our own needs," Gibbons explained. "At present there seems to be little inclination on the part of our young women to give themselves to religious life, especially such a missionary life as would be open to them in the institutions and schools cared for by your Order."[18]

One method used to increase the number of women entering the Sisters of the Blessed Sacrament was to recruit young women from Ireland interested in religious life. In 1913, the congregational annalist reported that two Irish postulants arrived at the motherhouse in September. When the Irish Provincial of the Holy Ghost Fathers, Rev. John Murphy, replied to the letter informing him of their safe arrival, he also asked the sisters to "tell Reverend Mother [Katharine] and Mother M. Mercedes that all the children there [in Kilkenny] are still enthusiastic about Mother's visit and I trust there will be tangible results in the course of time."[19]

Bringing young Irish women to the United States required the SBS to work with consulates and immigration personnel on a regular basis. In 1931, Sister Francis Xavier laid out the process by which the potential sisters would enter the United States in a letter to Drexel. Each young woman had to secure a copy of her birth certificate, six photos, and a letter from a member of the clergy attesting to her character. This material, along with a letter of consent from her parents, was taken to a "civic guard," and then to the Immigration Office in Dublin. When all of this was processed and approved, a passport was issued. The young woman then had to appear at the Consulate and answer a series of questions related to literacy and health. Despite the bureaucratic complexities involved in bringing Irish women to the United States, Sister Francis Xavier was optimistic. She expected to accompany twenty postulants to the United States if all went well at the consulate. The remainder of the letter is devoted to a description of several of the more promising candidates, one of whom was described by the Irish sisters as "all brains."[20]

Recruiting Irish women for the SBS was not an inexpensive proposition. At the same time that Sister Francis Xavier was enthusiastically describing the newest group of postulants, Mother Mercedes was informing Drexel that the consul at Dublin required a letter from Drexel and Company (the bankers for the congregation) testifying to the fact that the community was able to support the postulants, as well as a letter signed by Mother Katharine "bearing the corporate seal," and stating that she was able to act on behalf of the corporation and could sign any required documents.[21] In addition, the SBS agreed to educate the young women for a maximum of eight years in schools approved by the Department of Labor in Ireland.[22]

Most SBS—those born in the United States and those who grew up in other countries—did not come from wealthy families. An example of this is Katy Kiniry, who was given the name Sister Paul of the Cross. Kiniry, born in Sewickley, Pennsylvania, was the daughter of Irish immigrants, and worked as a seamstress before entering the Sisters of the Blessed Sacrament. "We are poor," she wrote in her letter seeking admittance to the community, "and I am obliged to sew for a living at $4.50 per week." Although she was sure she had a vocation to the SBS, Sister Paul was required to answer the questions that were asked of all candidates: Did she "object to tending and washing Indian and Colored Children?" and "Did she object to nursing these same children when they were sick 'even with contagious diseases'?" Drexel believed these questions were necessary because she needed her sisters to understand the work that would occupy them for the remainder of their lives.[23] If the congregation were to be successful, Drexel had to do her best to help her sisters understand what the work of the SBS entailed.

A Saint for Philanthropists

In addition to leading a new religious congregation, Katharine Drexel and Louise Morrell were able to distribute money to various charities as a result of the wealth they inherited from their father. Katharine Drexel took her role in the philanthropic process quite seriously and kept very careful account of any funds distributed. In addition to funding the work of the SBS among Black and Indigenous People, she also provided monetary assistance for schools and missions administered by other religious congregations, including the Jesuits and Franciscan priests and sisters. A 1904 document serves as an example of how she precisely recorded the donations made to Native missions in a specific time period. In that year, she funded schools and missions in twelve states, including St. Boniface Industrial School (California, $4737), Chippewa Boarding School (Michigan, $3620), and St. George's School (Washington, $4320). She also paid the salaries of several priests; one who served the pueblos in New Mexico received $800.[24]

Many of Drexel's financial contributions were funneled to the recipients through the Bureau of Catholic Indian Missions (BCIM). Although it is impossible to document fully the number of projects she funded (by 1907, according to one estimate, the Drexel sisters' donations to Indigenous ministries totaled not less than $1.5 million), she completely or partially funded churches, schools, convents and rectories; covered expenses related to the operating of the BCIM, and even purchased a house in Washington, DC, where the Bureau was located, and assigned three SBS to handle administrative and secretarial tasks. "For many years the Bureau owed its existence to the talents and treasure of the Sisters of the Blessed Sacrament."[25]

Although Drexel continued to fund schools and missions after founding the Sisters of the Blessed Sacrament, she made it clear that the money was no longer entirely hers to give away. Writing to the BCIM's Msgr. William Ketcham in 1911, she informed him that he had apparently misunderstood what she said about paying for some work that needed to be done. Drexel could no longer personally promise that a request for money would be approved; she had to present the proposal to her councilors. If she alone decided how the money would be spent, it would be—in her mind—a violation of her vow of poverty. The councilors, however, had approved the request and the money would be forthcoming.[26]

Drexel's philanthropy extended to other congregations of women religious. One congregation, the Mission Helpers of the Sacred Heart, was founded in 1890 to minister to the Black population in Baltimore; they expanded their work to include people of all races and nationalities in 1895. The SBS occasionally recommended students to the Mission Helper school in Baltimore, and the congregation received financial support from Drexel and Louise Morrell. In one instance, Drexel informed the superior that a student attending St. Francis de Sales School in Rock Castle, Virginia, was pregnant. The sisters removed her from school and took her to Philadelphia where she was placed in a "Maternity Hospital." The baby, now a month old, was in a foundling hospital. Would it be possible, Drexel asked, for the young women to be admitted to the Mission Helpers' Industrial School?[27]

Anyone accepting money from Mother Katharine and the Sisters of the Blessed Sacrament had to agree to the terms and conditions under which the funds were granted. She always stipulated that the money was to be spent on work devoted to either Black or Indigenous People; those who were unable to make this promise did not receive the requested funds. Anyone unhappy with the terms under which the money was offered found there was little room for negotiation. Shortly after being appointed archbishop of New Orleans in 1881, Francis Janssens expressed his concern over the number of Black congregants leaving the Catholic Church in Louisiana. The solution, he believed, was the establishment of several schools and a church designated exclusively for Black Catholics. The city's Black parishioners vigorously objected to Janssens's plan, believing it had more to do with enforced segregation than evangelization. As a result of their objections, Janssens moved the location of the proposed church from the Creole section of the city to a neighborhood populated by Black Americans and—despite the fact that he had already asked the Assumptionists—requested that the Congregation of Mission, or Vincentians, administer the new parish. The terms he gave the Vincentians were rather simple: (1) Black Catholics did not have to join this congregation (they could continue to attend white churches); (2) the Vincentians had jurisdiction over all of the city's Black Catholics; and (3) whites could have their confession heard at the new church but could not rent pews.[28]

The Vincentians turned to Mother Katharine Drexel when they began to raise money to renovate the proposed building designated for the new church, but she had some questions before committing any money. Drexel asked for an estimate for the cost of repairing and renovating the church. When told the cost would be $5675, Drexel was also assured that it would be the most beautiful church in the city and would surely attract Black Catholics. She originally offered only $2000 for the renovation costs but increased her offer to $5000 after Archbishop Ryan assured her of the project's importance. The money, however, was contingent on the Vincentians agreeing that "in the event of said church being abandoned for Colored purposes, the five thousand now given by us [Drexel and the Sisters of the Blessed Sacrament] shall revert to other Colored works in the diocese of New Orleans."[29] This was a standard clause found in many agreements in which Drexel agreed to fund a particular project and was meant to ensure that the money would actually benefit the people she hoped to help. After a series of negotiations that involved Janssens and the Vincentian provincial, the contract was amended to state that in the event that the parish failed and the property was sold for more than the purchase price, the Vincentians agreed to "pay over to the diocese an amount equal to the increased value of the property." Drexel finally agreed to the terms but stipulated that if the parish failed because of lack of interest or effort on the part of the Vincentians, the money would go to support other diocesan efforts to evangelize the city's Black residents. St. Katharine's Church was finally dedicated in 1895.[30] Despite the best intentions of Katharine Drexel, who wanted to use her money for the education and evangelization of the Black community, the church was segregated in the sense that Black New Orleanians were soon prohibited from attending churches designated for whites across the city.

In addition to the stipulation that any money she contributed was to be used for Black and Indigenous People, Drexel's financial support came with other conditions. She demanded what Amanda Bresie has called "painstaking record keeping practices in a church setting that was not always comfortable with a woman dictating the terms of business." It was not unusual for her to question reports, and letters to the BCIM frequently began with a rebuke, such as "according to my calculations there is a slight discrepancy" in a particular list of expenditures. In addition, Drexel expected to be notified about the progress (or lack thereof) of any building with which she was involved, and logged thousands of miles visiting missions to ensure that her money was being spent according to her agreement with the recipients. Bresie notes that people were happy to receive Drexel's money, but they were not always happy with the micromanaging that went along with it. Male clerical leaders could not have been happy to find themselves at the mercy of a woman religious for money they desperately needed.[31]

Bishops of dioceses that contained large populations of Black and Indigenous People continually bemoaned the fact that there were not enough women religious to staff all of the schools that were needed. Katharine Drexel's vast fortune could seldom solve the problem of personnel; but there were times when her relationship with the Sisters of St. Francis of Philadelphia allowed her to ensure that a particular school had enough teachers to open its doors. Founded in Philadelphia in 1855, the Franciscan sisters in Philadelphia had benefitted from the Drexel family's philanthropy throughout the congregation's history; it had even been one of the charities named in Francis Drexel's will. The sisters' philanthropic relationship with Katharine Drexel began as early as 1885, when she visited the community's motherhouse along with Father Joseph Stephan, director of the Bureau of Catholic Indian Missions, and learned that they were planning to build a novitiate. Two years later, when the plans for the novitiate were ready to be implemented, the Drexel sisters donated $30,000 on the condition that the Franciscans agreed to staff ten Native schools. The Philadelphia Franciscans began to honor their commitment to Mother Katharine almost immediately. In 1887, the same year that the Drexel sisters agreed to fund the new novitiate, the congregation sent four sisters to staff St. Louis Industrial School in Oklahoma. Funded by Drexel at the behest of Stephan, the school was intended to provide an education for children of the Osage tribe. In 1915, the Franciscans turned the school over to the Sisters of Loretto.[32]

Race and the Sisters of the Blessed Sacrament

Issues related to race and racism run throughout the history of Katharine Drexel and the Sisters of the Blessed Sacrament. Although Drexel founded a congregation to work with Black and Indigenous People, she also made a very conscious and troubling decision to prohibit Black women from entering the community. The place of race in the biography of Drexel and the history of the SBS will be discussed in several places throughout this book, but it is appropriate to begin the discussion with an account of Georgiana Burton.

The 1892–93 congregational annals detail the account of Georgiana Burton, "a Seneca Indian." A convert who believed she was called to religious life, Burton had applied to join a community of Indigenous women organized by Father Francis Craft but needed a safe place to stay until she received word of her acceptance. While Burton was staying with the SBS, she learned that Kraft's congregation had disbanded. According to the annalist, "The question was then taken up as to whether or not Miss Burton would be admitted as a member of our Community. A vote was passed by the members of the Community, and the majority was in favor of Miss Burton as a House Sister."[33] Sister Mary Elizabeth (the name given to her when she was professed) ministered at St. Francis de Sales school in Rock Castle, Virginia, until her death in 1909.

The next paragraph in the annals, however, sets a decidedly different tone. At the same time that a decision was made to accept Georgiana Burton into the Sisters of the Blessed Sacrament, two Black sisters from Savannah arrived at the motherhouse. Mathilda Beasley, a widow who had spent some time preparing to enter a religious congregation in England before returning to Savannah to form her own community known as the Sisters of the Third Order of St. Francis, was struggling financially to support the nascent congregation and its orphanage. Her worries over being able to provide for either the sisters or the orphans for whom they were caring led Beasley to attempt to "forge coalitions with white sisters laboring in the African American community."[34] Bishop Thomas Becker, who had arrived in Savannah in 1886, encouraged Beasley to approach Mother Katharine and ask for any help she could provide. Becker had already written to Drexel urging her to accept the women into the SBS in some way because he was worried that the new community might fail to prosper. "Why not try to have a sisterhood here which might envelop Sister Matilda [sic] and her poor assistants in some lowly grade and utilize them," he suggested. "This, or something similar might ward off the obloquy [public criticism] which is charged against the church that she either does nothing for the colored folks or does it in a very slovenly manner." Becker hoped that the women could at least make their novitiate with the SBS and that others would then follow them into the community. "Mathilda has two Black women as helpers and quasi-sisters to attend some thirty girls ranging from two to fifteen," he wrote. "If she had good sisters from the north whose heart would be in this work, in a few, a very few years, many Southern girls would join them."[35]

Perhaps because a member of the hierarchy had asked Drexel to accept Beasley and her sisters into the congregation, albeit on a lower level, "some consideration" was given to this idea, but despite the fact that the annals describe Beasley as "a very saintly Colored woman," congregational leaders "decided that such an action would be the death blow to the Sisters of the Blessed Sacrament as it now existed." Several reasons were given for refusing the request. First, the "strong racial feeling" among white Americans concerning Black and Indigenous People— in other words, racism—would make it difficult for the congregation to raise money and attract potential sisters. Second, "social prejudice would make it impossible to get recruits among white people"—white sisters might be willing to work among Black and Indigenous People, but "they would be unwilling to live in the close contact engendered by community life." Third, it was necessary to consider the "innate sensitiveness of both the Indians and Colored." If a Native or Black sister was reprimanded, for instance, she might decide it was based on race rather than her actions. This "would be most unjust to the Superior, who would see in the subject neither color nor class, but simply a soul dedicated to Christ's service." Finally, Drexel and members of the Council worried that if the SBS were to accept Black and Native women, it might impact the two "large and flourishing communities for Colored Sisters," the Oblate Sisters of Providence and the Sisters of the Holy Family.[36] Following this meeting, nonwhite women were prohibited from entering the Sisters of the Blessed Sacrament, a prohibition that persisted until the 1950s.

Although the SBS declined to work with Mother Mathilda Beasley and her fledgling congregation, Drexel did donate $4000 to support her work. Her financial support, however, was not enough to put the proposed congregation on a firm footing. Not only were her "efforts toward equitable sisterhood" unsuccessful, Shannen Dee Williams concludes, "[but the issue] precipitated the formal exclusion of women of color from the Sisters of the Blessed Sacrament for Indians and Colored People." Despite the decision to prevent Beasley and other Black sisters from affiliating with the Sisters of the Blessed Sacrament, the congregation reacted differently when the Franciscan Handmaids of Mary, a new Black religious community, were seeking a way to form their mistress of novices. Sister Dorothy spent time with the SBS at the motherhouse "learning" how to form and train novices for the Handmaids of Mary.[37] It would not be until 1952 that Sister Juliana Haynes would be the first Black woman to enter the Sisters of the Blessed Sacrament.

An official history of the congregation written by Patricia Lynch, SBS, offers a somewhat different account of the community's decision to admit only white women. In *Sharing the Bread of Service: Sisters of the Blessed Sacrament 1891–1991*, Lynch discusses the decision in light of Mother Mary of the Visitation's tenure as superior general and her decision to admit women of color to the congregation in 1950. The admittance of two Black women—both graduates of Xavier University in New Orleans—to the novitiate is described by Lynch as a "significant change." Citing a statement by Sister Consuela Duffy, Lynch claims that Mother Mary of the Visitation had been with Drexel when congregational leaders of the Holy Family Sisters in New Orleans asked her not to accept "young Negro applicants as the Holy Family Superior believed it would hurt the Negro congregations." Lynch simply states that by 1950 this was no longer considered an issue, and "the SBS have accepted such applicants ever since."[38] Lynch does not refer to the congregational annals in her discussion of the community's discrimination against candidates of color.

It appears that Beasley—and Becker—approached Drexel and the Sisters of the Blessed Sacrament because the congregation was firmly committed to missionary work among Black and Indigenous People. Anyone working with these two marginalized groups, they reasoned, should be open to expanding their membership in such a way that would support inclusivity. Drexel and her congregation, however, chose to neither challenge the prevailing norms regarding race in the late-nineteenth-century United States nor create what might have been a model of religious life that was truly inclusive and welcomed all women regardless of color. Following the decision of the SBS, Mother Mathilda and her sisters worked with the Missionary Franciscan Sisters of the Immaculate Conception until Beasley's death in 1903.[39]

The above story makes it clear that the Sisters of the Blessed Sacrament were not willing to challenge the status quo of late nineteenth-century America. Drexel did, however, believe that Black women should be encouraged to enter religious life. When Josephite superior John Slattery, SSJ, learned that several young women were leaving Holy Providence, a school located on the grounds of the motherhouse, to join the Sisters of the Holy Family in New Orleans, he suggested that although Black women should not join the SBS, they could be affiliated with the congregation as "Aids." The "Aids" would be sort of a "pious Society called by some colorless title." Instead of taking any sort of permanent vows, these young women would make annual promises of poverty, chastity, and obedience, and would wear uniforms rather than habits. If they wore habits, Slattery suggested, "some busybody might put it into their heads that they were Religious, and thereupon trouble might ensue."[40]

Drexel vehemently disagreed with Slattery's view and contended that Black women with a vocation should certainly enter religious life. Responding to Slattery's idea, Drexel informed him that she believed the young women should make vows. "Why should they not be religious?" she wrote,

> As I understand, they are sent to do the work of the religious without the graces of the protection of the religious. It is too much work and too exposing a work without the spiritual merit and protection the religious life affords. If it be possible—as seems to be the case—that the Colored girl may live in religion, why should she not do so, and enjoy its advantages?[41]

Drexel financially assisted the Oblate Sisters of Providence and the Sisters of the Holy Family as they struggled to complete their undergraduate degrees. The congregational annals of 1924, for instance, report that the Oblate Sisters of Providence were unable to gain admittance to Summer Schools for sisters hosted at various Catholic colleges and universities "simply because discrimination was exercised on account of their Color." When Father Francis Driscoll, OSA, president of Villanova University, agreed to admit qualified members of the congregation, two sisters attended, but the following year four Oblates enrolled in the summer school. In addition, Xavier University of Louisiana (see chapter 6), founded by Katharine Drexel and the SBS, was committed to supporting the educational goals of the Sisters of the Holy Family. Each year, two members of the congregation received a scholarship to complete their undergraduate degrees at the university.[42]

Immaculate Mother Academy, Nashville

By the dawn of the twentieth century, it was clear that Mother Katharine Drexel was holding down two jobs simultaneously. One job involved governing the Sisters of the Blessed Sacrament for Indians and Colored People, which not only meant developing rules and regulations designed to ensure that the congregation lived and prayed in accordance with church directives related to women religious, but also included other administrative duties such as making sure that each SBS ministry was appropriately staffed. Her second job was that of philanthropist; bishops and leaders of religious congregations did not hesitate to ask Drexel for money to fund projects relating to Native and Black ministries, and she had to decide which requests merited a donation. It can sometimes be difficult to separate these two roles when discussing Drexel, because there are instances when a school that she had agreed to help build was also staffed by members of the congregation. This, of course, often complicated negotiations between Drexel and the bishop or congregational leader. The story of the 1904 founding of Immaculate Mother Academy in Nashville is an excellent example of this situation.

When Thomas S. Byrne was named bishop of Nashville in 1894, he quickly concluded that a church and school were needed for the city's Black Catholic population, or they would be lost to the church. He met Josephite superior John Slattery on a visit to Rome and discussed with him the possibility of assigning a member of that congregation to work with Black Catholics in Nashville. After visiting the city in 1899, Slattery assigned Rev. Thomas Plunkett to work with the city's Black Catholics. Plunkett, however, had no church or school in which to meet his potential congregation. Byrne and Plunkett found a suitable building—the former Second Presbyterian Church—but did not possess the financial resources to purchase the building, or even make a down payment.[43] Slattery suggested that Byrne contact Katharine Drexel and ask for her assistance in building a church. He also gave the bishop some advice concerning the best way to approach her: "Have a poor mouth and ask for three times what is needed." Byrne should also, Slattery advised, get Archbishop Patrick Ryan's approval for his project. If Ryan were supportive of a church for Black Catholics in Nashville, Byrne would have a better chance of receiving a favorable reply from Drexel.[44]

In 1900, the bishop approached Mother Katharine and explained his need for a Black Catholic church. He had found a suitable piece of property, Byrne explained, but the cost was $8000, and he had only received $500 from the Commission for the Catholic Missions among the colored people and the Indians. Agreeing that Byrne's request was both worthy and reasonable, Drexel offered to contribute one-third of the cost, which would cover the down payment. Her donation came with the usual stipulation: if the building was not used exclusively for Black people, the money was to revert back to the Sisters of the Blessed Sacrament.[45] After a number of delays, the building was purchased in April 1902.

After buying the church building, Byrne almost immediately began planning a school for Black children. He expected to receive some criticism for this proposal because "many white Southerners saw the education of a Black child as the ruination of a good field hand."[46] Byrne had two initial ideas related to the school that he hoped would both counteract any opposition to the school and ensure its success. First, he planned to offer an industrial education; the school would not prepare young Black women and men for higher education. Second, he wanted the Sisters of the Blessed Sacrament to administer and staff the school.

Drexel did not have much of a connection with Nashville, but a 1904 Southern tour brought her to the city, and she and Byrne began to develop a relationship that was built on mutual respect. She did, however, disagree with the bishop's plan to offer industrial education and she was not at all sure that members of her congregation should teach in the school. Byrne insisted the school be staffed by Sisters of the Blessed Sacrament, however, arguing that congregations who taught primarily in white schools "would not put their heart into work for black students." Drexel finally agreed to put the issue of staffing before the congregation's council—a body responsible for making decisions that would impact the community—and informed Byrne that the SBS agreed to take responsibility for the proposed school. The council, however, had stipulated that in order for the school to operate under SBS auspices non-Catholics were to be admitted. The Sisters of the Blessed Sacrament were missionaries, members of the council argued, and one way to evangelize the Black community was through education. In addition, all children would be required to receive religious instruction.[47]

Drexel's firm conviction that postsecondary education should be open to the Black community led to a disagreement with Byrne over the type of curriculum that would be offered in the proposed school. Drexel wanted students in the schools that her congregation funded and staffed to be as well prepared as students attending all-white schools, and as a result insisted that they receive an education that would prepare them for either higher education or a successful career. In the end, the bishop agreed that an academic curriculum should be implemented, but some industrial courses would be offered for interested students.

After issues relating to staffing and educational philosophy had been resolved, Byrne needed to find a location for the school. Samuel J. Keith, one of the city's most prominent and wealthiest residents, owned the site he thought best suited for the school. Although the property was not for sale, Byrne suspected that Keith would soon be moving to a section of the city that was coming to be seen as a more desirable area for Nashville's upper class. In January 1905 Drexel traveled to Nashville in order to conduct a "covert evaluation" of the property with Byrne. Deciding that $25,000 was an appropriate price for the land, the bishop began the very complicated process of purchasing Keith's house and property.[48]

Byrne had been in Nashville long enough to know that Keith would object to his property being purchased by anyone affiliated with the Catholic Church, and he also suspected that the businessman would be unwilling to have his home converted into a school for young Black women. In order to circumvent any problems with the sale, W. P. Ready acted as the bishop's agent and arranged for Keith to sell his property to Thomas Tyne, a lawyer and friend of Byrne. The discussions and negotiations related to the sale of the property demonstrate yet again that Drexel was indeed a shrewd businesswoman. The congregational annals report that she originally only offered $18,000 for the property, and as a result the "phone was kept busy.... The owner, Mr. Keith would not hear of it." Drexel then offered $24,000 for the property and announced she would not give "another cent" toward the purchase. She finally agreed to purchase the land for $25,000 (the amount Byrne had suggested as a purchase price).[49] Keith agreed to the proposal and the check was drawn on Drexel & Co. bank; nobody would suspect anything was amiss when such a large bank was involved. When the sale was complete, Tyne immediately transferred the property to Mother Katharine Drexel and the Sisters of the Blessed Sacrament for Indians and Colored People.[50]

On February 13, 1905, the *Nashville Banner* reported on both the sale and the subsequent transfer of the deed. The Keith home, the paper reported, "will be used as an institution for the education of negro girls."[51] This was the first time that Keith understood what had actually happened, and he immediately tried to nullify the sale. In the end, the issue was race. Keith even told Byrne that if the bishop would agree to put any other Catholic building on the property—as long as it was intended to serve the white population—he would make a sizable donation to the institution. As James Summerville has written, "To the affluent white residents of the area, a black school on Vine Street threatened to crack the invisible but implacable wall separating their neighborhood from Nashville's black and poor, who ebbed and flowed around it."[52] When Byrne responded to Keith's concerns—and anger—he noted that the neighborhood was in fact in "the heart of a large Colored settlement," and that property values had already been lowered by a nearby railroad. In addition, he assured Keith that "the ladies [SBS] who are to take charge of that institution are women of good birth and breeding, of culture and refinement, and of a high and delicate sense of what is due to those by whom they are surrounded or with whom they come in contact."[53]

Keith also wrote to Mother Katharine to complain about the situation. He and his family had lived in the house for twenty-five years, he explained, and he would not have sold the property if he had known what Byrne and Drexel planned to do. "Moreover," he wrote, "my neighbors and those living in the near vicinity of the place feel deeply aggrieved; feel that their property is rendered almost valueless and that their homes are made undesirable by such use of this property."[54] Like Byrne, Drexel explained that she was sure the sisters and their students would not disturb the neighborhood in any way, and "gently challenged him to remember that the only real home for a Christian was awaiting him in eternity." The girls, she said, "will be only day scholars, and in coming to the academy and returning to their homes I am confident they will be orderly and cause no annoyance."[55] She also let Keith know that she understood that the core reason for his dismay at what had happened revolved around the fact that Black children would be attending school on property he had owned. "The Sisters of the Blessed Sacrament who have purchased the property are religious," she wrote, "who are the same race as yourself, and we shall always endeavor in every way to be neighborly to any white neighbors in our vicinity." In other words, Drexel saw no reason why the sisters, the students, and the neighbors could not get along with each other. Keith had her response to him published in a local paper without Drexel's permission.[56]

When Keith's protests failed to move either Byrne or Drexel, thirty-three white women petitioned Mother Katharine and asked her to consider the fact that by opening a school for Black students, she was causing their property to be devalued, and suggested that she could be held responsible for "stirring up racial strife." In her reply, Drexel expressed her "sincere hope that our present fears may not be realized, and that God may bless your homes even more and more."[57]

Immaculate Mother Academy, Nashville, Tennessee, July 16, 1908. Left to right: front row, Sister M. Aloysius, Mother Mary John (Allen), Sister Eucharia; back row, Sister Mary of the Assumption (Allen), Sister Mary Angela, Sister Margaret Mary, Sister M. Philip Neri, Sister M. Aquinas. Courtesy of SBS Archives, CHRC, Archdiocese of Philadelphia.

Keith and his neighbors were unable to prevent the school from opening, and on June 1, 1905, Byrne blessed Immaculate Mother Convent. Drexel traveled to Nashville in order to determine what work needed to be done to renovate the home and outbuildings to make them suitable for a school and convent. When she returned to the motherhouse, she announced that Mother Mary of the Sacred Heart had been appointed superior of the new ministry and that six additional sisters would join her. By August 19 all of the sisters had arrived in Nashville and were preparing to begin the school year. Immaculate Mother Academy opened the following month; it began as a school for girls from grades four through eight.[58] The school was different from others previously "undertaken by the Sisters in…that it was to be a day school rather than a boarding school and the pupils were required to pay a small sum for their tuition."[59]

Drexel informed Byrne that in the first days of the academy's operation thirty-two girls were in the academic program that would lead to a high school diploma and beyond, and eleven were attending to study music. Only one had expressed an interest in the program of industrial education that was offered; she was studying dressmaking. The school's enrollment grew quickly, and although more girls eventually enrolled in order to study industrial arts, most students were clearly attracted to the academic program.[60]

When the Supreme Court handed down *Brown v. Board of Education* in 1954, the future of both Holy Family School and Immaculate Mother Academy were called into question. In that year, the two schools had a combined enrollment of 172 students, only sixty of whom identified as Catholic. Nashville Bishop William Adrian decided that in light of the *Brown* decision, it made sense to integrate the parochial schools in the city as soon as possible. Male students attending Immaculate Mother were able to transfer to Father Ryan High School, and females could enroll at Cathedral High School. Holy Family students could either attend St. Vincent de Paul, a Black Catholic parochial school, or enroll in one of the formerly white parochial schools. The integration of Nashville's Catholic schools meant that there was no longer a need for schools sponsored and supported by Mother Katharine Drexel.[61]

Money Problems and Health Issues

By the early decades of the twentieth century, the richest nun in America began to experience money troubles. The first cause of Drexel's financial woes resulted from the implementation of a federal income tax following the ratification of the Sixteenth Amendment to the Constitution in 1913. A 1 percent tax on personal incomes above $300 was assessed and those with annual incomes over $500,000 were required to pay an additional 6 percent surtax. Because the tax code allowed exemptions for religious and charitable contributions, Drexel appealed for refunds and abatements since all of her income was going to serve Black and Indigenous People. Her appeals, however, were denied. By 1918 Drexel's tax bill was over $77,000; by 1924 she owed about $800,000. This meant, of course, that she had less money available to assist those seeking her help. Pennsylvania Senator George Wharton Pepper introduced an amendment to the Revenue Act of 1924 that exempted income used for "religious, charitable, scientific, literary, and educational purposes...if in the taxable year and in each of the ten preceding taxable years the amount...exceeded ninety per cent of the taxpayer's net income for each such year." Known informally as the "Philadelphia Nun Loophole," it allowed Drexel to continue funding work she believed was important to both the Catholic Church and the larger society. In 1940, Pennsylvania finally passed a similar version of the federal amendment.[62] The "Loophole" was not repealed until 1969.[63]

A second cause of financial worry for Drexel was the onset of the Great Depression. In the spring of 1929, several letters were sent to the Motherhouse explaining the difficulty sisters were having selling ticket books that were part of the money raised by the annual bazaar. Writing from New Orleans, Sister Mary Grace explained that the sisters in her convent were not able to sell their share of tickets; they had already "drained their nearest relatives and friends" to support a fundraiser "and in conscience, could not make [another] appeal to them now." Her explanation was not well received, and in a second letter, Sister Mary Grace gave a more detailed explanation of the situation she was facing. The people among whom they lived and worked were poor; they were not unwilling to contribute but they did not have the resources to help.[64]

Losses suffered by Drexel caused her to make difficult decisions relating to schools and churches she had been funding for a number of years. An archival document dated 1936, for instance, notes that the Indian Girls' Boarding School in Bayfield, Wisconsin, was not reopening after summer vacation. From 1900 until 1936, the school had received $1069 per year from Drexel through the "Catholic Indian Bureau" and $1620 from Drexel herself. In 1935, she informed the Franciscan priests administering the school that she could "not give the annual grant and had to cut her appropriation down to $600." It was impossible for the school to remain open under these circumstances.[65]

Drexel's interest in a church or school she had funded did not necessarily diminish over time. In 1937, she expressed her concern over the financial situation of St. Catherine of Siena parish in the Germantown section of Philadelphia. Writing to Father William Slattery, CM, the provincial of the Vincentians' eastern province, Drexel reminded him that the SBS had donated $18,000 toward the erection of the parish church and had paid for the building of the school and convent. In addition, the congregation "paid for all repairs in school and convent, contributed to the support of the Sisters and paid incidental school expenses." They could not, however, continue to provide this much financial support to the parish. The pastor, she told Slattery, insisted he could only pay for electricity, heat, water, and the sisters' salaries. This was simply not enough to support the school and the sisters assigned to St. Catherine of Siena. They could not be responsible, for instance, for expenses such as a retaining wall ($359) and new water pipes ($125). If the pastor would assume "debts of this nature," pay the cook's salary, and assume responsibility for school expenses and repairs, she concluded, "the Sisters can get along." Rev. Gerard Murphy, CM, pastor of St. Catherine of Siena, defended himself in a letter to his provincial, and listed a number of projects and repairs for which the parish had assumed responsibility, and explained that the parish planned a "lawn party" to raise money for other work needing to be completed. He drew the line at paying the cook's salary, however, writing, "I know of no pastor in the diocese who pays for the housekeeper in the convent."[66]

Even though she was forced to limit her contributions during the Depression, Drexel continued to fund work dedicated to Black and Indigenous People. From January 1928 until December of 1940, $1,703,679.18 was spent on Native missions ($843,816 of this was allocated to institutions that were not administered by Sisters of the Blessed Sacrament). Ministries devoted to Black Americans, including Xavier University, received $2,965,932.48; $464,047.43 was used for ministries not staffed by the congregation. Drexel also continued to keep meticulous records of her finances. In 1936, for instance, she spent $34,790 on "Colored Schools Outside the Congregation of the Sisters of the Blessed Sacrament." The Oblate Sisters of Providence received $400 earmarked for education and $5000 for a building; $16,630 subsidized teachers' salaries in Lafayette and Lake Charles, Louisiana; and $150 was allocated for missions in Atlanta and Macon, Georgia.[67]

Drexel's health began to decline when she suffered a slight heart attack in 1934. The following year, she undertook an extensive tour of Western missions that included stops at St. Catherine's, Santa Fe; St. Michael's on the Navajo reservation in Arizona; and St. Paul's in Marty, South Dakota. On her journey, Drexel realized that Sister Stanislaus, SBS, was facing serious health issues of her own, and took her to St. Louis to seek appropriate treatment. While in St. Louis, she suffered another heart attack and was forced to return immediately to the motherhouse in Bensalem.

Her deteriorating health led to Drexel's decision not to seek another term as superior general, and in 1937 Mother Mercedes O'Connor was elected to the position. Drexel was elected to the congregational council as Vicar General, and in this role served as Mother Mercedes's primary assistant. Her health, however, continued to decline and Drexel was able to spend less and less time on either congregational affairs or philanthropy. In addition, her ability to travel—even around the city of Philadelphia—was severely curtailed. Informed that she would be receiving an honorary degree from the Catholic University of America in 1939, Drexel informed Msgr. Joseph Corrigan that she was happy to accept this honor "provided the conferring of the degree does not require my presence in Washington."[68] Although her physical and mental health continued to decline, Drexel lived eighteen years after relinquishing her position of leadership, but her presence in the motherhouse served as a daily reminder of the congregation's beginnings and the visionary who made their ministries possible.

Chapter Three

THE PHILADELPHIA STORY

"*A*t last I'm on a real honest-to-goodness mission," Sister Albertine Wackerman wrote to Rev. Mother Katharine Drexel in 1936. "It certainly is all I dreamed it would be and more. I felt right at home the minute I put my foot in the front door....Everyone is well and happy here in our dear home and I can't tell you enough, Reverend Mother, what it all means to me." Sister Albertine's letter was included in a compilation of the congregation's annals as an example of a recently professed sister who was happy to—finally—be working outside of the novitiate. But Helen Wackerman, who grew up in St. Vincent de Paul parish in the Germantown section of Philadelphia and graduated from Hallahan High School in 1933, was, according to the annalist, missioned at St. Peter Claver School in "her own home city." Her "mission territory" was about fifteen miles from the SBS motherhouse.[1]

Most studies of Drexel, and by extension the Sisters of the Blessed Sacrament, focus on the congregation's work on Indigenous reservations and among Black Southerners. Neither Drexel nor her sisters, however, neglected the educational and spiritual needs of Black people living in the city in which she was born. As the founder and congregational leader until 1935, Drexel certainly made decisions related to any work the SBS might be asked to do in her native city, and she provided at least some funding for parishes and schools dedicated to Black Catholics. The story of Drexel's work in Philadelphia, however, is really the work of "her sisters." Sister teachers administered and staffed schools, and often found themselves involved in other ministries as well, such as nursing and social work. The same commitment and philosophy that formed their work in other parts of the country can be found in their Philadelphia ministries.

In some ways the story of the SBS in Philadelphia stands outside of the traditional narrative associated with the congregation. In her study of women religion and the American West, historian Anne Butler wrote, "The Sisters of the Blessed Sacrament demonstrated that Catholic women who wished to escape the confines of their own culture discovered in religious identity and social service the means to do so." These women, Butler explained, "established uncommon contacts among people of color, especially inside the West and the South."[2] Sister Albertine was certainly interacting with people of color, but at 12th and Lombard Streets in Philadelphia, not the American South.[3]

Philadelphia had become the most "important urban center of free blacks in the country" by 1824. The city was primarily segregated, however; 25 percent of Black Philadelphians lived in the Seventh Ward, an area that ran from Spruce to South Streets, and from 7th Street to the Schuylkill River. By 1854, the city's schools were segregated in areas where school directors counted at least twenty Black students.[4] In the 1850s, about one-half of Black children attended one of nine "colored schools"; others—but not all—attended private schools organized by various Protestant churches.[5]

Black Philadelphians primarily attended one of the city's many Protestant churches. W. E. B. Du Bois, in his now-classic study of the city's Black community, noted that Black churches in the city had increased from twenty in 1867 to fifty-five in 1897, thirty years later. In the Seventh Ward, home to many Black residents, the largest denominational groups were Methodists, followed by Baptists, Episcopalians, Presbyterians, and Catholics.[6] According to Du Bois, sixty-nine Catholic families lived in that section of the city at the time he was conducting his study. The local priest, he reported, estimated that between four and five hundred Black Catholics were attending Mass at various churches throughout the city. "The Catholic Church," Du Bois wrote, "can do more than any other agency in humanizing the intense prejudice of many of the working class against the Negro, and signs of this influence are manifest in some quarters."[7]

There is no evidence that Du Bois had any interaction with either Katharine Drexel or the Sisters of the Blessed Sacrament at the time he was preparing *The Philadelphia Negro*. The statistics related to Black Catholics included in the monograph, however, were connected to St. Peter Claver parish, located at Twelfth and Lombard Streets in the city's Seventh Ward. Prior to the parish's establishment in 1889, Black Catholics in Philadelphia worshiped in churches throughout the city, but often experienced discrimination; sometimes they were forced to sit in the choir loft or stand throughout the service.[8]

Before St. Peter Claver was formally established as a parish, Father Thomas Lilly founded a school for Black children in the vicinity of Fourth and Lombard Streets. Archbishop James Wood (1860–1883) invited a Black religious congregation, the Oblate Sisters of Providence (from Baltimore), to staff Blessed Peter Claver School in 1863. Three sisters were originally assigned to Philadelphia, but when it appeared that the school was flourishing, an additional Oblate was assigned to the congregation's first out-of-state mission.[9] The sisters, however, encountered a good deal of racist behavior in Philadelphia—at times they were even forced off of a sidewalk—and "were publicly insulted in the City of Brotherly Love."[10] In addition, the school struggled financially, and in December 1871, the annalist for the Oblate Sisters wrote, "Bishop (Wood) thought it best to close the school in Philadelphia."[11] Undeterred, the Oblates returned to Philadelphia the following year and attempted to again open a school. Because "they had little money to work with [they received no support from the diocese] and [were] under the constant display of prejudice, they were forced, once again, to close their school and return to Baltimore."[12] After the Oblates left Philadelphia, the Sisters of Notre Dame de Namur arrived and offered religious education classes for Black children. In 1878, they received permission from Wood to open a school for Black girls but closed it in 1882 because the school was struggling financially, and Black children were now permitted to attend Philadelphia public schools. Blessed Peter Claver reopened in 1886, thanks to the financial generosity of Katharine Drexel, who had not yet entered religious life, and was staffed by the Sisters, Servants of the Immaculate Heart of Mary (IHM's) and several laywomen. In the early twentieth century, after the SBS had been established, Drexel and her sister would become more actively involved in St. Peter Claver School, along with three additional schools located in the city of Philadelphia.[13]

Holy Providence School

During the course of its more than 125-year history, the Sisters of the Blessed Sacrament supported, administered, and staffed schools connected with four Black parishes in the Archdiocese of Philadelphia— Our Lady of the Blessed Sacrament (OLBS), St. Peter Claver, St. Catherine of Siena, and St. Ignatius—as well as a small residential school, Holy Providence, which was located on the grounds of the congregation's motherhouse in Bensalem.

Holy Providence, the first mission opened by Drexel and the Sisters of the Blessed Sacrament, was founded for two reasons: (1) the residential home and school was a way to immediately begin to serve the area's Black community; and (2) Drexel supported the idea of operating a "training lab" of sorts to help young sisters become competent teachers.[14] She reasoned that when sisters were living on reservations or in remote rural areas they would not have access to more experienced teachers when they needed advice or new ideas, and it was important that they learn from sisters who had been teaching for a while when they were living at the motherhouse. When the sisters moved into the unfinished motherhouse in Cornwells Heights, Pennsylvania—now Bensalem—fifteen Black children who had been living in Holy Family cottage on the grounds of St. Michel in Torresdale became the first students and residents at Holy Providence School. The new residential school was at least as unfinished as the motherhouse. There were no bolts, locks, or other hardware for the doors of the rooms, for instance, and "a Sister was appointed to sleep in the house with [the children]. Recognizing that the Sister should not be alone, two other sisters were to be appointed to sleep with the children."[15] When the school first opened, no age restrictions were placed on the children, and as a result, the sisters found themselves caring for boys and girls as young as six weeks old. When several babies died during very hot weather that first summer, Drexel, after consulting with several physicians, realized that administering a nursery for infants and babies was simply not feasible. The remaining very young children "were placed out with two colored women to board," and all survived.[16] Within one year of its founding, 150 children were living and learning at Holy Providence.[17]

Children residing at Holy Providence received both academic instruction and industrial training. Sisters Angelica and Dolores enrolled in classes in "Domestic Science and Art" at the Drexel Institute (now Drexel University—founded by Anthony Drexel), and "they, in turn, gave to the girls in an abridged way" lessons in dressmaking and plain sewing so they could support themselves when it came time for them to leave Holy Providence. Younger boys learned shoemaking and older boys worked on the grounds and in the dairy.[18]

In order to implement her plan to make Holy Providence a "laboratory" for the young sisters, who were also teachers in training, Drexel hired Mary Byrne, who had been granted a one-year leave of absence from her job as a normal schoolteacher in New York, in 1914. Byrne planned, with the help of Drexel, to structure Holy Providence in such a way that it could serve as a training school for young sisters who would soon be assigned to missions in other parts of the country with very little opportunity for mentoring. As a result of her work, the new sister teachers were given more time to prepare for classes, and required to submit reports detailing what they had accomplished during the previous week, and what they proposed to do during the coming week.[19] The curriculum developed for Holy Providence eventually served as the framework for other schools administered by the Sisters of the Blessed Sacrament; courses offered at the congregation's schools included Christian doctrine, penmanship, English grammar, reading, composition, physiology, arithmetic, U.S. history and geography, literature, church history, and Bible history.[20]

Not all of the children residing at Holy Providence were orphans. If a parent was alive—but unable to care for his or her child—the sisters obtained legal custody through indenture, which meant that the congregation was responsible for the care and education of the child until he or she turned twenty-one; if parents were able to prove later that they could provide for the child, the agreement became void. There were two reasons for seeking indenture rather than simply keeping the children at Holy Providence until they no longer needed or wanted to live in a boarding school. First, the congregation was concerned that a non-Catholic relative might try and gain legal custody of the child, which meant that he or she would no longer be raised Catholic. Second, students were not expected to leave Holy Providence until they were able to support themselves; the boys often went to a Josephite school in Delaware at the age of thirteen, but it was not unusual for female students to remain at Holy Providence until the age of twenty-one.[21]

Schools and Parishes

Drexel had been financially supporting St. Peter Claver church and school in a variety of ways for a number of years prior to founding a religious congregation, but Our Lady of the Blessed Sacrament, located on Broad Street in North Philadelphia, was also a ministry to which she devoted a considerable amount of time and money. The idea for a church dedicated to Black Catholics in this area first began to develop in 1907. The annalist for the SBS in that year noted,

> The Fathers of the Society of Jesus volunteered to take up the Colored work in Philadelphia. Father [Abraham] Emerick, S.J., who gave us our retreat some years before and who had a large experience in dealing with the Colored People of Jamaica, was appointed to take charge of the new mission.[22]

Drexel purchased a building that could be used as a convent, but acquiring something that was suitable for a church took longer. It was important that the new church be a place where Black Catholics would want to worship. As Sister Mary Mercedes O'Connor wrote to Drexel, the pastor [Emerick] "wants to make the new mission a thing to be proud of—an attraction to the Colored people."[23]

In a lengthy account written for *The Woodstock Letters*, Emerick claimed that the idea for what would become Our Lady of the Blessed Sacrament actually originated with a retreat he gave at the motherhouse in 1904. At that time, he recounted, Drexel had become very interested in his mission to Black people in Jamaica and offered him funds to implement some ideas related to catechetical work.[24] Returning to the motherhouse in 1906 to report on how the money had been spent, Emerick began speaking with Sister Mary John, who told him she was very discouraged by the fact that the sisters had little to show for the work they were putting into the Sunday School at St. Elizabeth's Church in North Philadelphia. Emerick remembered telling her, "You should not be disheartened. Who knows but your little colored Sunday School may someday be the foundation of a colored mission and colored church of North Philadelphia."[25]

According to a summary of the annals for Our Lady of the Blessed Sacrament, a primary advocate for a new mission to Black Philadelphians was Emma (Mrs. Coleman) Lewis, who had met Drexel during her novitiate with the Sisters of Mercy in Pittsburgh. After Lewis moved to Philadelphia in 1901, she began to organize a Catholic Sunday School for Black children and adults, and when she had enough interested students, she asked Archbishop Patrick Ryan for permission to organize a "mission." Ryan approved and by 1907, Our Lady of the Blessed Sacrament mission was informally operating in North Philadelphia. Emerick clearly did not like Lewis, describing her as "one of those characters, who when they get what they consider a good idea, make themselves and everyone else they come in contact with, uncomfortable until they have given birth to their idea." Lewis, he complained, gave Drexel "no peace" until her Sunday School was firmly established.[26]

Emerick and Drexel understood the difficulty of finding a suitable location for the new mission. Writing to Emerick, Drexel explained, "There seems to be some difficulty about locating [the new church]. The Gesu Parish [Jesuit] will not be anxious to have it in their limits, and St. Elizabeth's Parish will not wish it in theirs."[27] Despite reservations about where the new mission might find a permanent home, the Jesuit provincial and consultors, as well as the priests assigned to Gesu, decided to allow Emerick to staff OLBS under Jesuit auspices. In addition to having great respect for Drexel and her father—who had funded Jesuit churches and schools in Philadelphia and beyond—they believed the work was worthy of their time and attention. Jesuit leaders were also, however, clearly concerned about the potential location of any new church and decided that they had a better chance of keeping it away from Gesu parish if they were involved in the project. Emerick, in fact, did not reside at Gesu because it was feared his "presence would draw too many colored people around there."[28]

When Emerick was ready to search for a suitable site for the new mission, he discovered Drexel was in Rome seeking approval for the congregation's Constitutions. After locating a possible site, he met with Ryan to discuss what might be done in Drexel's absence. If Emerick's account is to be believed, Drexel's mentor and friend expressed some ambivalence about the new project and said that he "looked upon colored churches as a necessary evil." He was willing to support Drexel, who firmly believed that if missions were opened, converts would result, but was not especially optimistic about the outcome. Ryan then informed Emerick that only Drexel herself could make the final decision about the location for the new church. "We must allow her to do the negotiating," he reportedly said; "we must keep in the background; we must wait until she comes home."[29]

Determined to have settled on a site by the time Drexel returned from Rome, Emerick explained that he had created what he called a "black map" of Philadelphia; if he found a street that consisted of predominantly Black residents, he literally "marked it black." Emerick had four goals constantly on his mind: the new mission should be located on the best street possible; it should be central to many Black neighborhoods; the church should be as far away from Gesu parish as possible; and it should not be near any white Catholic churches.[30] In the end, he decided the new mission ought to be located on Broad Street, one of the city's main thoroughfares, because it was both busy and diverse enough that white residents of the area would not be upset to find that a mission for Black Catholics had opened.[31]

Emerick was involved with planning and ministering at Our Lady of the Blessed Sacrament for about eighteen months. All accounts of the story generally agree that neither he nor the Jesuit leaders in Philadelphia would consent to the terms Drexel demanded in exchange for a $50,000 gift to be used for the building of OLBS. Drexel—as always—stipulated that the money was given on the condition that the Jesuits

> will use said church property for specified spiritual services and administer the Sacraments and do the other spiritual services connected with a Colored Mission in return, and in case they fail to comply with these conditions the fifty thousand dollars, immediately, *ipso facto*, becomes due to the Sisters of the Blessed Sacrament.[32]

According to Emerick, neither he nor his Jesuit confreres would be allowed to minister at OLBS unless they accepted the money under the terms of the contract, making them "bound hand and foot, merely chaplains of the Sisters of the Blessed Sacrament."[33] The conflict was resolved when the Holy Ghost Fathers—or Spiritans—purchased a former Presbyterian church suitable for use as Our Lady of the Blessed Sacrament and assumed responsibility for ministering to the parishioners. Despite his disagreements with Drexel, Emerick was careful to avoid any harsh criticism of her. "Mother Katharine is always under all circumstances, favorable or unfavorable," he wrote, "a perfect lady, refined to her fingertips, with all the true nobility of an educated aristocrat without a trace of snobbery."[34] When the church was dedicated on February 6, 1910, it was "said to be the finest Catholic Church in the United States." The parish grew quickly and by 1941 was described by some as the "largest Colored parish in Philadelphia."[35]

Students and unidentified Sister of the Blessed Sacrament at Our Lady of the Blessed Sacrament School, Philadelphia, 1930s. Courtesy of SBS Archives, CHRC, Archdiocese of Philadelphia.

The Black community in the city's Germantown section came to Drexel's attention when a group of Black Catholics—including some who self-identified as nonpracticing—wrote to Ryan asking for their own parish, enclosing twenty-seven dollars as evidence of their willingness to raise any necessary funds. The reason for their request, they explained, was the attitude of the white members of St. Vincent de Paul's parish, who did not allow Black parishioners to attend the services of the Sodality of the Blessed Virgin Mary, or allow Black children to attend the parish school.[36] One particular manifestation of racism on the part of St. Vincent's occurred when Eleanor Tyler, a Black member of the parish, had to receive first communion behind all of the white children.[37]

Understanding that Drexel was supportive of the proposed parish, Ryan granted permission for the SBS to "to further [their] missionary work in Philadelphia," and the congregation contributed $18,000 toward the building of St. Catherine's, and erected a convent and a school, which opened in 1915.[38]

In addition to St. Peter Claver, OLBS, and St. Catherine of Siena, the SBS also assumed responsibility for a school in West Philadelphia. In 1924, Cardinal Dennis Dougherty (1918–1951) directed Rev. Vincent Dever to establish a parish for Black Catholics in West Philadelphia. Dever appears to have taken his assignment seriously, and at Drexel's request agreed to visit Jules Jeanmard, bishop of the Diocese of Lafayette, Louisiana, which at the time contained the greatest concentration of Black Catholics in the United States, to explore ways in which he might minister more effectively to his new parishioners. Prior to visiting Louisiana, Dever informed Dougherty that he had found "two… instances of exclusion from parish schools of colored children,"[39] but in a lengthy letter to the cardinal written after his return, Dever concluded that separate churches and schools for Black Catholics, although perhaps necessary, was not the ideal solution. "It does not seem that separate churches can be the final solution, for it would seem impossible to offer them [Black Catholics], for instance, a duplicate of our school system, and they are no longer satisfied with primary education alone," he wrote. "It would seem that the ultimate solution was to somehow make white Catholics realize that Christ having instituted the Church for all, its opportunities and energies should be given to all."[40]

Despite his reservations about separate parishes divided by race, Dever recognized that Black Catholics needed a church that offered them a welcoming environment, and in 1924 established Holy Savior mission within the boundaries of St. Ignatius of Loyola, a German national parish. It quickly became clear that the Holy Savior congregation was the larger of the two and would need both a church and school. By 1928, most of the German population had moved out of the neighborhood, and Dever was able to inform his parishioners that Dougherty had "turned over to us all the properties formerly used by St. Ignatius German parish." With the property came a new name. "Our parish," Dever wrote in the monthly calendar, "will now be called St. Ignatius. It will no longer be called Church of the Holy Savior."[41]

The SBS had been a presence in West Philadelphia since the beginning of the twentieth century when two sisters began teaching Sunday

School to the area's Black Catholics. The sisters temporarily left the area in 1918, but returned to offer religious education classes in 1924, when Dever opened Holy Savior Mission. One year later, in 1925, Drexel assigned three sisters to the new mission—two more soon joined them—and the school opened in 1926 with eight grades and fifty-six children.[42] By the end of the first year, seventy-nine children were enrolled in the school.[43]

A Ministry of Education

In many ways, the historical records of the SBS schools in Philadelphia read like those of any parish and parochial school in the Archdiocese of Philadelphia. One finds accounts, for instance, of graduations, first communions, and Mother's Club activities. At the same time, sisters teaching in the four schools designated for Black Catholic children had to adapt their work to address the realities of the situation in which their students were forced to live.

Young sisters—such as Sister Albertine—often wrote to Drexel and shared impressions of their work and of the people to whom they were ministering. After expressing her enthusiasm for finally being on a mission, for instance, Sister Albertine explained that she was spending a good deal of time preparing for the start of the school year. "We've been spending our afternoons at St. Peter Claver's," she wrote, "trying to make our rooms look respectable. Our pastor's motto seems to be 'Work hard, pray hard, and play hard,' so we must train his parishioners accordingly."[44] Writing from the same convent at about the same time, Sister Marie Michel, who was stationed at OLBS, informed Drexel that there were "forty-two little ones in my first and second grades and I expect more to come in next week." The doctor had visited her class the previous day, and although he was Jewish, "the darlings stood up very nicely and said, 'Good morning, Father.' It amused me, but I guess the Doctor is accustomed to it by now."[45]

One indicator used to gauge the quality of education that students in SBS schools were receiving was how many were accepted at Catholic high schools. As a result, historical records often single out those students for special mention. At the end of the 1929 school year, it was announced that four girls would be attending John W. Hallahan High School beginning in September. Eight years later, in 1937, the sisters were happy to report that all of the eighth graders had passed the diocesan exams and would be allowed to attend Catholic high schools. In 1967, two eighth-grade boys from St. Catherine's received full four-year scholarships to St. Joseph Preparatory School, a Jesuit high school.[46]

One goal of the Sisters of the Blessed Sacrament was to provide Black children in Philadelphia with a quality Catholic education, but they never discounted the importance of religious education, sacramental preparation, and attendance at Mass and other religious services. In 1954, the sister responsible for keeping an account of their ministry at St. Catherine's reported, "Non-Catholic boys are attending Sunday Mass regularly as a result of their contact with our children at our seasonal dances held in the school. One of these boys was baptized and has made his First Holy Communion."[47] Two years later, the sister teachers at OLBS touted the fact that the children being confirmed that year answered the questions asked by Auxiliary Bishop J. Carroll McCormick so well that they were granted a school holiday. A few years later, a sister noted that there was more to their work than the 3 Rs. "The most important work," she wrote, "is the reclaiming of Catholic parents who are coming back through the instruction of their own little ones."[48] When appropriate, they related liturgical events at the parish to what was going on in the country. The day after the death of President John F. Kennedy, the annalist commented, "The Church looked like it does on a Sunday morning. Almost all received Holy Communion."[49]

In some ways, the experience of SBS teaching in Philadelphia was different from what other teaching congregations may have considered normative—even those teaching in poor neighborhoods. Many of the school children in SBS schools, for instance, were living in abject poverty. During the 1930s, when so many Americans were severely impacted by the Great Depression, the children at OLBS often found themselves with nothing to look forward to at Christmas. In 1933, Drexel herself sent a box of wooden toys that had been made by the students at Xavier University in New Orleans, and her sister, Louise Morrell, sent clothes and shoes.[50] Because the sisters had visited the homes of most of their students, they knew who needed Christmas baskets filled with shoes and clothing, and they made sure families received what they needed to keep their children warm for the winter. Even after the Depression ended, families continued to need help providing Christmas gifts for their children. In 1960, for instance, Western Union suggested to local schools that during the Christmas season parents could send their children telegrams from Santa. The sister teachers at OLBS explained that the parents of the children in their school could not afford to send a telegram. The Western Union employees responded by collecting $82 to be used for the poorer children in the school.[51]

The sisters were keenly aware that their students often needed assistance to meet their basic material needs. Many children benefited when St. Ignatius School began serving a hot lunch and sandwiches each day during the 1954–55 school year.[52] Even sacramental celebrations could be a problem. In 1962, the sisters reported that twenty-six first communion dresses had been donated for children whose parents were unable to purchase appropriate clothing for their special day.[53] The sisters understood that working with marginalized populations in the United States meant ministering to those who were denied access to the nation's wealth; but they also realized they had committed to ministering to the poor and dispossessed when they took their vows as Sisters of the Blessed Sacrament. When sisters living at OLBS and teaching at St. Peter Claver wrote to Drexel, they noted that they "passed down dirty crowded streets and over broken pavements. Behind the walls of the school building, they can see God in the faces of a few hundred children who come from homes on these streets."[54]

In addition to the fragile socioeconomic status of many of the sisters' students, any history of the congregation's work in Philadelphia—and elsewhere, for that matter—is complicated by the complexities surrounding the issue of race in America. The children taught by the SBS in Philadelphia were—almost without exception—Black. And the sisters, children, and parents worried about some issues that their counterparts in other Catholic schools did not have to face. At the end of the 1923–24 school year, the OLBS annalist was pleased to report that the eighth graders had the grades they needed to attend Catholic high schools. This was especially important, she noted, because some people "had an idea that Catholic High Schools would not accept our children" because the children had not received an adequate education in elementary school.[55] By 1950, there was more very good news. Two graduates of OLBS, one male and one female, had received scholarships to Villanova University and Rosemont College.[56]

The sisters also confronted and responded to racial incidents that the schoolchildren (and their parents) experienced in other archdiocesan churches. When in 1938 they heard that some of the children attending SBS schools had been turned away from Mass at St. Francis

Xavier, located at 24th and Greene Streets, several sisters decided to find out for themselves exactly what was taking place in the church. They stood outside one Sunday and sent a child in to attend Mass. When the boy returned, he reported that the ushers told him about the eight o'clock Mass at Broad and Fairmount, Our Lady of the Blessed Sacrament. A year later, the sisters learned that white children at St. Columba's "plagued the Black children attending Mass at the parish," but noted with relief that one of the parish priests had put a stop to that sort of behavior. Although they deplored racial discrimination, the sisters made it clear that if Black Catholics felt unwelcome in their home parishes (based on geography), they should attend Mass at OLBS where they would surely feel welcome.[57]

More than Teachers

Although the Sisters of the Blessed Sacrament were not trained as nurses, they—like many congregations of women religious—were pressed into ministering to the sick during the 1918 influenza epidemic. The eighteen sisters transformed into temporary nurses, Drexel wrote, were caring for the sick in a variety of settings; some were at the Municipal Hospital (Philadelphia General Hospital), some at St. Peter Claver's (which was temporarily serving as a hospital annex), and some "have rows of 60 houses of poor." Although the SBS had taken a vow to "be the Mother and Servant of the Negro and Indian Races" and not to "undertake any work which may tend to the neglect and abandonment of the Indian and Colored Races," Drexel understood that they might be asked to perform other tasks in a time of crisis. Writing to Archbishop Patrick Ryan in 1891, Drexel explained that "'Indian and Colored' are to be our chief care: that our work must be for them: but that does not exclude our helping the white race in cases of necessity."[58] This was certainly the case during the 1918 influenza epidemic.

Other sisters worked in the Germantown section of the city, and nursed the "colored people, the Italians, and others of God's poor" in their homes, often discovering that the sick were suffering in appalling conditions. In one home, "there was no bedclothing, no fire, no food, no linens; as for dishes, there was a glass tumbler containing medicine prescribed by a doctor. All the patients were to take medicine from this glass."[59] The sisters did what they could with limited resources to make their patients as comfortable as possible.

When the flu epidemic had run its course, the sisters returned to their assigned ministries. Because evangelization was an important component of the work of the SBS, those assigned to the congregation's four parochial schools also did work that is sometimes associated with missionaries more than educators. Convent annals, for instance, often remark on issues related to church attendance and conversion. In October of 1920, the annalist reported that Mrs. West, a convert, came to visit; she "was prepared to make her Easter duty, but was afraid she could not remember the number of sins she committed." In addition, statistics relating to the number of children receiving the sacraments are mentioned consistently. In May of 1917, seventeen were baptized in one week; there were three first communions and fifty-seven received confirmation.[60]

Members of the congregation began visiting the homes of Philadelphia's Black residents at least partially in response to *Rerum Ecclesiae*, an encyclical issued by Pope Pius XI in 1926, which called for the development and promotion of a critical mass of Black clergy.[61] In response, the SBS designed an active program of home visitation of which the primary goal was to recruit children to attend a parochial school; they considered themselves to be "messengers of goodwill," and were not planning to "reproach evil-doers, but to observe, take record as to Baptisms, First Communions,...and any other information [they] could glean, but to ask no 'prying' questions." In addition to gathering information, they also found themselves helping people with a variety of problems. In 1937, sisters assigned to visitations in OLBS met an elderly couple who, although they both wore miraculous medals, had not been baptized. They were very poor, the sisters reported, and "often have no groceries at all." Although the written records are silent on how the sisters responded to this situation, in another instance they wrote of someone: "Not a Catholic....Wretched poverty. No food....We went over and put up some groceries." They were unable to meet all of the needs of everyone with whom they came in contact, but on at least several occasions, the sisters asked Wannamaker's, a large Philadelphia department store, to donate shoes that could be distributed to those in need. Along with material help, the work of the SBS was often combined with reflections or questions on the state of the souls of the people they were meeting. In one instance, sisters told parents who wanted to have their children baptized that they should receive the sacrament as well. Other comments from the records of their visitations demonstrate their hope that people would either convert or return to Catholicism. The annals are replete with comments such as the following: "Evasive about being a Catholic. But seemed to know too much to be anything else." "Promised faithfully to return to the sacraments." "A Baptist, but kindly disposed." "It would seem there would be no trouble getting this whole little family into the Church." And "Seems a very fine type, with deep faith in God.... Trust we are not too skeptical."[62]

Home visitations often meant that—even though their primary ministry was in the classroom—sisters sometimes assumed the role of social workers. In 1916, for instance, they placed a girl at the House of the Good Shepherd because of behavior issues, and a boy was sent to the Catholic Protectory because he was "truant and stays out all night," according to his mother.[63] Segregated archdiocesan institutions often complicated what should have been relatively simple problems to resolve. Writing to Dever from the OLBS convent, Sister Vincentia bemoaned the fact that Misericordia Hospital would not admit a Black woman to its maternity ward. Explaining that the woman in question was "respectable" and "married," she asked Dever if there was anything he could do to help the woman. "It is the same old story," she wrote. "Other religions can do for theirs and ours in spite of color but when in the providence of God our poor people happen to differ in color 'there is no room for them.'"[64]

Although the Sisters of the Blessed Sacrament did more than simply staff OLBS, St. Catherine of Siena, St. Peter Claver, and St. Ignatius, they were sometimes expected to do work that was not a part of their assigned daily tasks. In a letter to Dever, Dougherty noted that Rev. John J. Bonner, superintendent of schools for the archdiocese, had visited St. Ignatius and expressed some concerns about the school's physical condition, telling the cardinal that "the school part of the building... suffers from lack of care and systematic cleaning. The yard behind the house is in great disorder. The corridors and cloak closets have not been swept nor dusted for a long time. The drinking fountains are coated with dirt." The "superior" told Bonner that there was no one to care for the building. Although the sisters kept their classrooms clean, Drexel did not allow them to perform other custodial tasks because "as soon as class is over, they do settlement in the colored colony and visit the prisons." Dougherty ordered Dever to rectify the situation, writing, "It is unnecessary to say that sisters in charge of parish schools are neither obliged nor expected to attend to the cleanliness of the school and the schoolyard."[65]

Closing and Reimagining Schools and Ministries

During the 1960s and 1970s, SBS schools, including Holy Providence, found themselves faced with declining student enrollment, decreasing numbers of sister teachers, and financial difficulties. When it was no longer feasible for Holy Providence to serve as a residential school for Black children, the school became exclusively a day school for girls. In 1966, attempting to respond to changes taking place in U.S. society, the school began accepting white students. A 1969 article in the *Philadelphia Inquirer* reported that approximately two hundred girls were attending the school that went from first through eighth grade. Students included Black girls from "urban and rural poverty areas" and white girls who were considered middle class. The article quoted congregational leader Mother David Young: "What we now have is a school where black students are mixed with whites whose parents truly want integration."[66] Attempts to transform Holy Providence were unsuccessful, however, and the school closed its doors in 1971.

Congregational leadership informed Philadelphia Cardinal John Krol that they were planning to close Our Lady of the Blessed Sacrament School in 1967. Krol was not averse to the idea of closing a school or parish that ministered exclusively to Black Catholics. Writing to Rev. Arthur J. Nace, he explained,

> The parish actually is a segregated one and as such may prove a source of embarrassment. It is possible that, if the school is closed, the attendance [at Mass] will decrease and we may have little choice but to close [the parish] within a short period of the closing of the school.

He further noted that the Holy Ghost Fathers—or Spiritans—were willing to go along with any decisions made by the archdiocese concerning the school and the parish. When OLBS parents were notified that the school was closing and the property was being sold, they were "surprised and saddened."[67]

In an article published in the *Catholic Standard and Times*, the closing of OLBS was attributed to a shortage of personnel and diminishing financial resources. Two hundred and fifty students would transfer to either Our Lady of Mercy or St. Augustine, but—ironically—fifty students would attend Gesu school, the very parish Emerick had hoped to prevent Black Philadelphians from attending during the first decade of the twentieth century.[68] When the parish itself closed in 1972, older parishioners deplored Krol's decision, remembering that they had been turned away from the city's predominantly white churches and had found a "home" at Our Lady of the Blessed Sacrament.[69] The remaining sisters officially departed OLBS convent on August 10, 1967, but as the annalist noted, "We had turned the keys over so we never really did lock the door!"[70]

At the same time that Krol was scrutinizing parishes for financial and demographic viability, the Sisters of the Blessed Sacrament—like other congregations of women religious—were faced with declining numbers and aging members, causing them to make difficult decisions about the future of their ministries, including Germantown's St. Catherine of Siena. The congregation considered withdrawing from St. Catherine's as early as 1948, informing Krol that the school did not have many students, and members of the congregation were needed at other parochial schools in the city, particularly Sts. Peter Claver and Ignatius.[71] At that time, the SBS choose to remain at the school, but the situation did not improve. In 1960, only four sisters were assigned to St. Catherine's and the grades were doubled, making it "difficult to give individual help to our poor readers."[72] The school's Parent Teacher Association tried to help by paying the salary of a lay teacher assigned to second grade for the 1970–71 school year. The situation remained untenable, however, because—in addition to double grades—the physical plant was deemed inadequate. Mother Elizabeth Fitzpatrick, congregational president, informed Krol that she could think of no way to rectify the situation involving the building itself, and the archdiocese was unable—or unwilling—to make the necessary improvements.[73] The Vincentian Fathers, who administered and staffed St. Catherine's, were not interested in acquiring the school that had been built by Drexel and her sisters, and in January 1972, the annals report that Mother Elizabeth and Sister Alma visited the convent and informed the sisters that the school would be closed.[74] A month later, a letter went home to the parents, and in May the notice of the school's closing appeared on the front page of Philadelphia newspapers. In a 1972 statement, Krol praised the work of the SBS, writing, "At this time, I publicly thank the Sisters of the Blessed Sacrament for their dedicated service to the faithful of St. Catherine's parish these many years. May God bless and reward these good sisters for their unselfish labor in behalf of our children and the entire parish."[75]

In 1970, changing demographics and declining numbers led to the merger of St. Peter Claver School with St. Theresa of Avila, which was located at Broad and Catherine Streets. In that year, the SBS annals referred to the parish's smaller population: "The older members of the parish who are in the area are still faithful to the parish and school. But very few younger people are involved. Many are non-Catholic, many live at a great distance from the school and it is difficult to have close association with them." At the same time, the number of SBS available to staff congregational ministries was decreasing, and the result was that the community withdrew from St. Peter Claver in 1972 and was replaced by sisters from several congregations and lay teachers. In a letter to parents, SBS president Mother Mary Elizabeth Fitzpatrick explained that the congregation had decided that no ministry would be maintained if they could not provide a "qualified, efficient and adequate staff." As a result, she continued, "we must withdraw from 12 of our centers of service. St. Peter Claver School is one of them."[76] The school was closed in 1984 and the parish suppressed in 1985.

St. Ignatius School has survived into the third decade of the twenty-first century. A 1971 feasibility study described the school as "the heart of the Parish" and noted that it set "the tone for Black hope and aspirations in West Philadelphia." St Ignatius, the report continued, was "in some way quite typical of SBS institutions and in some ways is quite advanced." Some members of the parish and neighborhood expressed the hope that the sisters assigned to the school would become more involved in relationships and events taking place outside of St. Ignatius, but the study noted that the sisters seemed "fulfilled and happy" to be part of the parish community."[77] Sister Caritas Allen, a member of the St. Ignatius School community in 1975, proposed that the school be a "model" for "SBS newcomers, for others who really want to learn to love and work with Black children, and as a potential source of religious vocations." An SBS presence in West Philadelphia was vital because there were very few "other than SBS who truly believe in the unique potential of the Black community." Sisters of the Blessed Sacrament differed from other congregations and members of the laity working with African Americans because they believed Black children "have the same potential, the same weaknesses and strengths as white children," and stressed that their own lives were better for the "privilege" of working with them.[78]

During the 1980s, the sister teachers at St. Ignatius worked to immerse themselves in Philadelphia's Black community by attending Black Catholic celebrations at the cathedral, visiting residents of the neighborhood, and facilitating Black History celebrations in the school.[79] When Sister Maureen Emmanuel was appointed principal of St. Ignatius in 1985, she began to develop the Imani Center that would focus on the two ideas of Black and Catholic. The center was to "be a room for prayer, religious studies, and activities of a religious nature, where the culture of the people was reflected." Several years later, the Imani Center continued to prepare children to receive the sacraments, help teachers design activities for Lent and Advent, and assist students and teachers with Mass preparation.[80] In 2005, as a result of a merger, the school was renamed Our Mother of Sorrows/St. Ignatius of Loyola School, and as of this writing is classified as one of the archdiocesan Independent Mission Schools. In 2018, it described itself as the only remaining mission of St. Katharine Drexel in Philadelphia.

The Sisters of the Blessed Sacrament remain a vibrant part of Philadelphia Catholicism in the twenty-first century. Although there are few sisters actively working in the area, the congregation's headquarters remain anchored in the archdiocese and many retired members of the community reside in Philadelphia or its suburbs. Most of the congregation's work, however, took place outside of Philadelphia, and many American Catholics view the Sisters of the Blessed Sacrament primarily through their ministries to Indigenous People and Black Americans in other parts of the United States. The work of the SBS on reservations and in Black communities throughout the country primarily involved establishing, staffing, and supporting schools, including Xavier University of Louisiana. Although Katharine Drexel's fortune financially supported the schools—her money was often the *only* source of support—the congregation helped decide what projects would be funded in addition to administering and staffing the schools. As the following chapters will demonstrate, Drexel's vision could not have been implemented without the Sisters of the Blessed Sacrament.

Chapter Four

HEADING WEST

Founding and Funding Ministries to Indigenous People

*M*other Katharine Drexel and a companion, Sister Evangelist, left St. Elizabeth's en route to Santa Fe, New Mexico, on April 9, 1894. This was the first of many times that Drexel would leave the community for an extended period of time, and "there was not a dry eye when the time for final parting came," the annalist wrote. As the train carrying the two sisters left Bensalem for a trip that would last several weeks, the SBS gathered to see them off "waved their handkerchiefs until the answering wave was little more than a tiny speck of white borne farther and farther away by the fast flying train until it was suddenly lost to sight in the bend of the track."[1] Although the sisters left behind felt Drexel's absence keenly, they were heartened by letters she sent informing them of her thoughts and decisions.

The trip itself was for business; the two sisters wanted to determine if the situation at St. Catherine's Indian School was as dire as they had been told. Drexel had funded the building of the school, but she and the SBS had received reports from several Catholic clerics involved in western missions, including Rev. Joseph Stephan of the Bureau of Catholic Indian Missions, indicating that it was possible the school would have to close for lack of personnel. The reports turned out to be true; and given the mission of the Sisters of the Blessed Sacrament, using members of the congregation to staff the school appeared to be a logical choice if they could gain the approval of Philadelphia archbishop Patrick Ryan. When Mother Katharine and Sister Evangelist returned to Philadelphia, they stopped at Ryan's residence to describe the state of St. Catherine's and remind him of the souls that would be lost if the school was closed. After hearing their story, Ryan informed Drexel that the SBS could take the mission.[2] This was good news to Mother Katharine and all of the Sisters of the Blessed Sacrament, who began preparing to staff and administer St. Catherine's Indian School in Santa Fe when the school year opened the following September. The nine sisters assigned to the New Mexico school— the annalist referred to them as the "chosen ones"—would be the first among many missioned to Native and Black communities.[3]

Drexel had been interested in Indigenous People since she first traveled to the western United States with her father and sisters after her mother's death in 1883. "To these visits," she wrote, "I owe, after God's grace, my religious vocation as an Indian missionary."[4] In addition, Nebraska Bishop James O'Connor had nurtured her desire to help Indigenous People through letters that described the abject state of poverty in which they lived, as well as their need for churches and schools. Shortly after Francis Drexel's death, Bishop Martin Marty and Father Joseph Stephan visited the Drexel sisters in hopes of soliciting their financial and moral support. Both men ministered to Indigenous People; Marty would become the first bishop of Sioux Falls and Stephan would go on to head the Bureau of Catholic Indian Missions (BCIM). Their trip to Philadelphia was designed to raise funds to subsidize their efforts to evangelize Indigenous communities. Clearly swayed by their presentation, Katharine Drexel donated $500 to the cause. Her generosity would continue until the Great Depression forced her to decrease her contributions to Black and Indigenous People, two groups that have been systematically excluded from church and society.[5]

In addition to substantial monetary donations, founding a religious congregation served as another way to manifest Drexel's commitment to Black and Indigenous People. The history of the Sisters of the Blessed Sacrament is—in many ways—the story of a missionary congregation. Women entered the congregation fully expecting to spend the remainder of their lives working with those who had been marginalized by white society—sometimes in remote parts of the country—as teachers, catechists, and home visitors. Some sisters spent most of their adult lives with one group or the other; others were assigned to work in a variety of settings and moved between the two communities.

It is impossible to discuss every mission—and there were well over one hundred—that Katharine Drexel and the SBS founded, funded, or staffed. Some, as might be expected, were more successful than others. In 1909, for instance, St. Augustine's Indian Mission in Winnebago, Nebraska, was founded. Drexel's spiritual advisor, Bishop James O'Connor, had not been able to provide any educational support for members of the Winnebago and Omaha tribes prior to his death, and efforts to realize his wish were unsuccessful until Mother Katharine agreed to provide monetary and personnel support. By 1946, however, SBS leadership decided to withdraw the congregation from St. Augustine's. "The field," the chronicler reported, "had never been promising, and failed to provide, at any time, any promise of lasting good for the future." The sisters assigned there "could do greater good for God and the Church elsewhere."[6]

Mother Katharine Drexel spent millions of dollars building churches and schools for the Indigenous community, including some that were staffed by the SBS. Although there would never be enough sisters in the congregation to staff all of the schools in which she took at least some financial interest, three in particular—St. Catherine Indian School, St. Paul Indian School (now the Marty Indian School) in South Dakota, and St. Michael Indian School in Arizona—would play an integral role in the history of the SBS. Several sections of this chapter will be devoted to an examination of these three schools to allow us not only to discern how Mother Katharine and her sisters operated them, but also to view a host of sometimes disturbing issues such as challenging economic and social contexts, power politics with the federal and local governments, gender tensions, abuse of students, and racial prejudice.

SBS and Schools for Indigenous People

Katharine Drexel's memories of how she began supporting ministries to Indigenous People began before she founded the SBS. She wrote that with Monsignor Stephan's approval "I built two Indian schools, one for fifty boys, another for as many girls, among the Osage Indians, in the hope that with boarding schools for them the Indians would become civilized, marry and settle down to live good Catholic lives."[7] As this chapter demonstrates, the story is more complex, but the fact remains that Drexel donated a substantial sum of money over a period of approximately fifty years to build and staff Native churches and schools, but to a certain extent the success of her work was contingent on government policies related to the education of Indigenous People. When Ulysses S. Grant was inaugurated president in 1869 there was widespread agreement in Washington that the federal Bureau of Indian Affairs (BIA) was mired in corruption. The new president made a number of changes intended to improve the situation, which became known as Grant's "Peace Policy." A Board of Indian Commissioners was established to advise the BIA and make sure funds allocated to the agency were appropriately spent. In an attempt to further minimize corruption, the administration of a number of agencies designed to assist Indigenous People was turned over to various Christian denominations. Catholic leaders were upset and angry when they discovered that they would only be given jurisdiction of seven out of about seventy-five agencies; according to their calculations, they should have assumed responsibility for at least thirty-eight. One result of what Catholic leaders believed were unjust—and even anti-Catholic—actions on the part of the government was the 1874 creation of the BCIM, originally known as the office of the Commissioner for Catholic Indian Missions.[8] BCIM leaders discovered almost immediately that the organization could not survive unless it became financially self-sufficient. The money the Bureau received from the federal government and the annual Lenten collection for Black and Native missions was not sufficient to build and support the number of churches and schools the BCIM hoped to establish.[9] When Katharine Drexel began to contribute substantial amounts of money to the BCIM, Catholic missionaries to Indigenous People finally had a chance to build and staff the churches and schools they desperately needed.

Although church officials did not think they had been "given" enough schools under the terms of Grant's Peace Policy, the situation began to change by the 1890s as Protestant denominations moved away from sponsoring schools and began advocating for these institutions to be run by the government. The result was that Catholics began to staff and administer those schools from which other denominations had decided to withdraw. More schools meant that they received more federal money to support the educational process, and would perhaps save more souls by leading Indigenous People to the Catholic Church. In 1874, for instance, Catholic schools were only receiving a total of $8000; by 1890 that figure had increased to $50,000. The allocations, however, also led to heightened tensions with both Protestant denominations, that—despite the fact that they had withdrawn from those schools—did not want to see them administered by Catholics. In addition, Catholic disagreements with the federal government exacerbated when Thomas Jefferson Morgan, who was well known for his anti-Catholic sentiments, was appointed Commissioner of Indian Affairs, and the situation continued to escalate until the outbreak of World War I as "Protestants and Catholics engaged in a battle for funding and cultural hegemony."[10]

Congress began to cut federal funds to Catholic Indian schools in the late 1890s as a number of groups, including the anti-Catholic American Protective Association, argued that the government should bear sole responsibility for educating and assimilating Indigenous People. In order for the BCIM to maintain its system of schools despite this financial loss, Katharine Drexel's continued support was essential. Although it is difficult to determine how much money Drexel contributed to missions dedicated to Indigenous People in total, it is possible to get some sense of the philanthropist's largesse. In order to keep Catholic Indian schools viable, Drexel agreed to pay schools what they lost in government funding provided they maintained a certain level of enrollment. In 1899, for example, that difference was $99,046, and did not include the cost of staffing and maintaining SBS schools or any churches she agreed to subsidize. "Between 1895 and 1928, Drexel estimated that she supplied almost $6,000,000 to the Indian missions."[11]

Drexel and the SBS did not limit their ministry to schools founded by their own congregation, but "made assisting in religious education at government schools a significant part of their undertaking."[12] As a result, the SBS conducted religious education classes at several government schools, including the Carlisle Indian School in Pennsylvania. Carlisle is only about 130 miles from the motherhouse in Bensalem, and most women entering the SBS probably did not think they would be assigned to catechize Indigenous People in central Pennsylvania. When Rev. Henry Ganss was assigned to St. Patrick Church in Carlisle in 1891, he realized that his parishioners included Catholic students at the Carlisle Indian School, and he argued for their right to attend

Mass and catechism classes on Sunday. School administrators agreed and Ganss then tried to persuade Katharine Drexel to send a few SBS to the parish. Their job, he explained, would be to provide religious education—assuming Richard Henry Pratt, the director, agreed—for the school's Catholic students and operate a small school for the city's Black children.

Although Drexel supported Ganss's efforts to catechize students at the Carlisle Indian School, she was unable to send SBS sisters at the time of his original request. Harrisburg Bishop John Shanahan was able to convince the Sisters of St. Joseph (SSJ) to staff the school, however, and Drexel willingly provided the funds needed to sustain a convent. The SSJs did not remain in Carlisle for long and were replaced by the Sisters of Mercy. When that congregation announced their intention of leaving Carlisle in 1906, Drexel was finally able to send members of the congregation to provide religious instruction for Catholic students at the Indian School. When the new ministry was announced on July 11, 1906, many of the sisters were somewhat "surprised" because they did not think of Carlisle as a place ripe for the evangelization of Blacks and Indigenous People.[13]

The sisters assigned to Carlisle arrived on August 27, 1906, and provided catechetical instruction for forty-three students on their first day. They devised an evening schedule in which older boys attended catechism classes on Monday; younger boys came on Thursday, and girls received instruction on Wednesday. Students from the school also came to the parish on Sunday mornings for Mass, and classes were offered at the Indian School on Sunday afternoons. The sisters did not teach Catholic doctrine in any sort of systematic way; classes consisted of learning and reciting the Lord's Prayer, reading from the New Testament, and lessons related to the life of Christ and the Ten Commandments. Students were also prepared to receive confession and first communion. Those who could not speak English confessed their sins with the help of a translator who went into the confessional with the child but did not face the young person making his or her confession. The priest would ask the penitent a question that would be translated, and the answer would be given by a shake of the head or—if the question concerned the number of times a sin was committed—holding up fingers.[14]

Residential schools for Indigenous People, including the one located in Carlisle, are difficult to discuss in positive terms. Richard Henry Pratt, the founder of the school, believed that Indigenous People needed to be completely assimilated into white American society. Carlisle Indian School purported to assist in this process by removing children from their homes and tribes, transporting them to a school located hundreds of miles away, and "educating" them to be Americans. "Kill the Indian, Save the Man," was a statement Pratt often made to explain his views on education and assimilation. The removal of the children from their culture often meant that when a student died their bodies were not returned to their families but were buried on the grounds of the school.[15] The Sisters of the Blessed Sacrament stationed in Carlisle were not employed by or officially connected to the school in any way and had no formal process to challenge Pratt's views or policies. Their job was to make sure the school's Catholic students received at least a basic religious education and they took their responsibility very seriously.

The sisters' concern for the souls of the Catholic students extended to those who lived outside of the school. Some students, for instance, were sent to live with and work for families in the area. Pratt developed the program, known as the Outing System, because he believed it provided job training for the older students and contributed to their assimilation into mainstream society. Boys who participated in the Outing System worked as farmers and blacksmiths; girls were usually placed as housekeepers or domestic servants. They received a modest salary that was deposited in a bank account.

There were, of course, negative components of the Outing System. Because the children were placed with families in Pennsylvania, for instance, they were only able to speak English, and there is no doubt that many students were mistreated, abused, or taken advantage of by the families with whom they lived. The Sisters of the Blessed Sacrament accepted the Outing System as part of the educational program at the Indian School, but they did advocate for Catholic students being placed with Catholic families whenever possible and that they be allowed to attend Mass on Sunday.[16]

The sisters' ministry to the Black community in Carlisle involved a good deal of outreach, as well. In September 1906, a flyer announced that a "Select Free School for Colored Children" was opening in St. Katharine's Hall, which had been built with funds provided by Katharine Drexel, who saw "the need of equal educational facilities for the Colored Race in Carlisle." Throughout the years of the school's existence, the sisters provided reports of their visits to the area's Black families as well as the academic and spiritual progress of their students. In 1914, for instance, Sister Justin shared some good news: "Father Welsh has promised to baptize a number of our Colored pupils in about a week." She also explained that some students who had expressed an interest in being baptized were unable to obtain the consent of a parent. Oscerean Davis, for instance, "says his mother is willing for him to be a Catholic but his father says if he mentions it again he will take him away from our school." Although he came to Mass without his father's knowledge, the sisters would not baptize him because they would not go against Mr. Davis's wishes.[17]

The SBS ministry in Carlisle came to an end in 1917 for two reasons. First, only seventeen Black students enrolled in the sisters' school for the 1917–18 academic year. U.S. entry into World War I meant that Black people were able to find jobs in the country's larger industrial cities for more money than they could earn in Carlisle. At the same time, the War Department, in whose buildings the Indian School had been housed for thirty-eight years, needed the space for a hospital. Since the great majority of Indigenous People lived west of the Mississippi River, it made sense from an economic perspective that residential schools should not be located in the eastern part of the United States. The Carlisle Indian School transitioned to General Hospital No. 31 on August 15, 1918. As a result of these two factors, there was no longer a need for a SBS presence in Carlisle.[18]

Drexel and Indigenous People

Mother Katharine Drexel was not a political activist as the term is used in the twenty-first century, but she did believe the government was responsible for the poverty in which the overwhelming majority of Indigenous People lived. In addition to her western travels where she observed the marginalization of Indians for herself, Drexel had been heavily influenced by the 1881 publication of Helen Hunt Jackson's *A Century of Dishonor*, which was a very serious treatment of the U.S. government's policy toward Indigenous People. Jackson was not especially interested in issues related to social justice, but she began to study this subject after meeting a group of Indigenous People in Boston who were trying to explain how poorly the federal government was treating them. *A Century of Dishonor* consists of historical sketches of seven tribes and the ways in which they were mistreated by the government, a chapter describing four massacres of Indigenous People, and a final chapter. When the book was published, Jackson made sure a copy was sent to every member of Congress as well as President-Elect James A. Garfield.[19]

Drexel occasionally used both her money and her influence to advocate for Native interests with either the U.S. government or the BCIM. Her influence was a result of her wealth, prestige, and relatives. She had two well-placed brothers-in-law: Edward Morrell (Louise's husband) served several terms in Congress, and Walter George Smith, who married Elizabeth, was appointed to the Board of Indian Commissioners by President Warren G. Harding. When the Cupeño and Digueño tribes were fighting removal from their traditional lands in California in 1903, Drexel donated $6000 to defray legal expenses. Although both the California and U.S. Supreme Courts ruled against the tribes, she maintained an interest in their situation and several years later paid for three tribal representatives to come to Washington, DC, and lobby for their cause.[20]

Drexel also pressured Monsignor Joseph Stephan, who led the BCIM from 1884 until 1901, to persuade the government—in this case the Department of the Interior—to improve the living conditions of some Native tribes. Stephan's lobbying met with some success. In 1899, the Indians living at San Ildefonso Pueblo received additional funding as a result of Drexel's interest in their predicament. She had less luck garnering support from Stephan's successor, Father William Ketcham, when she voiced her agreement with a radical proposal in a 1904 bill calling for the removal of all white people from Native lands. Ketcham argued against Drexel's support of the bill, writing, "[Y]ou could as easily remove the Atlantic from our eastern coast as you could remove the hundreds of thousands of white people from the Indian Territory." Drexel's support for this bill demonstrates that although her views on the rights of Indigenous People may have focused more on structural change than has been previously suggested, as a woman religious she was not expected to express her opinions on issues such as this in a public venue.[21]

Drexel's decision to refrain from speaking publicly about proposed federal legislation is not unusual when viewed within the history of U.S. women religious prior to the mid-1960s. Although sisters were a visible manifestation of the Catholic Church's presence throughout the United States, they were expected—and often required—to maintain a low profile in the world outside of the school, hospital, and convent. Matters related to government policy—even if they impacted parochial schools on reservations—were the purview of ecclesiastical authorities, not women religious, and sisters were expected to defer to the males who supervised and approved their work. Although there were exceptions to this general rule, women religious, including Drexel, understood that a good working relationship with local bishops and pastors depended on the willingness of women religious to accept their place in the hierarchical structure.[22]

Unlike most women religious, Drexel's willingness to use her wealth to establish and sponsor churches and schools gave her the ability to exercise some authority when it came to deciding how her money would be spent. She was adamant, for instance, that any schools dedicated to the education of Native children that benefited from her generosity were not to admit white students. In 1892, Sister Mary Ruth informed her that the Franciscan Sisters teaching at St. Elizabeth Indian School in Purcell, Oklahoma, were honoring Drexel's stipulation and only admitting Native children to the school. Ten years later, on a 1902 visit to St. Elizabeth's, Drexel wondered why there were so many "white girls" enrolled. Sister Patricia, a Sister of St. Francis of Philadelphia, helped to answer her question by allowing Mother Katharine to move from room to room asking, "Surely you have no Indian blood in you?" The replies were similar. "Yes, my mother was a Creek, half breed." "My grandfather was a Choctaw." These answers came from "children with light hair and blue eyes." The "bleached Indians" in Oklahoma, as Drexel sometimes referred to them, were entitled to the same amount of land and money as other Indigenous People as long as they could prove they were partially Choctaw or Chickasee. This concerned Drexel because, in her opinion, the lighter-skinned Choctaw or Chickasee, some of whom had received an excellent education on the East Coast, would control the tribal governments and push others aside until they "learn to think and become more civilized." Her solution was to ensure that the schools she funded provided Indigenous People with a "first class education."[23]

Clerical Authority and Drexel's Money

Women religious traditionally have not had a significant voice in the U.S. Catholic Church, and they have been expected to follow the directives of bishops and priests in almost every instance. As Carol Coburn and Martha Smith wrote, "Women religious who challenged male authority often found themselves labeled 'unladylike' and their very sanity questioned."[24] Drexel did not actively challenge the male hierarchical structure of Catholicism, but her vast wealth allowed her to set the terms under which her money was given and dictate how the money earmarked for Indigenous People might be spent. Her ability to assert financial authority in a patriarchal church made her somewhat of an anomaly; the great majority of women religious had virtually no say in how parish or diocesan funds were allocated.

Simply put, the Bureau of Catholic Indian Missions was financially viable only because of Katharine Drexel's contributions. In an 1899 letter to Drexel, Monsignor William Ketcham thanked her for the "great and most liberal donation of $83,000" that had supported Native schools during the previous school year. Ketcham understood that Drexel could not be the sole source of BCIM support, but he was having difficulty convincing the U.S. hierarchy of the importance of promoting special collections for this work. He gently reminded Drexel that other communities of women religious were able to help support themselves through teaching and nursing. The SBS were faced with a different situation: the people with whom they worked were poor and American Catholics did not seem particularly willing to support the work of the congregation.[25]

Priests seeking donations from Drexel and the SBS were often disappointed—and angry—when they realized Drexel would not change the terms under which the money was given. Only projects related to Black and Indigenous People received funding, and there were no exceptions. Urban Catholics, some argued, also needed help building churches, schools, hospitals, orphanages, and other institutions that were founded in the late nineteenth and early twentieth centuries to meet the needs of what has been termed the "immigrant church." When Paulist Father Walter Elliott, a white priest ministering in New York City, asked Drexel for $500, he was dismayed to discover that she would not change her terms under any circumstances. Writing to a friend, Elliott complained, "she said in effect 'no poor white trash need apply.' Only black and red are the team they [Drexel and her sisters] will back."[26]

Overseeing Investments

Drexel funded the building of churches and often paid the salaries of priests stationed on a reservation, but her real interest was the education of Indigenous People. "Without Anglo schooling," she believed, "the Indians had no chance to extricate themselves from the dreary arrangements imposed by a disdainful white society nor, by her thinking, to enjoy Christianity." As a result, she made the decision to distribute her wealth in ways that would allow Indigenous People to receive the education to which they had been denied access for far too long. The education offered in the schools Drexel funded, as well as those staffed by the SBS, would hopefully allow members of both groups to achieve socioeconomic equality within the dominant white power structure. The classroom, according to Anne Butler, would "elevate humankind."[27]

During the Great Depression, Drexel often had to tell those depending on her support that she could no longer fund some schools and projects. In 1934, Sister Macaria, who was working at St. Mary's Indian School in Odanah, Wisconsin, learned that Drexel was "obliged to withdraw" her support. She had been giving the school about $5000 per year between her own donations and BCIM allocations, and that was no longer sustainable. Around the same time, Monsignor William Hughes, director of the BCIM, sent several letters to Drexel indicating his concern about what her reduced contributions would mean for work with Indigenous People. In 1933, Hughes expressed his disappointment that Drexel was no longer contributing $1000 per year for expenses incurred by the BCIM. One year later, he wrote asking how much her payments for three Indian schools would be reduced; in 1935 Hughes wanted to know if she would be decreasing her contributions to fifteen schools or ceasing to support them completely.[28] The once wealthy heiress did what she could, but the economic crash had deeply depleted her resources.

An SBS Ministry:
St. Catherine's, Santa Fe

Residential schools, in which Native students from a fairly large geographic area lived in dormitories on school property during the academic year, are problematic for several reasons. First, children attending these schools were uprooted from their families. They were removed from the reservation and forced to adapt to a strange culture in the hopes that they would assimilate into mainstream American society. Second, there are many documented instances of children being physically, emotionally, and sometimes sexually abused at a number of schools founded in the United States and Canada to educate children from Indigenous communities.[29] Third, many schools did not receive adequate funding, and as a result, the living conditions were less than ideal. At times, children did not even have enough to eat. Fourth, the education the children received did not always prepare them to either enter the work force or gain admittance to a college or university.[30] Schools administered by the Sisters of the Blessed Sacrament faced all of these issues to one degree or another.

Brian S. Collier describes St. Catherine Indian School as the "first modern era Catholic Native American boarding school," and notes that it demonstrates Drexel's "deep commitment and personal spiritual mandate for serving others in the name of her religious ideals."[31] Katharine Drexel donated the money used to build St. Catherine's on land owned by the Archdiocese of Santa Fe. Originally designed as a residential school for girls, the new edifice was dedicated on June 16, 1886, five years before the founding of the Sisters of the Blessed Sacrament. From its inception, St. Catherine's struggled to find enough teachers to provide adequate staffing. In 1893, Archbishops Placide Chapelle of Santa Fe and Peter Bourgade of Tucson expressed their desire for the SBS to assume responsibility for St. Catherine's, but Philadelphia's Archbishop Ryan refused permission on the grounds that the SBS needed more formation before they would be ready to work such a distance from the motherhouse. As a result, St. Catherine's was forced to close for the 1893–94 academic year. After receiving Ryan's permission, the Sisters of the Blessed Sacrament took over St. Catherine's in 1894 as a permanent ministry of the congregation.[32]

The first four of the nine sisters assigned to St. Catherine's left Philadelphia on June 13, 1894. Although it was the first time that members of the congregation had been assigned a ministry in the western United States, it was not an unexpected assignment. The second group of SBS left for Santa Fe on June 24. Their journey was interrupted by a Pullman strike and took much longer than expected. It took the five sisters ten days to journey from Philadelphia to La Junta, Colorado, because strikers stole the train's engine twice. When the sisters finally arrived at St. Catherine's, they wrote to the motherhouse praising the work that had been completed by the four sisters who preceded them, describing it as "marvelous." The floors, one commented, had been "scrubbed almost as white as our refectory tables."[33]

The sisters' next task was to find parents willing to enroll their children at St. Catherine's by convincing them that their daughters and sons would receive a good education and be kept safe in the residential school. Their job was made more difficult because the parents spoke little, if any, English, and the sisters did not speak Pueblo. Drexel, who had traveled to Santa Fe to be present for the opening of the school year, was disappointed when only five boys enrolled on the first day. By the end of the school year, however, eighty-four boys and girls were attending the school. Some of them lived more than one hundred miles away from Santa Fe.[34]

The SBS assigned to St. Catherine's were part of a larger congregation of women religious and were governed by the Rule of the order as well as by their vows of poverty, chastity, and obedience. The distance between New Mexico (and other missions) and St. Elizabeth's—the motherhouse in Bensalem—often meant that a local superior had many questions about how to handle those placed under her authority. In a 1903 letter, for example, Drexel was asked a number of questions of varying levels of importance, but in the end, no question was considered minor or frivolous. Could one ask questions of another in the secular entry, between the parlor and breakfast rooms? "No,...unless a Sister be in the parlor or breakfast room with company and a Sister knocks at [the] door and asks her a question." A more serious question concerned whether a Sister might speak or shake hands with Native visitors. The answer was clear. "In passing, any of the sisters may speak a few cordial words, and shake hands with Indians. For a prolonged conversation—say more than five minutes—permission should be asked."[35]

During the summer months of 1918, the sisters who remained at St. Catherine's were expected to visit the pueblos in order to check on their former and current students, making sure they had remained committed to the Catholic Church and its teachings. In addition, the sisters were instructed to offer catechism to those who were interested in learning more about the tenets of the church. "So much good was accomplished that year by year afterward sisters went out for a week or ten days at a time and worked among the Indians, going from house to house gathering the children and instructing them." It was not easy to spend the summer ministering in the pueblos, but the sisters chosen "did not mind in the least," because they believed they were truly acting as missionaries and saving the souls of those with whom they worked.[36]

St. Catherine's goal was to provide a better than average education, and the staff continually worked to revise its program and curriculum to meet the changing needs of students. The school was founded as an industrial Indian school, which meant that both academic and vocational tracks were offered, and the faculty and staff hoped the students would achieve success after graduation. In 1935, six boys and two girls constituted the first high school graduating class. Over the years, the lower grades were eliminated, and St. Catherine's became a school for students in grades seven through twelve. By the 1960s, the curriculum's focus was on general studies, business, and preparing students for college.[37]

By 1937, Mother Katharine Drexel had been succeeded as Mother General by Mother Mercedes O'Connor. Sisters, of course, continued to write "home" to the motherhouse informing those in leadership positions about the successes and failures of each mission. Writing to Mother Mercedes in that year, Sister Tarcisius provided some sacramental statistics related to the sisters' work in the Santa Fe area. Thirty-five students were enrolled in the high school at St. Catherine's and another 240 attended the grammar school. High School students could choose from several clubs moderated by the SBS, including the Junior Holy Name Society, a Library Club, a Science Club, and the Children of Mary. Five children had been baptized, she reported, three students had been confirmed, and sixty-three had received first communion. The Indian children living in the pueblos are baptized and confirmed as infants, she noted, so the numbers listed in her report referred to children from other tribes who did not have a priest living among them. Almost fifty years after the SBS arrived in Santa Fe, the sisters—those assigned to New Mexico and those in leadership positions at the motherhouse—continued to emphasize their role as missionaries as well as teachers.[38]

The routine at St. Catherine's has been described as "quasi-military." The day began with reveille at six a.m. and ended with the playing of "Taps" at night. This was similar to many other residential schools for Indigenous children, however, and some parents—even those who were non-Catholic—preferred to send their children to St. Catherine's instead of the government school in Santa Fe, seeing it as the "lesser of two evils."[39] The school expanded its facilities over the years to accommodate a growing number of students. In 1917, a recreation hall for students and a building to house boys were built. Nine years later, in

1926, a new classroom building allowed the SBS to increase the number of students attending the school.[40]

The SBS hoped the young men and women in their classrooms would return home and spread Catholicism among their friends and relatives. In addition, the sisters taught catechism and prepared children to receive the sacraments at the government school in Santa Fe. The 1911 annals report that seventy-three children attending the government school made their first communion that year. On that same day, about sixty children went to confession; two girls were baptized; and 130 children at the school received communion during Mass. The first communicants were treated to a "lovely breakfast," and the SBS provided candy and cake for a special treat. The chronicles also note that the children attending the government school were not allowed to talk during meals, including this one to celebrate their reception of a sacrament, "on account of the large number of children, over three hundred, all dining in the same room."[41] The SBS, of course, also prepared the children at St. Catherine's for first communion and confirmation, and religion played a prominent role in the school's curriculum. Students were encouraged to join sodalities; the Holy Name Society allowed boys to attend Communion as a group once a month, and girls were able to join the Sodality of Mary.[42] At least during the early years of the school, the sisters seemed to have had little interest in Indigenous religion. In 2003, Patrick Toya, remembered that the sisters never mentioned Indian religion. "They stressed their Catholic religion and evangelized us in the Catholic way." He went on to say that "there was no conflict [about teaching Catholicism] at all because nobody made any issue of it."[43]

By 1994, synopses of St. Catherine's that appeared in material designed to promote and raise money for the school stressed its historical connection with the Sisters of the Blessed Sacrament in language reflective of liberation theology and twentieth-century views of native education. One document, for instance, claimed, "For over one hundred years, St. Catherine Indian School has been implementing Katharine Drexel's goal of bringing the liberating message of Christ and the enabling power of education to Native Americans." By the 1990s any school hoping to raise significant amounts of money had to provide evidence that students were achieving the goals set by the faculty, and St. Catherine's could boast that recent graduates had received scholarships from the University of Notre Dame, Georgetown University, and Dartmouth College, and were enjoying successful careers in education, law, medicine, and engineering. The promotional material went on to explain why the school depended on outside donations to help it survive: tuition did not come close to covering the expenses related to operating and staffing St. Catherine's. In addition, a number of students' families could not afford to pay any or all of the tuition and were receiving various forms of financial assistance. "For the additional funds required in offering an educational program to prepare students for an increasingly complex and technical society, St. Catherine's looks to individuals and organizations who have a concern for the quality of life and economic opportunity of Native Americans and other minorities."[44] Although every attempt was made to keep St. Catherine's operational, the lack of SBS personnel to staff the school required the hiring of lay teachers, along with the added financial burden of salaries and benefits. For several years, SBS and others committed to St. Catherine's sought ways to keep the school financially viable but were unsuccessful. Four years after the 1994 fundraising appeal, St. Catherine's announced that the school was closing. Its final graduation ceremony was held at the close of the 1997–98 school year.[45]

Patrick Toya, a former student at St. Catherine's, remembered that "academics was number one" at the school, but "by the same token, discipline was there." His published reminiscence claims he never observed any physical abuse at the school. "Official SBS policy prevented sisters from using corporal punishment without special approval from Mother Katharine herself, [but] it is difficult to say whether this ban held up in practice."[46] Brian S. Collier, however, suggests there were indeed "abuses and brutal assimilation," but notes that the school's faculty "took some measures to meet people where they were, a lesson they [the sisters] learned from the Gospels."[47] Despite this, the SBS expected their students from Indigenous communities to participate in the process of Americanization as soon as they arrived at St. Catherine's. They were immediately bathed, given a haircut, and dressed in "American" clothes.

Students at St. Catherine's certainly ran away—a common occurrence at Native boarding schools in general—for reasons related to abusive treatment, homesickness, and as Collier notes, "because they could." Being forced to attend a residential school was sometimes described as being sentenced to prison. One was not free to leave and often had to work long and hard outside of school hours. Students were assigned tasks, for instance, that involved keeping the school clean, working on the farm, and taking care of the grounds.[48]

Drexel's concern for Indigenous People and her contributions directed to their education does not mean that she stepped outside of the box on issues related to their forced assimilation. She believed that schools founded or funded by the Sisters of the Blessed Sacrament would help raise Indigenous People out of poverty and allow them to move into the mainstream of society. This, of course, was not always the case, and Native boarding schools are now viewed "as places of oppression which failed to live up to the lofty promises [of those] who started the movement." It is difficult, especially in a work of this nature, to attempt to describe any residential school as normative because so much depended on those administering and staffing the school, but it is important to place Drexel and the Sisters of the Blessed Sacrament within the context of the era in which the schools were founded as well as critically examine their work in these facilities.[49]

Native Sisters

St. Paul Indian School, Yankton, South Dakota

When Benedictine Father Sylvester Eisenman opened a school for the Yankton Sioux in Marty, South Dakota, in 1919, he quickly concluded that a day school was not a feasible option. Children who lived twenty miles from the school—or more—found it impossible to get from their homes to the school during inclement weather when the roads were impassable. Eisenman asked Mother Katharine for sisters to staff his planned residential school, but she told him there were none available to send to South Dakota. After her initial refusal, Eisenman spoke to the sisters living at St. Elizabeth's and managed to convince them of his project's importance. All of those present expressed an interest in working in South Dakota, and Drexel agreed to send four sisters to staff St. Paul's Indian School. Unlike St. Catherine's, the SBS did not own the school, although Drexel did help to defray some of Eisenman's expenses. The number of sisters assigned to St. Paul's at any one time, however, made the school one of the largest of the SBS ministries to Indigenous People.[50]

One way to convince students and their families that the SBS were genuinely concerned about their spiritual and physical welfare was to develop relationships, and the faculty assigned to St. Paul's were expected to devote part of their time to visiting the families of their students who lived on the reservation. Sister Liguori, who spent many years at Marty, learned how to drive so that the sisters could reach out to families who lived some distance from the school. In 1943, the sisters started a sewing class in one town "for the purpose of keeping in touch with the Indians and with God's help bring back the lost sheep."[51]

The importance of St. Paul's in Marty for any study of Katharine Drexel and the Sisters of the Blessed Sacrament lies in the religious congregation that was founded to work at the mission. When, under the guidance of Benedictine Father Francis Craft, Sister Mary Catherine Sacred White Buffalo (Josephine Crowfeather) was professed in 1890, the first community of Indigenous women religious, the Indian Congregation of the Order of St. Benedict—the name was later changed to the Congregation of American Sisters—was formally established. Although Drexel occasionally contributed to Craft's work, she did not play a part in the new congregation. Unfortunately, the Congregation of American Sisters did not survive and had ceased to exist by 1901.[52]

According to the recollections of Sister Mary of Lourdes, SBS, the Oblate Sisters of the Blessed Sacrament began when a female student at St. Paul's was asked what she planned to do when she finished her education. She replied that she did not know because she wanted to become a sister but did not think there was a congregation suitable for her. "Our Indian girls go to white communities and they don't stay," she said. "If I went to be a Sister, I'd want to be an Indian Sister." When the young woman's comments were reported to Eisenman, his response, according to Sister Mary of Lourdes was, "That's just what I've been waiting for. I want to start an Indian Community but I don't want it to come from me, I want it to come from the girls."[53] After canvassing the students, twelve girls expressed an interest in entering religious life.

Mother Liguori began meeting with the young women once a week and after she had been instructing them for about a year, Eisenman requested that Drexel assign someone to form the young women into sisters. Drexel agreed, but when Sister Mary of Lourdes arrived in Marty, she discovered only one girl interested in even thinking about her vocation. Despite her best efforts, no other students stepped forward. Seven girls eventually expressed their desire to enter religious life. Sister Mary of Lourdes concluded her recollections by reminding others that they "were taken out of high school and were isolated just like postulants were in the early days. They weren't allowed to talk to the other sisters that were there, and they weren't allowed to talk to the other children without permission. It was terrible."[54]

The Oblate Sisters of the Blessed Sacrament (OSBS) was formally founded in 1935 by Eisenman and supported by Mother Katharine Drexel and the Sisters of the Blessed Sacrament. In a 1935 letter to Drexel, Eisenman explained that there were fourteen young women interested in the OSBS, but "four or five" were still in grade school; the others were in high school. Two young women were about to finish high school, but Eisenman thought it best for all of them to return home for the summer "after giving them a word of counsel about those precautions necessary to protect their vocations." If some were unsure of their vocation, going home for the summer would allow them to drop out of the process. Eisenman suggested that candidates for the new congregation spend two years in the novitiate because it will "take a longer time to put the Religious Spirit into these children as they have no traditions such as we have when we come to the Religious Life."[55] Drexel may have been at least somewhat worried about Eisenman's idea of a congregation composed entirely of Indigenous women. One account notes that Eisenman first asked her to accept some of these women into the SBS, but she refused. "Her answer was negative as she felt in early years when others from the West had entered, they had not persevered or were unsatisfactory."[56] The convent chronicles do not expand on this statement, but it is safe to say that Drexel was hesitant to admit young women from Yankton into the congregation.

The purpose of the OSBS was to "aid in the works of the Mission of Marty, South Dakota." They were to carry out this goal by (1) assisting the Sisters of the Blessed Sacrament; (2) teaching and assisting in the classroom; (3) instructing children in the "industrial and domestic words of the Mission"; (4) caring for sick children; and (5) visiting the Indians at home to "instruct them and help them in their spiritual needs." Sister Mary of Lourdes, who was responsible for forming the new sisters in religious life, recognized that they were expected to work hard, and informed congregational leaders that they were also taking classes. She suggested that if there were enough children at the school to do some of the work of the OSBS, the sisters could take two courses during the 1937–38 academic year. These courses would be in addition to a course on apologetics and instructions on vows.[57]

The first profession ceremony for the OSBS took place in 1938. The two newly professed sisters, Sister Mary of Lourdes wrote, were transformed by the experience. "Truly, one can see the effects of the grace of Profession in them." Eleven years later, in 1949, Mother Mary of the Visitation informed the Sisters of the Blessed Sacrament that the Oblate Sisters of the Blessed Sacrament were now a "fully constituted Religious Community 'of the Diocesan Rite.'" At the time, there were seven professed members of the OSBS. The SBS, however, remained integral to the life and governance of the new community, and the community's council consisted of two members from each congregation. Two years later, when the bishop of Sioux Falls made a canonical visit to the OSBS, he announced that the congregation would now be completely independent. During this same visit, the question of higher education for the sisters was broached. The bishop was not averse to them receiving college degrees and supported two sisters going to the SBS motherhouse in Bensalem each summer in order to earn college credits. The congregation, composed entirely of Indigenous women, was now being encouraged to earn college degrees in order to gain proficiency as teachers, moving in the same directions as other congregations of women religious.[58]

During the second half of the twentieth century, changes in both the Catholic Church and U.S. society led missionary congregations on reservations to begin the process of turning over the administration of churches and school to local tribal leaders. The governance structure at what was renamed the Marty Indian School began to change in 1970 when the Benedictines—who had administered the school since Eisenman founded it—announced that all of their schools serving Indigenous People should be transferred to the appropriate tribe. Although the Benedictines would continue to serve as missionaries in the area, they would no longer control the schools. The following year, as the number of women entering religious life continued to decrease, leaving communities—including the Sisters of the Blessed Sacrament—with a shortage of personnel, the congregation announced that no sisters would be assigned to the high school for the 1971–72 academic year, but some would be teaching at the elementary school level. By 1975, the school had been officially transferred from the church to the tribe, and the four SBS working in Marty had moved to smaller quarters.[59]

Oblate Sisters of the Blessed Sacrament, South Dakota, 1947. Courtesy of Marquette University Archives, Bureau of Catholic Indian Missions Records, ID 10472.

Sister Marjorie Everett, one of the last SBS to teach at the school, arrived in 1971 after spending four years at Xavier Prep in New Orleans (see chapter 6). One result of the Second Vatican Council (1962–1965) was that women religious, including SBS, were now able to request an assignment to a particular ministry. Everett had requested an experience at an "Indian mission," and offered some reflections on how her experience at Marty differed from her time in New Orleans. The students in South Dakota, she observed, were cooperative but "did not have aspirations for higher education." Realizing that she had to adapt her teaching methodology to reach her new students, she created what she described as a "safe" way for students to ask questions and receive help. Instead of asking, "Does anyone want me to go over it again?" which meant a student might be singled out, she began to say, "How many of you want me to explain that again?" In addition, Sister Marjorie allowed her students to work in pairs because this approach seemed to provide some sort of moral support. Overall, she concluded, these students "were like any others," and they all responded to personal attention. She was unhappy to learn that her first year would also be her last because the SBS withdrew all teachers from the school at the end of the year.[60]

In 1980, the Sisters of the Blessed Sacrament announced that diminishing financial resources and numbers would no longer allow them to commit to providing staff for the Marty Indian School. Sister June would continue the community outreach work she was doing, but no members of the congregation would be associated with the school. The announcement noted that Sister June would live with the OSBS community who "welcomed the opportunity to help our Sisters as we had them in their founding years." About a year later, while studying at Xavier University in New Orleans, a priest identified only as "Father Tom" suggested that Sister June consider other ministries where she might be needed, telling her it was time "to let the people go." If the community needed her, they should ask her to stay. "We should not be catering to them or forcing anything on them."[61]

SBS and the Franciscans

St. Michael's, Arizona

Hoping to find a way to work with the Navajo tribe, the Bureau of Catholic Indian Missions managed to secure property just south of the reservation's Arizona border in 1895. Three years later, with the financial backing of Mother Katharine Drexel, three Franciscan friars arrived with the goal of educating and evangelizing the Navajo living in that area. Drexel agreed to pay for the land, build a school, and financially support the friars. This included all of the costs involved in opening the mission, including any necessary renovations, furniture, wine to be used at Mass, and a horse and saddle. When Drexel asked the Franciscans for an estimate of their living expenses, however, the provincial refused. The friars would, he told her, follow their vow of poverty and live on whatever she saw fit to donate to their mission. She suggested a contribution of $1000 annually to support three missionaries. All major purchases and any dealings with businesses had, as usual, to be approved by Mother Katharine.[62]

The Franciscan approach to missionary work involved learning the language and culture of the people among whom they ministered. Their first project was an informal school for boys living in the immediate area;

this allowed the friars to begin educating some children at the same time they were learning Navajo in order to better communicate with their neighbors. When Drexel visited the friars shortly after they began their work, she had no trouble understanding how important this ministry was to the education of Indigenous People. In 1901, she began to implement her vision of "a complete, thriving Catholic Navajo community" centered around St. Michael's School, by financing and planning the construction of a three-story building that included a chapel.[63]

When Anselm Weber, OSF, traveled the reservation to recruit students for the planned school, he encouraged them to send their children to St. Catherine's in Santa Fe until the new school was ready to accept students. His message to parents was that the Sisters of the Blessed Sacrament would be responsible for educating their children at St. Catherine's and St. Michael's. The sisters would treat the children as their own, Weber explained, and he even brought Mother Katharine with him to meet tribal leaders. Drexel offered her assurances that parents would be allowed to visit at any time, but she would not allow the children to be taken to a medicine man when they were sick. When eleven sisters arrived to staff St. Michael's in 1902, they immediately understood the necessity of allowing children to help their families with the autumn harvest; the school formally opened in December of that year with twenty-one students enrolled. By the end of the spring term, Weber had recruited an additional twenty-five children.[64]

St. Michael's was a bit more progressive than other schools and its curriculum was "locally pragmatic": it was not necessarily designed to push students to be successful in white society. Mornings were devoted to a traditional academic program with students receiving instruction in English (grammar, reading, and vocabulary), science, U.S. history, geography, and music. During the afternoon, students received instruction in practical or industrial skills. Girls received training in cooking, sewing, and nursing; boys worked on the farm or in the bakery. All classes except catechism were conducted in English, but students were allowed to converse with each other in the Navajo language outside of the classroom. In addition, the sisters focused on ensuring that the students honed some of the traditional skills of the Navajo community such as basket making and rug weaving. The academic calendar took the children's need to work on the autumn harvest into account, and as a result, school was held irregularly from April until November.[65]

While on extended tour of SBS missions in 1905—including some that were financed but not staffed by Drexel and the congregation—Mother Katharine wrote to the sisters at the motherhouse and expressed her pleasure with what she observed at St. Michael's. "It rejoiced me to see at St. Michael's the evidence of the good work done through the instrumentality of our sisters," she told them. As she often did, her letter included comments on how many children had received the sacraments because it was a clear demonstration that the SBS were doing more than simply teaching material that could be found in almost every American classroom. Forty-six had been baptized and instructed, "a better showing than Our Lord gave Himself at the end of His three years of active life for the conversion of those for Whom He was called." Sister M. Evangelist, in a report to the Commissioner of Indian Affairs, praised the children at St. Michael's, claiming they were "intellectually above the average Indian." If they were fluent in English, she continued, they would be equal to white students in the classroom.[66]

Children sometimes became ill and died while they were living and studying at St. Michael's, and stories about this are found in letters written by sisters stationed in Arizona. In 1911, the school experienced an outbreak of measles and at least two children died. Sister Mary Josephine wrote to the sisters at St. Elizabeth's, informing her readers that "Little Bart," age six, "winged his flight to heaven last night at 8:30 o'clock." Bart had apparently been associated with St. Michael's since he was a baby, and both Mother Katharine and Louise Morrell had met him on their visits to the school. In addition to Bart, a student named Paul had also died and Sister Josephine made sure to let the sisters in Pennsylvania know that the sermon preached at the funeral had led one man to return to the sacraments for the first time in five years. When she wrote the letter, fifty-eight students had been diagnosed with measles; only Paul and Bart had died. She closed by asking Mother Katharine to "pray if it be God's holy will we may lose no more."[67]

The influenza epidemic of 1918 had a great impact on those living on the Navajo reservation. Benjamin R. Brady and Howard M. Bahr have called the epidemic "among the most fateful events in tribal history," explaining that many died because they had no one to take care of them when they fell ill due to the "size and desolation of the reservation and the physical isolation of some of the camps." When Weber realized that the epidemic had reached Fort Defiance in the fall of 1918, he immediately quarantined students, faculty, and staff. They were not allowed to leave the school and "no one, neither red nor white, could visit the school." Because of this action, and as Weber noted, the prayers of the Sisters of the Blessed Sacrament, the school was "completely protected from the influenza." Although the school did not escape a later wave of influenza, it was far less deadly than the version that hit the rest of the Navajo tribe—and the country as a whole—in the fall of 1918.[68]

In 1946, Santa Fe Archbishop Edwin V. Byrne wrote to Mother Mary of the Visitation to tell her about his visit to St. Michael's. He was shown the plans for the proposed new high school and was pleased that the sisters were trying to provide the Navajo with an education that would help them escape poverty. In her response, Mother Mary of the Visitation informed Byrne, "The condition of the Navajo at the present time is of great concern to us." As the men who had fought in World War II returned to the reservation, it was clear that the conditions under which they were forced to live had to change. The SBS hoped to erect a new building and make other improvements to the St. Michael's complex, but the price to complete all this work would be very high. In addition, a shortage of building supplies was making it difficult to think about starting any new construction. In a statement that reflected the work and contributions of Katharine Drexel, she told the archbishop that because the church and government had done so little for the Navajo—and other tribes—"by almost force of necessity and at a point of sacrifice, our Congregation is urged to try to do something for the Navajos; hence the resolve to erect a High School building and try to win as many souls as we could through the mission for God and his glory." Not much had changed since Miss Katharine Drexel had made her first donation to advance the education of Indigenous People. There was still little hierarchical commitment to the Indians of the United States.[69] Despite financial struggles, St. Michael's High School opened in 1946.

SBS and Indigenous People

Joining the Sisters of the Blessed Sacrament did not mean that one had any knowledge of the history, culture, or current situation of Black or Indigenous People, and until the 1960s sisters were not able to choose the ministry in which they hoped to work. Sisters working with Indigenous People could be assigned a position in a day school or a boarding school as a teacher; some served as catechists and visited families and individuals in the surrounding community; and a small minority were assigned tasks related to housekeeping. There is no way of knowing how many members of the congregation had read *Century of Dishonor*, the book that impacted Drexel's view of the way Indigenous People had been treated by the U.S. government, and even if some had read Jackson's work, there is no way of determining whether they shared her views.

It is likely that some women who were interested in the Sisters of the Blessed Sacrament were readers of the *Indian Sentinel*. Published between 1902 and 1962, the magazine focused on stories about Indigenous People and the church's efforts to convert them to Catholicism. Most of the articles were written by missionaries—various Sisters of the Blessed Sacrament are listed as contributors in the table of contents— and tended to be firsthand accounts of activities and events the authors had experienced or observed. It would be difficult for subscribers to miss the role the SBS were playing in the evangelization of Indigenous People. The 1907 issue (only one issue was published that year) featured a lengthy article on Katharine Drexel and the work of the congregation. The final paragraphs exhorted readers to remember that although there were 111 members of the SBS, that was not enough for "the vast fields awaiting the harvesting." More sisters were needed if Indigenous People would ever be brought to the Catholic Church. Articles such as this indirectly advertised the work of missionary congregations—including the SBS—for young women determining if they had a vocation to religious life.[70]

There is some indication that the sisters who were first missioned to work with Indigenous People developed an appreciation for and knowledge of the culture in which they were immersed. Writing in the *Indian Sentinel* in 1924, Mother Katharine stated that one of the best ways to win over Indigenous People was through home visitation. Rev. Sylvester Eisenman accompanied her on a visit to the home of Amos and Lucy Yellow Eyes during a trip to Yankton, South Dakota, and Drexel was quite taken with the ancestral tribal clothes, describing one item as a "superb war bonnet. The effect," she wrote, "was quite startling in its grandeur."[71] Later that same year, Sister Stanislaus recounted a visit the sisters living at St. Catherine's had made to the pueblos. Traveling with a priest, who celebrated Mass, heard confessions, and even performed a wedding, the sisters held classes every night at 6:30 to instruct those interested in Catholicism.[72]

At least some Sisters of the Blessed Sacrament occasionally attended religious ceremonies that took place in the area where they were missioned. Sister Philip Neri described her experience at a Medicine Dance for readers of the *Indian Sentinel*. It was not a scene, she suggested, with which most twentieth-century Americans would be familiar. "Boiling caldrons, mysterious incantations, lurid flames from campfires, and shadowy figures of women wrapped in shawl[s] of gorgeous colors, moving noiselessly from caldron to caldron, suggested a scene from Macbeth, rather than a present-day picture of life in our own United States," she wrote of her experience with the Winnebago tribe in Nebraska. Although she was not at all familiar with the ceremony she had been invited to witness, Sister Philip Neri recognized that it was an important part of the Native religious experience and suggested that the way the participants and witnesses behaved "might be an interesting and instructive object lesson to Christians in their devotions."[73]

The Second Vatican Council called for women religious to examine what had inspired the founders of their congregations to begin their work and to think about how that inspiration might be transmitted to members of their communities in the second half of the twentieth century. The documents of the Council on this subject certainly related to Sister Francis Mary Riggs's work on the SBS and Indigenous People. When Riggs was conducting research for her doctoral dissertation in the 1960s, she discovered that the sisters studied did not know a great deal about Native culture. By 1964, only about 10 percent of sisters were working in missions focused on Indigenous People; forty-nine were either faculty or staff at residential schools, twelve sisters were assigned to day schools, and four were associated with catechetical centers.[74] The opinions of the 162 sisters she surveyed—about 24 percent of the congregation in 1964—covered a wide range of views. One sister expressed the paternalistic view that Indigenous People "do not wish to adopt the white man's way. But we should try to make them as it is best for them." Another took a bit of a softer approach, saying, "We should improve their manners and education. But I do not think we should obliterate their ceremonies."[75]

Many sisters, according to Riggs, admitted that they were unfamiliar with Native culture. One way that sisters assigned to a ministry for Indigenous People were able to learn more about their students was by visiting their homes, but reactions to this approach were mixed. One sister agreed with this idea, commenting, "You can't know the child until you see him [sic] in his [sic] own environment." Another vehemently disagreed. "Stay away!" she exclaimed. "Visits seem fruitless. Anyway, they should come to us, not us to them."[76] In addition, there were few resources available at the motherhouse that would adequately prepare SBS for this work. Most sisters, Riggs reported, were still reading works that had influenced Katharine Drexel—such as Helen Hunt Jackson and even James Fenimore Cooper—as their source of knowledge for Indian history and culture. "Most books are at the Motherhouse. Real interest begins on the missions where books on Indians are fewer or outdated. They are outdated at the Motherhouse." Most admitted that they had never learned the language of the people with whom they lived and worked. "Navajo is too difficult," one said. "We could never learn it."[77]

Riggs concluded, "The majority of respondents were unaware of the nature and function of culture as a possession of society and therefore of the true character of the mission situations." Most of the SBS that participated in her study saw that the role of the missionary was to teach. Catechesis and visitations did not really enter into their view of what they were called to do to minister to Indigenous People. The sisters also did not support the right of Indigenous People to self-determination. Some of this was related to the age of the sisters interviewed; the younger sisters involved in the study—who were more educated than the older members of the congregation—took a more holistic approach to working with Indigenous People.[78]

Where Are We Now?

The history of residential schools, including those founded by Katharine Drexel, who is often considered the patron saint of racial justice, is incomplete because we still do not have a grasp of the many issues related to abuse at U.S. and Canadian schools. In 2021, Kathleen Holscher, writing for the *National Catholic Reporter*, informed readers that the guiding principle behind Catholic and government residential schools was "to claim and control young people so entirely: in body as well as soul, in life and also death." To demonstrate this claim, Holscher explains that the sisters and priests in charge of these schools enforced rules, with vicious punishments, about how students should bathe and cut their hair. They issued them clothing to wear. They monitored them when they slept at night. They prohibited certain forms of kinship and friendship. They decided who should and should not receive medical care. And they buried students when they died.[79]

This statement may be at least somewhat true for schools operated by the SBS—they certainly cut students' hair, issued them clothing, and assigned sleeping spaces—although there is no evidence as of this writing that children were inappropriately buried at any schools sponsored by the congregation. The stories of what took place at residential schools, including those connected with the SBS, have not fully come to light (this issue will be more fully addressed in chapter 7).

St. Michael's School, located on the Navajo reservation, is the only SBS school for Indigenous People still in operation, and is currently a bright spot in a landscape dotted with stories of churches that failed to honor their commitments to a group that has been historically and systemically excluded from mainstream U.S. society. It remains faithful to the vision of Katharine Drexel, but in the twenty-first century the number of SBS working at the school has decreased dramatically. In 2009, twenty SBS were connected with St. Michael's; by 2021 that number had dwindled to one member of the congregation living and working at the school. The school accepts students from all faiths, but everyone is required to take four years of theology. Two sisters serve on the board of directors and the SBS leadership team is described on the school's website as "Managing Members."[80] St. Michael's remains focused on Katharine Drexel's vision as it works to provide an excellent education that will allow students to succeed in college—95 percent of its graduates attend some form of postsecondary education—and beyond, as well as "providing a haven for students on the reservation, where life is not always easy."[81]

Drexel demonstrated her concern for the way in which Indigenous People had been treated by establishing and sponsoring schools and churches on tribal lands throughout the United States. In addition to establishing their own schools, including St. Catherine's and St. Michael's schools, the congregation was associated with St. Paul's Indian School in South Dakota for a large part of the twentieth century and staffed countless schools connected with missions devoted to Indigenous People. Because most American Catholics were uninterested in the education of Indigenous People, Drexel spent a significant amount of her own money to ensure that these schools and churches were built, staffed, and maintained. In addition to Indigenous People, the Sisters of the Blessed Sacrament and Mother Katharine Drexel believed Black Americans deserved the opportunity to receive an education that would allow them to succeed in U.S. society. In order to implement that idea, Drexel and the SBS founded schools designed to provide Black Americans with the tools they needed to improve their socioeconomic status in a society in which the odds were stacked against them. The next two chapters are devoted to their story.

Chapter Five

FROM RURAL SOUTH TO URBAN NORTH

SBS Ministries to Black Americans

$\mathcal{S}$ister Benedicta had never been in the "far South" until she was appointed superior at St. Edward's School in New Iberia, Louisiana, in 1936. School had only been in session one day when she wrote her first letter to Mother Katharine describing her experiences. The anecdotes she recounted in her letter reflected the faith and dedication of the Black Catholics living in the area. When she was talking to a woman enrolling her three children in St. Edward's, for instance, Sister Benedicta discovered they "got up at *four* o'clock every Sunday, in order to be in time for *six* o'clock Mass. The little ones walk *five* miles to our church!" In addition, she was "pleasantly surprised" that about 150 received communion at the 6:30 a.m. First Friday Mass. "They have practically no money to contribute to the church," Sister Benedicta wrote, "and it's good to see that they have come in spite of it."[1]

Unlike the Sisters of the Blessed Sacrament's work with Indigenous communities, which took place on or very close to reservations, the SBS ministered to Black people throughout the United States. In addition to founding a number of schools for rural Black Louisianians, Drexel and the SBS staffed and sustained important ministries in large urban centers, such as New York and Chicago, as they responded to pastors and bishops concerned about the need for Black children to receive a Catholic education. As *Brown v. Board of Education* slowly began to be enforced throughout the South, the SBS found that in many instances their schools were no longer needed, so they sought other ways to minister to the Black community.

As we examine the work of Katharine Drexel and the Sisters of the Blessed Sacrament among Black Americans, it is important to remember that the congregation did not admit Black women until 1950. Drexel and the majority of the SBS believed they had made the right decision because in their view an integrated religious community would distract from the work Drexel was trying to accomplish and possibly put the sisters in danger when they were assigned to ministries in the South. Despite their desire to minister to and fund projects related to Black people, there is no evidence that Katharine Drexel ever considered taking any sort of leadership role as an advocate for racial justice. That her work was important is demonstrated by the number of Black women and men who received an education as a result of her vision and financial commitment, but it did not lead to integrated Catholic schools and churches throughout the United States. Drexel and the Sisters of the Blessed Sacrament were involved in many schools dedicated to the education of Black children from elementary school to Xavier University in Louisiana (which is the subject of the following chapter). Since it is impossible in a work of this nature to discuss every school in the 130-year history of the congregation, this chapter will focus primarily on SBS schools in rural Louisiana and the cities of Chicago and New York because Mother Katharine and her sisters devoted a good deal of time and money to the education of Black children in these areas.

The situation of Black Catholics was not high on the American bishops' list of tasks nor was it a primary focus of white Catholics. When the Second Plenary Council—a meeting of all of the bishops in the United States—opened in Baltimore on October 7, 1866, the subject of how the Catholic Church might deal with those who had been formerly enslaved was the last item on the agenda. New Orleans archbishop Jean-Marie Odin, who had arrived in the Crescent City in 1861, was charged with leading a discussion related to Black Catholics in the United States. Archbishop Martin Spalding, who was chairing the council, informed Odin that the bishops "shall especially want the benefit of your experience in devising the most effectual means for saving the poor emancipated slaves."[2] Although several proposals were put forward for the bishops to consider, including establishing schools and orphanages for Black children and recruiting priests and women religious to work with the newly freed women and men, Odin persuaded those in attendance "to postpone any specific requirements to create separate missions or churches." The council adjourned without approving any systematic plan to evangelize and assist Black people. Whether or not Black Catholics in a particular diocese would receive any assistance from the Catholic Church was left up to the individual bishop.[3]

When the Third Plenary Council opened in Baltimore in 1884, very little progress in this area had been made, despite the fact that the Josephites had been ministering to Black Americans since 1871. At this council, the bishops in attendance called for the creation of separate schools and churches for Black Catholics, making "separation an official strategy."[4] By the time Katharine Drexel founded the Sisters of the Blessed Sacrament about seven years later, it was clear that the American institutional church had other concerns than the needs of Black people, Catholic or not. In addition, annual collections on behalf of missions focused on Black and Indigenous People attracted little interest. White ethnic Catholics, often struggling to find their own way in the United States, deliberately chose not to contribute to these collections. According to historian Nicole Farmer Hurd, "Dismal collection receipts point to racism at all levels of Catholic life." Drexel's commitment of money and personnel for schools and churches for Black people was necessary for those working in these ministries to receive any help at all.[5]

Katharine Drexel and the Complexities of Race

Mother Katharine Drexel's thoughts and actions on issues related to race and racism are—as has been previously mentioned—complex. For her, anyone who adhered to Catholic teachings could not support racial injustice of any sort. She wrote in the congregational newsletter entitled *Mission Fields at Home*,

> After all, if we look at the facts clearly in the face, we must admit that from the viewpoint of complete Catholicism there is no race problem. We are children of the one Father, creatures of the one Creator forming part of His Mystical Body

in the Church Militant here below and destined to continue that membership in the Church Triumphant above.[6]

Other Catholics—and non-Catholics—clearly disagreed vehemently with this sentiment. Drexel and the Sisters of the Blessed Sacrament were sometimes referred to as "'nigger sisters' for choosing to identify so fully with African Americans and build first-class schools for them."[7]

In at least one instance, Drexel did not hesitate to correct someone who described Black people in a way she believed was simply wrong. Writing to Rev. Joseph Coulombe in Montegut, Louisiana, she explained that she disagreed with his view that the SBS spent their lives "in behalf of the two *most dejected* races of North America." She continued by pointing out that "were our colored brethren to hear themselves called the 'most dejected of races' their feelings would be very much hurt." Drexel softened her criticism by telling Coulombe that she understood that he may not have been thinking about the situation from "this angle" when he formulated the phrase but insisted that the congregation did not think they were involved in an "ungrateful mission." She still hoped Coulombe would support the mission of the SBS and encourage young women to consider joining the congregation when speaking with students at Catholic colleges and high schools.[8]

Drexel's one-on-one interactions with individuals, of course, do not tell the whole story. As noted in previous chapters, Mother Katharine Drexel was not an anti-racist, a term that was not in use during her lifetime but is important when discussing her life and work from the perspective of the twenty-first century, but she did support groups actively working for racial justice. In addition to her commitment to the education of Black children, Drexel was "deeply involved" with the work of the NAACP by the 1930s. She willingly contributed to the organization but stipulated that her name not appear on newsletters. Until the 1960s, women religious were not expected to be visible or vocal advocates for societal change, and Drexel did not attempt to distinguish herself from other nuns in that regard.[9]

Like other congregations of women religious in the 1960s and 1970s, the Sisters of the Blessed Sacrament heeded the directives of Vatican II to examine their founder and develop an understanding of her importance for their present situation. When the SBS looked at the life and work of Drexel closely, they could relate what they discovered to issues related to race in U.S. society. Many of the sisters concluded that if one looks below the surface, there is evidence that Drexel did advocate an end to racism in the United States In 1985, thirty years after Drexel's death, the SBS produced a "Directional Paper on Racism," in which they stated that one of the reasons for the founding of the Sisters of the Blessed Sacrament was "to help eradicate the effects of racism." This statement was supported in a brief paper written by Sister Patricia Marshall, SBS, entitled "Katharine Drexel on Racial Justice" that enumerated several examples demonstrating the truth of this statement. Sister Patricia claimed that Drexel "dealt with racism seriously and systemically over the long haul. She put building blocks in place that would act, interact, and energize long after she would be physically gone." According to Marshall, Drexel promoted racial justice in the Catholic Church and U.S. society in several ways. First, she advocated for the integration of Catholic schools and universities long before most other bishops, priests, sisters, and educators. As a result of her labors, for instance, two Oblate Sisters of Providence—graduates of Xavier University—were able to enroll in a summer session at the segregated Catholic University of America.

Second, Marshall suggests that one of the "most longlasting ways in which Katharine Drexel addressed the church on racial justice" was through her work with Jesuit John La Farge, a vocal proponent of racial justice. She first met La Farge when he asked Mother Katharine and her sister, Louise Morrell, to support the Cardinal Gibbons Institute, a residential school for Black children, which was struggling financially. La Farge and the Drexel women developed a productive working relationship, and the Jesuit would go on to support the Federated Colored Catholics of the United States. In 1932, Mother Katharine strongly suggested that all of the Sisters of the Blessed Sacrament listen to La Farge's radio program, *The Interracial Hour*, and asked them to recommend the program to their students.[10]

Marshall also documents several ways in which Drexel used her money to "combat racism," including a project developed by Roy Wilkins (who at the time was the assistant secretary for the National Association for the Advancement of Colored People) and journalist George Schuyler in 1933. Wilkins and Schuyler conducted an investigation of "racist conditions in the deep South" by traveling throughout the region dressed as workers or laborers to visit Black workers on the levees of the Mississippi River. Despite harassment by local police, the two men visited more than twenty work camps located on the levee, as well as some riverboats, and discovered unsurprisingly that people were "savagely exploited." Their investigation piqued Drexel's interest in the substandard conditions and dangers under which the workers on the levee labored and led her to send a telegram to President Franklin D. Roosevelt, in which she protested "the discriminatory provisions of the Contractors' Code...because it [would] not in any way benefit or improve the condition of the thirty thousand Negro laborers on the Mississippi Flood Control Protection project."

Marshall's final example concerning Drexel and advocacy for racial justice is her willingness to protest the lynching of Black people by white mobs. She was a member of the American Scottsboro Committee, an interreligious group of clergy and laypeople formed to protest the way in which the Scottsboro "Boys" had been arrested and were being tried. This rather short-lived committee was dedicated to publicizing the "truth about these boys clearly and properly to create public opinion in their favor apart from any propaganda for radical or other movements and to secure their freedom as speedily as possible because they are innocent." In addition, Drexel asked the superiors of SBS convents to contact their congressional representatives and urge them to vote in favor of the Costigan-Wagner Bill, which was designed to end lynching in the United States. Her efforts were ultimately unsuccessful; the bill was never passed.[11]

When examining Katharine Drexel and her role in advocating for racial justice, it is helpful to discuss Louise Morrell and her willingness to support her sister's work founding and funding schools and churches for Black people. Morrell dedicated a portion of her inheritance to the education of Black and Indigenous People, and she supported the Catholic Church in its efforts to provide spiritual sustenance for Black Catholics. When her will was read in 1945, the Catholic Interracial Council, of which La Farge was a prominent member, learned that it would receive $3500 a year for two years. The Council would receive an additional $1500 per year for the following two years, which meant Morrell had left the organization a total or $10,000 to be used for the benefit of La Farge's *Interracial Review*.[12]

In a radio address, Morrell extolled the work of the Sisters of the Blessed Sacrament but emphasized that their dedication and effort was not enough. The laity needed to be more involved in the work of Mother Katharine and the SBS. "Our lay folk," she said, "appear too indifferent or detached from the spiritual as well as the material needs of the negro," but she hastened to add that it was because they simply didn't understand the nature of the congregation's work in this area. One solution to this problem could be found at St. Michael's Shrine in the Torresdale section of Philadelphia, which had been founded by Morrell with the enthusiastic support of Cardinal Dennis Dougherty, whose "earnest desire" was that "the clergy and the laity of this great diocese should make frequent visits to the Shrine...to receive instruction and inspiration regarding the missionary work among the members of the colored race." At the end of her address, Morrell noted that she was speaking for her sister, Mother Katharine Drexel.[13] There is no way of knowing how many people were convinced to help the SBS as a result of Morrell's radio address, but with or without additional support, Katharine Drexel and the SBS would found and finance Black ministries—particularly those related to education—as long as they were able.

The schools established throughout the South by Drexel and the Sisters of the Blessed Sacrament were certainly segregated. In fact, Southern schools funded and staffed by the SBS were founded because of the larger segregated system of education that existed throughout the region. Some scholars have persuasively suggested that segregated Catholic schools actually contributed to the "problem" of segregation. Historian James Bennett, for instance, argues in his 2005 book, *Religion and the Rise of Jim Crow in New Orleans*, that the parallel school system for Black students implemented by New Orleans Archbishop Francis Janssens "instituted structures that reinforced the segregationist practices occurring in the secular realm, from railroads to public schools, rather than offering a viable alternative to the racism he claimed to oppose."[14] In addition to the archdiocese's segregated parochial school system, Bennett explains, only congregations that worked "exclusively among the city's Catholics of color could teach in black Catholic schools." This meant that the Sisters of the Blessed Sacrament and the Sisters of the Holy Family—a Black congregation founded in New Orleans—were the two communities that parish priests depended upon to staff Black parish schools. Drexel, of course, would not allow her sisters to teach in any schools that were not dedicated entirely to Black and Indigenous People.[15]

Bennett acknowledges that prelates like Janssens thought their decision to build churches and schools for Black Catholics allowed the church to serve those with whom white racists refused to associate. Although Janssens never considered integrated churches and schools as a possibility in his archdiocese, in the end, his "commitment to separate institutions advocated the same response as the white supremacists he deplored." For Janssens, "separation [of churches and schools] was a temporary means to a very different end; for white supremacists, segregation was the end itself."[16] Although Katharine Drexel and the Sisters of the Blessed Sacrament certainly believed that Black children were entitled to and deserved an education that was equal to whites—as did white orders of priests such as the Josephites—Bennett claims these communities "contributed to the segregated and inferior position of the black church members that were the focus of their ministries." Recruiting congregations from outside of Louisiana (and the South) to minister to an area's Black residents demonstrated that Black Catholics stood outside of the mainstream Southern white Catholic Church and were not considered equal to whites.[17]

On the one hand, Bennett's assertions are valid and need to be seriously considered when discussing this issue. The other side of the story, however, is that many of the students enrolled in SBS schools (and those of other religious congregations) would not have been able to attend elementary and secondary school on a regular basis if it were not for the system of Black Catholic schools that were funded primarily by Drexel and the SBS. Colette Madeleine Bloom, for instance, reflected on her educational experience with the SBS in a 2010 essay published in *Catholic Southwest*. The sisters Bloom knew in New Orleans in the 1950s and 1960s were all white and well educated. Drexel herself, Bloom writes, "had it all—whiteness, prestige, social standing, financial clout and the freedom to do anything she desired." Despite this description, Bloom admired what the SBS in New Orleans were accomplishing in their attempts to provide quality education for Black children. "Perhaps the women of the SBS order," she wrote, "had no personal experiences with disenfranchisement and exclusion from any other position besides gender, but these women had a higher calling to make the 'dispossessed ones' well armored in their struggle for full citizenship rights."[18]

Starting Out in Virginia

The Sisters of the Blessed Sacrament began working with Black children almost as soon as the congregation was founded. Holy Providence, a residential school for children whose parents were either deceased or unable to care for them, opened on February 2, 1893, on the ground of St. Elizabeth's in Bensalem.[19] "The second missionary venture of the Sisters of the Blessed Sacrament" was St. Francis de Sales, a school for Black girls located in Rock Castle, Virginia. Drexel made the decision to open a boarding school for girls shortly after Edward and Louise Morrell purchased Belmead Plantation in order to open a school dedicated to providing Black men with an industrial and agricultural education, a "Catholic Tuskegee."[20] Located about forty miles outside of Richmond, the Morrells named the school, which opened in 1895, St. Emma's after Emma Bouvier Drexel. St. Francis de Sales, named in honor of the women's father, was located near St. Emma's, and was planned as "a boarding school for Colored Girls of the South,...to give higher education and to prepare them for the work of teachers."[21]

Although it was apparently rumored that St. Emma's would educate Black and white boys, Edward Morrell stated that he and his wife had "chosen the Brothers of the Christian Schools to conduct [St. Emma's] for the benefit of colored boys, and for colored boys only." "Its object," Morrell explained, "is to give many colored boys of the South a good, practical education, it is to teach them to use their hands and brains properly."[22] During the early years of St. Emma's, students were taught a number of skills, including wheel wrighting, carriage and wagon painting, horseshoeing, carpentry, shoemaking, and masonry. Classes devoted to auto repair were introduced in 1919.[23] Students were not charged tuition but did pay two dollars per month for clothing and a fee for board and medical care.[24]

In order to be eligible to enroll at St. Emma's, students had to be at least fifteen years old and live below the Mason-Dixon Line and east of the Mississippi River. In addition to vocational instruction, the young men also were required to follow a schedule of traditional academic courses taught at the secondary level, including Christian doctrine and Bible history. During the 1920s, there were two distinct faculties at the school; "those teaching academic subjects were white while Black teachers were responsible for courses related to industrial and vocational education."[25]

The Christian Brothers administered St. Emma's until 1924 and were succeeded by a lay faculty and administration until 1929. The Benedictines assumed responsibility for the school in that year and remained at St. Emma's until 1947. The Congregation of the Holy Spirit—also known as the Spiritans or Holy Ghost Fathers—who followed the Benedictines in managing and staffing St. Emma's, transformed it into a military school. For many years, students graduating from St. Emma's received three diplomas: a traditional academic diploma, a diploma certifying they had completed courses in industrial education that was accredited by the Department of Labor, and a third recognizing the military training they had received from the National Defense Cadet Corps school. Until it closed in 1972, St. Emma's Military Academy was the only Black military school in the United States.[26]

The Sisters of the Blessed Sacrament opened St. Francis de Sales in 1899, several years after St. Emma's was founded. Located on a former plantation that had been home to enslaved people, the first student to enroll was Mary Boyd, who had attended St. Stephen's mission school on the Wind River Reservation in Wyoming. She was followed by "Miss Gertrude Canneville, and her baby sister, a girl of sixteen." Other girls soon joined them, "many of them from the best families in Richmond, a great many being non-Catholics." A total of thirty-nine girls enrolled in St. Francis de Sales when it opened. As they had with the children enrolled at Holy Providence in Bensalem, the SBS required parents or guardians to sign an indenture, which meant that the students were placed under the care of the SBS until they were twenty-one. The indenture system, which was commonly used in U.S. orphanages during these years, made sense for children who were orphans or whose parents could not care for them because the congregation could legally care for children with no other visible means of support. The students who enrolled at St. Francis de Sales, however, were not orphans and, not surprisingly, a number of parents refused to agree to the terms of indenture and the sisters "lost some of [their] best children." As a result of parental refusal to allow their daughters to be indentured, the SBS began to modify the system, and Sister Patricia Lynch notes that the last indenture was signed in 1910.[27]

When St. Francis de Sales opened, students were required to take courses in "domestic economy," such as cooking and sewing, but the school was also intended to be "a house of higher studies, and…a normal school, for Colored girls could readily find employment as teachers in the Colored schools of the South." Students who attended the school had to demonstrate competence in a variety of academic subjects, including U.S. history, geography, literature, physiology, "civil government," algebra, and "note singing." Despite the presence of an academic curriculum, Sister Patricia Lynch wrote, "Not everyone was expected to complete the entire academic program." Students who focused on industrial classes were often "assigned to work in the kitchen, bakery, housekeeping, sewing, and nursing departments."[28]

Although Katharine Drexel and the SBS welcomed girls from non-

Catholic traditions as students at St. Francis de Sales, the curriculum of the school included courses in Catholic doctrine and mandatory attendance at Mass and retreats. Congregational annals for 1900–1901 report that in that year about 50 percent of the students were non-Catholic, "all very strong Baptists." The Catholic students came from Maryland and "Creole portions of the South." In what is certainly an understatement, the annalist noted, "Neither class was very tolerant of the feelings of the other."[29]

Journalist and author Ellen Tarry was one of the students at St. Francis de Sales who converted to Catholicism. Raised Congregationalist in Birmingham, Alabama, a friend convinced Tarry to attend St. Francis de Sales. "When Lena [her friend] added a description of the many beautiful cherry trees on the campus of Rock Castle, the strawberry patches where the girls could pick as many berries as they pleased and told me about the handsome brown boys at Belmead (St. Emma's Military Academy) who came calling regularly," Tarry remembered, "she was sowing seeds on prepared ground." Her father allowed her to attend St. Francis de Sales on the condition that she not convert to Catholicism, and she entered the school in 1921.[30] Tarry enjoyed her years at St. Francis de Sales and remembered meeting girls from New York, Philadelphia, Washington, DC, Georgia, and Florida. After attending a retreat conducted by Abraham Emerick, SJ, and reading a book by Father F. X. Lasance entitled *The Prisoner of Love*, Tarry found herself drawn to Catholicism. "Instead of being a God I worshipped on Sunday," she wrote in her autobiography, "He had become a God I wanted to worship every minute of every day."[31]

In addition to hoping that Protestant students would find their way to the Catholic Church, the SBS also prayed that some graduates of the school would realize they had a vocation to religious life. Although St. Francis de Sales graduates were not allowed to enter the Sisters of the Blessed Sacrament because the congregation did not accept Black women (see chapter 2), at least fourteen women entered a religious congregation between 1899 and 1941. The first student to enroll at the school, Mary Boyd, entered the Sisters of St. Francis of Philadelphia; thirteen others entered the Oblate Sisters of Providence, a Black congregation.[32]

The SBS in Louisiana

The need for ministries to Black Catholics in Louisiana was driven by the fact that Black children were not welcome in white Catholic churches and schools. If they did attend a "white" church, Black congregants were usually assigned to sit in a specific section, and their children were not allowed to attend the parish school. When Francis A. Janssens was named archbishop of New Orleans in 1888, Katharine Drexel was already distributing some of the money she and her sisters had received from their father's will to assist Black Catholics in Louisiana in the face of this reality. She contributed to the schools and orphanages administered by the Sisters of the Holy Family and paid the salaries for teachers at schools staffed by the Sisters of Perpetual Adoration.[33] In addition, she helped support Janssens's plan to establish St. Joseph's parish, which was designated for the city's Black Catholics (see chapter 2). Most of Drexel's early work in New Orleans, however, took place during the administration of James Blenk, who was named archbishop in 1906. Although the primary ministry of the SBS in New Orleans was to Xavier University of Louisiana, which is the subject of the next chapter, the Sisters of the Blessed Sacrament were involved in a number of schools in the city, including Holy Ghost, Blessed Sacrament, Corpus Christi, and St. Peter Claver.

New Orleans Archbishop James Blenk began the process of establishing a parish designated solely for Black Catholics in 1909 when the members of Mater Dolorosa moved to a larger church and voted to exclude Black Catholics from attending services at the parish. The old church was turned over to Black Catholics, and Josephite Father Peter LeBeau became pastor of what became St. Dominic's, New Orleans's first Black territorial parish. The parish included a school, and Le Beau often turned to Katharine Drexel and the Sisters of the Blessed Sacrament for help. In 1911, for instance, the pastor wrote to Drexel and requested financial assistance because the church and school were in need of repairs. "The whites around here don't care much for us and [our] work," Le Beau wrote, "but that gives me courage to work for our poor and colored people." When Drexel asked for more details about his proposed work, Le Beau told her that he needed $800 to repair the church and school. He tried to explain that the members of St. Dominic's could not help because they could not find jobs that paid them a living wage, writing, "On account of prejudice they cannot get [a] clerkship or even work as waiters."[34]

Although Katharine Drexel certainly believed that New Orleans's Black citizens needed schools and churches, she was very concerned about the lack of educational opportunities for Black children in rural Louisiana, and began to focus on the Diocese of Lafayette, which had been carved out of the Archdiocese of New Orleans in 1918. During the early decades of the twentieth century, the diocese boasted the largest population of Black Catholics in the United States. Jules Jeanmard, the diocese's first bishop, was concerned that Black Catholics would simply leave the church if they were not able to worship freely or attend a parochial school.[35] Mother Katharine would eventually devise a plan that involved building two-room schools in small communities where Black girls and boys had little or no access to schooling. Before this project began, however, Jeanmard asked Drexel for help building churches and schools as needed—Drexel usually supported a school being built before the church—and asked her to consider assigning sisters to teach in the diocese. In 1920, Drexel provided funds to replace Sacred Heart School in Lake Charles. SBS were assigned to the school about two years later, joining lay teachers Eleanora Figaro and Mary Ryan. Within a few years, Sacred Heart was providing teacher education so that its graduates were prepared to teach in elementary school. "By 1933," Amanda Bresie writes, "[the SBS] linked Sacred Heart with SBS run Xavier University and offered extension classes at the Lake Charles campus."[36]

St. Jude's School, West Point à la Hache, Louisiana; built by Mother Katharine Drexel and the SBS. Teacher is an unidentified graduate of Xavier University of Louisiana. Courtesy of SBS Archives, CHRC, Archdiocese of Philadelphia.

The reality of segregation in Louisiana led Jeanmard and Drexel to attempt to provide Black children with an education while preventing them—and their parents—from leaving the church. When the Spiritians, for instance, agreed to staff a new parish, St. Edward's in New Iberia, they hoped that the Sisters of the Blessed Sacrament would agree to serve in the proposed school. St. Edward's was established as a parish specifically for Black Catholics who had been attending Mass by sitting in a separate section designated for them at St. Peter's Church. Rev. Francis Lichtenberger, pastor of St. Edward's, was charged with building the church and school, and discovered "to his disappointment" that the white Catholics in New Iberia would not give any money at all to the project. Drexel supported Lichtenberger and encouraged him to build a combination church and school. She would, Mother Katharine assured him, commit the SBS to staff the school.[37]

The school was ready for the 1918–19 academic year, and true to her word, Drexel assigned three members of the congregation to St. Edward's. Because influenza was sweeping through the area, St. Edward's School did not finally open officially until November when forty-two students enrolled. The school grew quickly and when Drexel visited St. Edward's in April 1919, she promised to send an additional two sisters for the following school year. On the first day of the new school year, 150 students were present, and that number quickly grew to 186. In 1924, the parish opened a high school, which included a Teacher Training Institute to prepare graduates to teach in schools Drexel was planning to establish throughout the diocese. According to Sister Patricia Lynch, "From 1925–1927 the small high school trained a pool of leaders from numerous small towns around New Iberia....From 1930 to 1936, the Teacher Training classes prepared students for a First Grade [class] Teaching Certificate." Between 1927 and 1938, Lynch notes, seventy-five students graduated from St. Edward's High School; by September of 1938, seven were teaching in rural schools founded by Drexel and the SBS. Because there were not enough members of the congregation to staff all of the schools needed in southwestern Louisiana, Drexel had to find other ways to ensure that there were enough teachers for all of the schools. The Teacher Training Institute at St. Edward's, along with a similar program at Sacred Heart, as well as Xavier University graduates, ensured that there were a dedicated group of lay teachers working alongside the Sisters of the Blessed Sacrament.[38]

In 1921, Drexel toured the area where she and Jeanmard believed schools were most needed and shared her thoughts in a letter written "home" to the motherhouse. After visiting a school that the SBS had helped build in Point à la Hache, forty-four miles from New Orleans, she explained that the local priest had done some fast thinking in order to secure enough teachers for all the children desiring to attend. Black children were only allowed to attend school three months a year in Louisiana, and the priest wanted to make sure that they received the best education possible during that time. When he and the "school supervisor" arrived at the building, "which, by the way, had not been painted, but is a much better schoolhouse than the whites have in this part of the country... Father asked the supervisor how he would like to use this school for his county public school." The only condition was that the supervisor would guarantee the salary for two teachers. "'Teachers!' said the supervisor, 'You haven't enough "niggers" here to borrow two teachers.'" The priest then showed the supervisor the 120 Black children arranged according to the grades they would be in if they were able to attend school. The supervisor agreed to pay two teachers' salaries for three months, and Drexel added, "The Colored people are so anxious for education that he [the priest] expects to raise money enough for some further months' instruction." After visiting several additional schools and scouting potential sites for others, the sisters arrived in Jesuit Bend, a community that was in need of a school for Black Children. In order to get there, the sisters had to take a boat. After a series of mishaps, they arrived but the water was so high they had to go the opposite side of the river in order to land.[39] Visits to rural Louisiana communities convinced Drexel and the SBS of the importance of the schools they were building and helping to staff; without them a significant number of Black children living in the Diocese of Lafayette would not be able to attend school.

Beginning in 1923, Drexel and the Sisters of the Blessed Sacrament—with Jeanmard's enthusiastic support—embarked on a campaign to build schools for Black children throughout the Diocese of Lafayette. It was important to the congregation that any schools they financed or staffed be located in communities "with large numbers of unschooled African-American children" so that they could educate as many students as possible in one school. In addition, sisters assigned to the Diocese of Lafayette selected and trained Black women, often graduates of Xavier University, to teach in the schools. These teachers received a modest stipend, and it was arranged for them to board with a "respectable Colored family" living in the area.[40] They planned to build "some sturdy two- or three-room schoolhouses where graduates of Xavier or other normal training schools would be able to teach." Between 1923 and 1955, Drexel paid the salaries for at least forty-two Xavier University graduates teaching in fifteen schools in rural Louisiana. Staffing the schools primarily with laywomen meant that the Sisters of the Blessed Sacrament would not have to be responsible for teaching in all of the schools in the diocese designated for Black children.[41]

In 1982, Agnes G. Lagarde remembered her experiences as a lay teacher in one of the rural schools. Her first teaching job had been at a rural public school in St. Charles parish, Louisiana, but while attending summer school at Xavier University, Lagarde was asked by Mother Mary of Grace to teach at St. Ann's School in Mallet. The school, which opened in October 1931, was a two-room building, and—like most Southern rural schools at that time—was only in session from October until May so that students could help their parents with planting and harvesting. In a written account of her memories teaching at St. Ann's, Lagarde told readers that her students spoke only French, and some traveled to school in wagons and buggies or on horseback. Most of them, she explained, came to school barefoot, saving their shoes for Mass on Sunday. Lagarde only taught at St. Ann's for one year; she left to get married. Her daughter, Sister Roland Lagarde, SBS, was later assigned to St. Ann's in Mallet as a member of the congregation.[42]

As always, certain conditions had to be met before Drexel would commit to financing and staffing a school in a particular community. It was important, she believed, that the local pastor be involved in the supervision and maintenance of any school financed by the SBS. "We felt it would be absolutely useless to do anything with regard to rural schools unless they were well and properly supervised," she wrote to Jeanmard in 1923. Drexel had hoped to be able to assign two SBS to supervise the construction and maintenance of the schools, she explained, but was unable to spare anyone. "Therefore," she continued, "the responsibility and burden of the supervision of these schools, if they are undertaken at all, must devolve upon the pastors." She asked Jeanmard for his assurance that pastors would be able to supervise the building and maintenance of the schools and that their successors—should they be reassigned—would continue the work. Drexel then informed the bishop that the congregation was currently trying to start five schools but could not do more than that during the coming year because their "funds [were] exhausted." Even though this was an informative letter rather than any sort of legal contract, she added a postscript reminding Jeanmard, "Any help above spoken of is 'if I live.' If I die the Congregation of Sisters of the Blessed Sacrament could not assume the debt."[43]

By August 1923, Drexel and the SBS had a tentative plan for the rural schools being built throughout the area surrounding Lafayette. Writing to Sister Eucharia, Drexel informed her that the congregation would be able to pay the salaries of eight teachers assigned to five schools as long as the salaries were reasonable. Since the priests in charge would depend on someone from the congregation hiring lay teachers, Sister Eucharia was charged with this task, but Drexel offered her some suggestions for completing her assignment as easily as possible. The school at Rayne would need just one teacher, for instance, because only thirty students would be enrolled, and she hoped that two Sisters of Divine Providence would be willing to teach in Broussard.[44]

St. Elizabeth's in Prairie Basse, Louisiana, is an example of the way in which Drexel and the SBS decided where to build a rural school. In 1923, Father James Hyland wrote to Mother Katharine and asked for financial help for his school; he could not afford to pay the salaries of the two teachers he would need for the 200 students he thought might enroll. Drexel agreed, but as she always did, stipulated that any assistance Hyland received would end upon her death; the SBS would not be responsible for continuing to support the school. She also reminded the pastor that if the school closed or the building ceased to be used for the Black community, the money would have to be repaid to the Sisters of the Blessed Sacrament. Drexel understood that a new building was needed if St. Elizabeth's was going to thrive, and in 1925 found an anonymous donor willing to contribute $2000 to finance construction of the school; she also agreed to help support one teacher assigned to St. Elizabeth's. The school's sole faculty member taught kindergarten through seventh grade, and covered all subjects, including religion, music, drawing, and physical education.[45]

The project to build schools and ensure they were staffed continued into the 1930s. Notre Dame School in St. Martinville, for instance, was the last of the rural schools opened by Drexel and the SBS. The school opened in 1931 staffed with lay teachers. When Drexel heard that the teacher assigned to the lower grades was responsible for nearly two hundred students, she decided that a third teacher needed to be hired. Since there were only two rooms in the school, it was necessary for the pastor to find a way to house the additional class. According to notes compiled by Mother Agatha Ryan, the pastor "was instrumental in obtaining a hall from one of the Colored Catholic Societies, free of rent." In order to furnish the classrooms, the three teachers started a "Parents' Club" to help raise money for necessary furniture and supplies. The club organized a fair, which raised enough money to "purchase the various necessities needed to commence the school year," including desks, tables, and benches.[46] The SBS began teaching at Notre Dame in 1942.[47]

The Great Depression created difficulties for the rural schools that the SBS had agreed to support. Sister Gabriella, who was assigned to Sacred Heart in Lake Charles in 1932, told Drexel that the sisters were helping to feed the "under nourished children" attending the school. A butcher had agreed to supply the sisters with soup bones, and the cook—with the help of some of the eighth-grade girls—was making soup. "We are selling the soup at .03 [cents] a cup to all who want it," Sister Gabriella wrote, "and giving it to those who cannot pay for it." Worried that some of the families who needed the soup had not yet come for their share, she planned to visit her students' families to tell them soup was available to those who were hungry. "The leftover soup comes in handy for the 'tramps.'"[48]

In addition to trying to find a way to feed hungry students and their families, Drexel and the SBS were forced to make difficult decisions about what ministries they could continue to fund. Writing to Jeanmard about St. Edward's in New Iberia in 1937, Drexel reminded him that the congregation had always paid the lay teachers' salaries, a total of $1,170. The four sisters assigned to the school received a total of $900 in salary from the pastor, "which is utterly and completely inadequate to support the Sisters, pay the salaries, pay the wages of the domestic, and keep the little convent in repair, so the deficit always falls on our Motherhouse."

In addition to their work at St. Edward's, Drexel continued, the sisters were supporting other schools as well as Xavier University, paying salaries for rural schoolteachers, and supporting missions dedicated to Black and Indigenous People throughout the country. The financial losses Drexel suffered during the Great Depression meant that she had to reallocate funds for schools. The result was that schools and parishes were informed that they would be receiving less money. She told Jeanmard, for instance, that she had informed St. Edward's pastor that the congregation could no longer provide the financial assistance he had come to expect.

The pastor's response was that if the SBS withdrew financial support, the high school would be closed. The remainder of the letter constitutes a plea to keep the high school open:

> Can Your Excellency think of any way by which this school may be financially aided and so keep in existence? If Father [the pastor] could obtain, say at least $1,000 toward the salaries of his teachers, I think he surely ought to try to obtain the rest, and on our side, when we can send more Sisters to New Iberia, Your Excellency may be sure we shall be happy to do so.[49]

Sacred Heart High School remained open despite challenging economic times and did not close until 1967 when Black students were able to attend St. Louis High school.

The rural schools remained open, however, despite the congregation's financial difficulties. In 1943, the congregation reported that SBS ministries could be found in twenty-one dioceses throughout seventeen states; this did not include any schools or churches that had benefited from Drexel's willingness to fund other ministries devoted to Black and Indigenous People. The report notes that in 1942, twenty-one rural schools were operating in Louisiana. By 1943, however, four had been "given up" because "the State now pays the salaries of the teachers there."[50]

SBS Ministries to Black Americans in the North

Ministries to Black people supported by the congregation were located in many major U.S. cities, including Chicago, New York, and Boston. In 1882, Black Catholics in Chicago, who had been attending Mass in the basement of St. Mary's Church, began to raise funds to build a church where they could worship in the main sanctuary. St. Monica's parish in Chicago was built through their efforts and funds raised by Father Augustus Tolton, the first Black priest ordained in the United States. As part of his initial fundraising campaign in 1889, Tolton asked Katharine Drexel for financial assistance. By the time of Tolton's death in 1897, Drexel had contributed about $30,000 to help build St. Monica's.[51]

Following Tolton's death, St. Monica's did not have a resident pastor for eleven years when Father John Morris, a white priest, was assigned to the parish. According to a pamphlet published by St. Elizabeth's Church in Chicago to commemorate the Silver Jubilee of Father William Brambrink, SVD, the SBS agreed to staff St. Monica's School after a laywoman named Elsie Hodges convinced Morris to ask Katharine Drexel for sisters. Hodges, so the story goes, visited Morris, and asked where she could find the convent. When told there was no convent because there were no sisters, Hodges told Morris, "Ask the Blessed Sacrament Sisters. They'll be glad to come." Whether the story is true or not, what is clear is that Morris and Drexel agreed that the SBS should staff the parish school. St. Monica's grew from 150 students in 1913 to almost 1000 in 1925.[52]

According to Sister Patricia Lynch, the sisters assigned to St. Monica's did more than simply teach during the week. Weekends were devoted to moving furniture, painting, cleaning, and making tickets for raffles being held to support the school. In addition, they visited patients at Provident Hospital, prepared children for baptism or first communion, and directed their students in a "Christmas entertainment" to which family members of the school children were invited.[53]

The *Chicago Defender*, the most influential Black newspaper in the United States at the time, criticized the opening of St. Monica's, claiming it was a segregated school. "Why can't Colored children go to St. James' or to the School at 41st and State Street?" The newspaper encouraged parents to "remove their children [from the school] if they don't want the wrath of the Race heaped on their heads. Just think, we are fighting 'Jim Crow' Laws and they [are] upholding them by sending their children to such a school." Some Black Catholics defended the school and claimed those fighting St. Monica's were nothing more than anti-Catholic.[54]

Although only Black children were enrolled in St. Monica's school, the parish itself was integrated. That would change in 1917, however, when Archbishop George Mundelein informed Rev. Adolph Burgmer, provincial director of the Society of the Divine Word, of his plan to change the way in which the archdiocese had been ministering to Black Catholics. Morris was reassigned to another parish and the Society of the Divine Word assumed responsibility for St. Monica's. "I desire St. Monica's to be reserved entirely for the colored Catholics of Chicago and particularly of the South Side"; Mundelein wrote, "all other Catholics of whatever race or color are to be requested not to intrude. It is, of course, understood that I have no intention of excluding colored Catholics from any of the other churches in the diocese,...but simply of excluding from St. Monica's all but the colored Catholics."[55] Mundelein claimed that two nearby churches could minister to the white population of the area, but also noted that because of religious congregations such as the Society of the Divine Word and the Sisters of the Blessed Sacrament, the Black Catholic population needed less support from the archdiocese. "In essence," according to historian Timothy B. Neary, "Mundelein turned over responsibility for African American Catholics to specialists from the Society of the Divine Word and Sisters of the Blessed Sacrament."[56]

Chicago's changing demographics meant that the Sisters of the Blessed Sacrament were soon asked to assume additional responsibility for the education of the city's Black children. In 1922, the SBS began teaching at Chicago's St. Elizabeth School. Founded in 1881 to serve Irish Catholics, by the second decade of the twentieth century as white Catholics fled from the area, the parish school was serving as an "overflow" for students from St. Monica's. In 1924, the Divine Word Fathers took over the pastoral duties at St. Elizabeth's, and the two schools merged as St. Elizabeth's School in that same year. In 1926, St. Monica's officially closed and all Black Catholics living in the area attended St. Elizabeth's. Because Chicago parochial schools generally did not welcome Black students, St. Elizabeth's filled an important role in the city's Catholic school system. Although the establishment of the school allowed the segregated network to remain in place, St. Elizabeth's also, according to Neary, "offered a unique benefit to African-American families—an educational alternative to the Black Belt's substandard public schools."[57]

When Mundelein asked Drexel for sisters to staff St. Elizabeth's, he told her that he needed ten SBS for the coming academic year (1922–1923). Eight sisters would be assigned to the grammar school and two others would teach at the high school. She gladly designated eight SBS for St. Elizabeth's because she believed that "the Most Reverend Archbishop of Chicago is a Leader amongst all the Archbishops in donating a school for elementary and secondary education for the Colored Race." Drexel asked the cardinal if he would agree to have two lay teachers assigned to the high school because she wanted members of the congregation studying at Catholic University to be able to complete their education in a timely manner. She was, Drexel told Mundelein, "trying to prepare for the needs of the near future." If the cardinal would agree to her proposal, she would be happy to make up the difference in salary that a laywoman would receive.[58] As the city's demographics continued to change and Black people moved into neighborhoods that had been populated by white Catholics, the Society of the Divine Word also assumed responsibility for St. Anselm's parish in 1932, and five Sisters of the Blessed Sacrament arrived in that same year to administer and staff the school.[59]

In a 1936 letter to the motherhouse, Sister John Vianney admitted that she was worried when she found out she had been assigned to St. Elizabeth's, but her fears were unfounded. "Would you kindly tell [Mother Philip Neri]," she wrote, "that there isn't a chance of getting mixed up with gangsters." Sister John Vianney described St. Elizabeth's as a "darling mission," and thanked Mother Katharine Drexel for sending her to Chicago. She understood that St. Elizabeth's was "one of our large missions," but explained that seventeen sisters did not seem like a very large number compared to the fifty-one she had lived with in the novitiate. Her companion, Sister Alma, teaching at St. Anselm's in Chicago, agreed with Sister John Vianney. In a letter to Mother Katharine, she wrote that she "was just in love with this place already and [was] anxiously looking forward to the opening of school on Tuesday next."[60]

In addition to an academic curriculum, students at SBS schools were required to attend religion classes and—if Catholic—prepare for first communion and confirmation. They were encouraged to go to Mass and to try and convince their parents to attend as well. The congregational annals for 1937 include comments from a sister assigned to St. Elizabeth's on the topic of religion and faith. In what appears to be an excerpt of a letter written to Mother Katharine, the sisters described the parish children as "real good material for a future generation of staunch Catholics,...not the type that grow wings, Oh, no! but an energetic, wide-awake group, with plenty of mischievous tricks, a desire to succeed; and a good fund of the love of God!"[61]

The Sisters of the Blessed Sacrament differed from many white teachers teaching Black children in Chicago's public schools because they "dedicated their lives to serving African Americans." In addition, as Neary explains, "The rigorous discipline of the convent and missionary work directed their lives, which they passed on to their students." "St. Elizabeth Grade School," one student remembered, "was a place [where] you knew what you were supposed to do. The nuns at the grade school taught and you learned—you actually learned something there....You had to do what you were required to do."[62] Drexel and the SBS worked to provide their students with a quality education that would allow their students to succeed when they moved on to either higher education or the work force, but they did not usually discuss Black history or culture at the elementary and secondary school level. "'One thing I will say about the nuns: they instilled in us a sense of pride in ourselves,' remembered Marie Davis, but 'I don't recall it having anything to do with race.'"[63]

By the 1960s, a decrease in numbers coupled with an aging population meant that the SBS did not have enough sisters to staff all of their schools. In 1968, St. Anselm's PTA challenged Mother David Young's decision to remove three sisters from their classrooms in the middle of the school year in order to respond to vacancies in other schools caused by sisters leaving the community. The sisters, they told Mother David, were "all superior teachers in classrooms with much less than ideal conditions." The PTA asked the Mother General to allow the sisters to return until the end of the school year, and that "unilateral decisions effecting the lives of our children on the part of the mother house immediately end." A third request called for a policy to be developed that prohibited transferring sisters at any time other than the end of the school year. In her reply to the PTA, Mother David indicated that she understood the parents' concerns, and explained, "An isolated action never sets a precedent nor establishes a policy." The problem was simple: "There is a crying need for Sisters." The congregation's leadership was doing their best to provide sisters where they were needed, but Mother David clearly did not have enough personnel to give the parents of St. Anselm's what they wanted.[64]

In addition to maintaining a presence in Chicago, the SBS staffed parochial schools in other large urban centers. When the Spiritan Fathers agreed to staff St. Mark's parish in Harlem in 1912, they asked the SBS to open a school. The congregation agreed, and Drexel traveled to New York City to find space suitable for a school and convent. Finding two houses on W. 134th Street, Drexel designated the one described as being "in very good repair" as the school. The other house, which would serve as the convent, "was badly in need of every kind of repair—painting, papering, fumigating. The floors were almost destroyed—it has been used as a sort of tobacco factory." Despite the condition of the convent, the sisters assigned to St. Mark's moved in prior to the beginning of the 1912–13 school year. When they arrived, accompanied by

Mother Katharine Drexel, "they found that the beds which had been ordered from a Philadelphia firm, had not come, so for over a week they used the floors."[65]

The congregational annals report, "Everything struck the new Sisters [assigned to New York] as being very novel and interesting." The blinds in the refectory, for instance, were "scrupulously kept down" to prevent any of their neighbors from seeing the sisters eating. The SBS at St. Mark's also were very aware that they were among the very few whites living and working in Harlem. "There are Colored folks to the right of us, Colored folks to the left of us, and Colored in the front of us, and also in the rear of us," the annalist wrote. The sisters also commented on the music they could hear from neighboring homes and businesses but placed their remarks within the context of a negative stereotype often leveled at Black Americans. "When a dance starts up, you can hear the whole program distinctly. Our Colored brethren in the rear seem to be the happy possessors of every kind of musical instrument, and they have been blessed with voices, so they sing and play and enjoy themselves, as only the happy-go-lucky Negro knows how to do."[66]

Katharine Drexel was proud that St. Mark's—a parish to which she had contributed a good deal of money—became very successful in a relatively short period of time. Writing to Cardinal Patrick Hayes in 1925, Drexel rejoiced, "God has blessed the work at Saint Mark's so that now we have over six hundred pupils there, and every classroom available is crowded to its utmost capacity." She worried that if something were not done, the students being promoted at the end of the current school year would have no opportunity to receive "the blessings of a Catholic education." The school building would eventually be expanded, and the Sisters of the Blessed Sacrament would expand their ministry in New York City to include All Saints, St. Charles Borromeo, St. Thomas the Apostle, and St. Joseph.[67]

Although Katharine Drexel and the SBS believed that Black people were equal to whites in every way, their students did not always think that they acted in a way that demonstrated this conviction. Rev. Lawrence Lucas, who had been educated by the SBS at St. Mark's in Harlem, remembered in his memoir that the sisters who taught him did not teach the students to celebrate their Blackness. He wrote,

> One might expect that under these circumstances—an all-colored school with nuns dedicated to the colored work—my ego would be restored. This was not the case. The colored kids were yearning to be white because they already knew it was better to be white. The sisters were white and were part of the system that reinforced our belief.[68]

Lucas admitted that he did not "experience the blatant racism that some do even today," but he did transfer from St. Mark's and enrolled in All Saints School, which was staffed by the Sisters of Charity until they left and the SBS assumed responsibility for the school.[69]

Diane Nash, one of the student leaders of the Civil Rights Movement of the 1960s, remembered her uncomfortable conversation with an unnamed member of the congregation when she was a student at St. Anselm's in Chicago. Although a devout Catholic when she became involved in the struggle for civil rights—she had once considered entering religious life—her memories of this particular sister were not positive. During the course of a conversation, the sister told Nash, "You *know* that we love God in our order [SBS], because we deal with the least of God's people." Cecilia Moore writes, "The spiritual merit the sister felt she was gaining by serving in the black community and the implied racial superiority in the statement stung and remained with Nash."[70]

Other students recounted very different experiences. Mabel Landry Staton, who attended St. Elizabeth's in Chicago, claimed the SBS instilled "self-esteem and confidence in their students." "I'll never forget the time I raised my hand in first grade," she remembered. "'Sister, why are we different from everyone else?' I had asked. The nun replied, 'God gave you color because he loves you more.' There wasn't any stopping me after that." Lucas, Nash, and Staton clearly remembered both negative and positive encounters with the Sisters of Blessed Sacrament that stayed with them for many years.

During the second decade of the twentieth century, Drexel and the SBS began the process of opening a ministry in Boston that involved settlement work rather than staffing a school. In 1914, the annalist for the congregation wrote, Cardinal William O'Connell "summoned" Mother Katharine and Mother Mercedes O'Connor to the city because he "wished that the Sisters of the Blessed Sacrament take up settlement work among the Colored people there." As a result of the meeting, which included O'Connell's dog pulling the sisters' lunch out of a bag that had been placed under a chair, Drexel agreed to open a settlement house but suggested that the sisters live in a rented house temporarily in order to let the work "slowly develop." O'Connell, for his part, agreed to pay the living expenses for the sisters assigned to work in Boston. Blessed Sacrament Mission Center "administered to the sick, instructed the 'ignorant,' and provided 'food and clothing for the poor, besides conducting a sodality and sewing circle'" for Black women.[71]

Shutting Down

The SBS were forced to close a number of their ministries beginning in the 1960s. As congregational numbers declined, and Black parents chose to send their children to integrated schools—public and Catholic—it was simply not viable to sustain all of the schools they had been sponsoring and funding for many years. The SBS closed St. Francis de Sales in Belmead, for instance, in 1971. Despite some courses in home economics, St. Francis had touted its academic curriculum for many years. In an article that appeared in the *Washington Post* in 1993, Hattie Toppins Delgado, a graduate of the class of 1941, remembered, "St. Francis girls have always had a strong tradition of academic excellence," but that accomplishment could not change the reality that there were not enough students enrolled to keep the school operating. St. Emma's Military Academy closed at the end of the 1971–72 school year, after a significant drop in enrollment that began in the late 1960s; during the last year the school was open, ninety-three students were enrolled at St. Emma's, forty of them scheduled to graduate that year.[72] Because St. Emma's buildings were in a state of disrepair, the SBS decided to raze the school's buildings in 1974 and the sisters who had been living there to oversee the process of shutting down the property moved to St. Francis de Sales. Several members of the Sisters of the Blessed Sacrament remained at Belmead until 2017, when SBS leadership announced the property would be sold and the sisters—who had been working with local youth and several other ministries—relocated.[73]

Decisions to close schools Katharine Drexel and the Sisters of the Blessed Sacrament founded throughout the South were made for a variety of reasons. The very gradual integration of public and parochial schools meant that the schools the congregation founded were no longer necessary in southwestern Louisiana, New Orleans, and other

Southern locations. In 1970, Mother Elizabeth Fitzpatrick wrote to the congregation on the subject of school integration. Telling her sisters that school integration was a top priority for the SBS, Mother Elizabeth reminded them that their "dedication to the Black community, begun by Mother Katharine Drexel, is vibrantly alive and active among us today." Two obstacles to integration, she explained, were racism and issues related to money and facilities. Any manifestation of racism or racist attitudes that hindered integration was "inimical to the teachings of the Church on the Mystical Body of Christ." "We, SBS," she continued, "pledge ourselves to the position of supporting unitary education for the Black People of Louisiana." Although Mother Elizabeth did not mention the possibility of SBS schools closing as a result of integration, this would clearly be a result of policies and laws dismantling the system of segregated education.[74]

In some instances, members of the congregation found themselves remaining within the environs of a particular parish, but no longer teaching. By 1979, Our Mother of Mercy School in Church Point, Louisiana, was no longer being used as a parish elementary school. All students attending parochial school in Church Point were enrolled at Sacred Heart—the "white school"—and many Black parents had transferred their children to the town's public schools. Three SBS assigned to the parish were involved in pastoral ministry, religious education for students in elementary school, and youth ministry. The Sisters of the Blessed Sacrament remained a presence in Our Mother of Mercy until 1993.[75]

In 1965, Mother David Young wrote to Chicago's Cardinal Albert Meyer on the subject of St. Elizabeth's High School. Students attending St. Elizabeth's could now "be accepted in other schools,...[and] in all fairness to them, they should be given the opportunities that can be provided by schools with larger enrollments and better facilities than it is possible to offer in small high schools." Katharine Drexel, she explained, used her money and resources to provide an education to Black students who were unable to attend Catholic—and sometimes public—schools because of policies related to segregation and discrimination. "Now that these barriers have been removed, she [Drexel] would want them to be given every possible advantage." Because the congregation was struggling to finance and staff schools that had been founded by the SBS, she asked Meyer to "accept the withdrawal of the Sisters of the Blessed Sacrament from St. Elizabeth High School, Chicago, as of June 1965."[76]

In 1971, a sister described St. Elizabeth's elementary school as "the last hope for learning in the community." Compared to other elementary schools in the area, the school was "doing a good job," but was limited by issues related to money and facilities. Although there were ten SBS assigned to the school, the principal, described as "energetic and intensely involved with the Apostolate," had been forced to be "more of a debt collector than an educator." The church planned to take over that responsibility, however, and there was hope that the principal could begin to focus on providing students with a quality education. The SBS were able to maintain a presence at St. Elizabeth's—the last school with which they were affiliated in Chicago—until 2006. Cardinal Francis George responded to the news of their withdrawal in a letter to Sister Patricia Suchalski, herself a Chicago native, writing, "Countless students, parents, faculty members, parishioners and neighbors have benefited from your witness of faith and service." That sentiment was echoed by bishops in dioceses throughout the country as the congregation either closed schools or withdrew sisters from its many missions. The pattern of withdrawing from ministries repeated itself throughout the late twentieth and early twenty-first centuries. Boston's Blessed Sacrament Mission Center was "taken by eminent domain in 1967." The Sisters of the Blessed Sacrament moved to St. Paul's in the city's Dorchester section and remained there until they left the archdiocese in 1981. Sister Mary Jane O'Donnell notified Monsignor Joseph O'Keefe, vicar general of the Archdiocese of New York, that the SBS would no longer be a presence at St. Mark's after June 1982.[77] Closing some schools and withdrawing sisters from others did not mean that the Sisters of the Blessed Sacrament were abandoning their commitment to work with Black and Indigenous People.

From the 1890s until the second half of the twentieth century, the Sisters of the Blessed Sacrament ministered to Black people throughout the United States. Working primarily in the field of education, they founded and staffed a variety of schools from small, one-room buildings in rural Louisiana to larger urban parish schools in Chicago and New York. Many of the students educated by the SBS in the South would have only had access to a rudimentary education if not for the sisters' presence in their community, and Northern black children often only received access to the parochial school system as a result of Drexel's willingness to fund and staff schools in urban areas. Despite Drexel's ability to use her wealth to offer Black children access to an academic and religious education, her money could only go so far. Her schools received little, if any, support from either bishops or wealthy lay Catholics. In addition, as a woman religious—even one with a fortune at her disposal—who was expected to defer to the local ordinary, Drexel and her sisters were unable to challenge structural segregation in either church or society. As we will see in chapter 7, however, some SBS living and working in the South were active observers of and participants in various aspects of the Civil Rights Movement; they were especially involved in helping to determine the best way to ensure that Black and white students attending newly integrated parochial schools received a quality education. As they made painful decision to close or withdraw from ministries, the congregation continued to sponsor and help staff its most enduring legacy, Xavier University of Louisiana, an institution important enough to this story that it deserves its own chapter.

Chapter Six

AN ENDURING LEGACY

Xavier University of Louisiana

"That afternoon," the SBS annalist wrote, "we learned that [Hurricane] Katrina had changed course and was headed for New Orleans. The evacuation order went from voluntary to mandatory. A decision was made to stay." The seven Sisters of the Blessed Sacrament who decided to remain in the Crescent City were living in the convent on Xavier University's campus in August 2005 and knew how to prepare for hurricanes. They had plenty of drinking water, flashlights, and batteries, and they filled bathtubs and taped windows. Some of the sisters attended a Saturday vigil mass and were asked if they planned to evacuate. Their response was a resounding no.

Most of the university's resident students left campus, but about 350 students out of a total population of approximately 4,000 chose to remain along with about forty staff members. The campus, including the convent, lost electricity about 4:45 a.m. on Monday, August 29, but the sisters stayed informed of the storm's course with battery-operated radios and televisions. When the storm began to subside on Monday afternoon, they cooked meat and other frozen items that would not survive the loss of electricity. After feeding faculty and staff who had taken refuge in the administration building, administrators delivered the food to students who had waited out the storm in several dormitories. The sisters went to bed Monday night hoping that the worst was over.

While the sisters slept, however, the levee broke, causing water from Lake Pontchartrain to flood the city. "The campus," the annalist reported, "looked like a lake...[and] we knew we would have to evacuate for no one knew when the water would stop rising." By Thursday, the sisters were able to evacuate; each was able to bring one small bag with her. It was not until November 18 that Sister Mary Anne Stachow could return to campus and begin the arduous process of cleaning the convent. Other sisters gradually joined her, and on January 17, Xavier University officially reopened. At the request of President Norman Francis, the sisters agreed to house a number of women faculty and staff who would be unable to return to the university without housing.[1]

When the Sisters of the Blessed Sacrament were forced to evacuate their convent during Hurricane Katrina, it was the first time that the campus had been without members of the congregation since Mother Katharine Drexel founded the university in 1915. Established to provide higher education for Black Catholics—although non-Catholics were never excluded from admission—Xavier is perhaps best described as the flagship of the ministries of the Sisters of the Blessed Sacrament. The university is the only Catholic institution in the group known as Historically Black Colleges and Universities (HBCU) and remains the only university in which the SBS have been involved as a congregation.

Xavier University is an essential cornerstone of the work of Katharine Drexel and the Sisters of the Blessed Sacrament. As smaller ministries, such as elementary and secondary schools, closed due to declining numbers of sisters and changing demographics, the university has remained a congregational mainstay and an important part of the U.S. Catholic educational landscape. In addition, any discussion related to race and racism and Katharine Drexel and the Sisters of the Blessed Sacrament cannot discount or omit the fact that Drexel and the congregation invested millions of dollars, assigned many sisters to serve as professors, staff, and administrators, ensured that SBS on the faculty possessed the appropriate terminal degrees, and worked to make sure that students graduated with the tools and credentials needed to succeed in American society. Xavier is a crucial component of the larger history of the Sisters of the Blessed Sacrament and should play an important part in any scholarly conversations about the SBS and Katharine Drexel.

Ministry in New Orleans

Many of the segregated schools established for Black Americans in the aftermath of the Civil War were under the auspices of a Protestant denomination or missionary association. Catholic students were admitted to and enrolled in these institutions, but church leaders often expressed concern that living in a non-Catholic environment might cause some Catholic students to leave their church for another that they found more hospitable. New Orleans Archbishop James Blenk (1906–1917) insisted on the establishment of separate parishes for Black and white Catholics despite objections from New Orleans's Black community and developed a plan to create a system of segregated territorial parishes. At the same time, Blenk supported the idea that the Black Catholic population of New Orleans should have access to a Catholic education under the condition that the schools were segregated. SBS congregational annals credit Blenk with informing Drexel that Southern University, "a State Institution for Colored boys and girls," had been ordered by the state of Louisiana to relocate from New Orleans to Baton Rouge, and the property was currently for sale. The archbishop thought the land "could be secured at a big bargain," and he invited the SBS to consider purchasing the property in order to begin an educational ministry in New Orleans.[2]

Accompanied by Mother Mercedes O'Connor, Drexel arrived in New Orleans in April 1915, and conducted a thorough inspection of the property. With the assistance of the mayor and several local politicians, the property was purchased at a public sale for $18,000. In a letter to her councilors, Mother Katharine explained that she needed between $3,000 and $4,000 for repairs and renovations. "We are going to visit the Baptist and Strait Institute and Public Schools to see what we must compete with," she reported at the close of her letter.[3] Drexel and her sisters shared Blenk's concern that younger Black Catholics were in danger of leaving the Catholic Church for one of the city's many Protestant churches. Protestant denominations—Mother Mercedes O'Connor referred to them as "sects" in the parlance of the era—offered young Black men and women the option of private schools and high schools, and the Catholic Church had to provide children with an alternative.

"Who shall account to God for this terrible loss, who shall answer for these souls?" she worried.[4]

On August 16, 1915, Mother Mercedes and Sister Mary Frances left Pennsylvania for New Orleans. (Mother Mercedes, however, simply accompanied Sister Frances; she did not remain in New Orleans.) Within a week, five other Sisters of the Blessed Sacrament began the journey south. The sisters lived with the Sisters of Charity—a very common practice when a religious congregation moved to a new area—until they were able to move into their own quarters.[5]

Almost as soon as the sisters arrived in New Orleans, the hurricane of 1915—storms of this severity were not yet given names—passed twenty miles west of New Orleans at the end of September. Writing to Mother Katharine to explain how the storm had impacted the planned ministries, Sister Mary Paul of the Cross reported that the sisters "feared our ceilings would fall; the rain came through the walls (not so much through the walls, but through the ceilings of [the] temporary chapel), our dormitories, all the windows through the building had rain pouring in underneath,...and worst of all, was the heavy torrent of dirty, black, sooty rain through the chimneys opening onto the class room." Property damage was fairly extensive: a tree fell on the domestic science building, furniture was strewn along the street, and the fence was blown down. But the sisters were grateful no lives were lost.[6]

Despite the hurricane, "Southern University of Louisiana under the protection of St. Francis Xavier," renamed Xavier University Preparatory School, opened in the fall of 1915. Although Drexel planned to open a university, she began by following a pattern established by many Catholic colleges, especially those founded by women religious, by establishing a high school to meet the needs of Black students who hoped to attend college, and then founding a college when that became a viable option. (The university would be formally established ten years later.) The SBS originally planned to welcome students in grades seven through ten, but so many students enrolled that the sisters expanded the school's offerings and opened an eleventh grade as well. One year later, Xavier added grade twelve. (The school was not yet a university, despite its name.) The sisters almost immediately found themselves somewhat overwhelmed with students. Sister Mary Frances reported that they were "at our wits end trying to take care of [the children] we have at present. In some classes we can *keep* them but not *teach* them." She herself was teaching two Latin classes but was only able to do so because the domestic science classes had not yet begun.[7]

As Sister Frances's letter reveals, the philosophy of what came to be known as Xavier University Prep called for a combination of classical and vocational education. Courses offered included sewing, typing, carpentry, English, mathematics, Latin, church history, physics, plane geometry, and normal (teacher) training.[8] The SBS also believed that "since virtue...is the chief end of education, the formation of character is greater than the mere acquisition of knowledge." Their emphasis on the development of character led to attaching "a special value to many things not mentioned in the curriculum—to a sense of honor, to self-respect, to courtesy, to gentleness, to reverence, to right values, [and] to a recognition of personal duty." Although the new high school was clearly conducted under Catholic auspices, the SBS welcomed "to its advantages pupils of every denomination, and anything like an attempt to force religious convictions of [sic] non-Catholics shall be scrupulously avoided." All students were required to attend "religious exercises and... catechetical instructions, but non-Catholic students" could be excused from these requirements.[9]

In June 1916, Sister Frances reported that twenty-six students graduated from the "High School Department of Xavier University." Twenty-two of the students were Catholic; four were converts.[10] Three years later, in 1919, the SBS responded to the growing need for Black teachers and established a Normal School. In 1925, they expanded their operations and formally opened Xavier University.

Founding a University

Prior to the outbreak of the Civil War, several colleges and universities for Black students had been established in the North, including Wilberforce University in Ohio and Cheyney and Lincoln Universities, both located in Pennsylvania. In 1865, Shaw University was founded in North Carolina; and during the twenty-five years following the end of the Civil War, approximately one hundred institutions of higher education were founded for Black men and women in the South. Many of these were funded by Protestant denominations such as the African Methodist Episcopal Church and the Disciples of Christ, but they also received support from a number of missionaries and northern philanthropists.

Although these schools originally focused on "basic skill development, including instruction on social skills (i.e., etiquette and dress), manual trades, and religious education," two models of education eventually emerged. The first focused on vocational training; the second offered students a more traditional liberal arts education.[11]

Enrollment at what are now known as HBCUs increased in the years immediately following the Civil War until the 1930s. In 1900, for instance, 3880 Black students were enrolled in southern colleges and professional schools; by 1935 that number had increased to more than 29,000. The men and women who received an education at these institutions often became teachers, doctors, and lawyers, and as a result, entered the Black middle class. Since higher education was mostly segregated, the task of preparing Black women and men for professional careers fell largely to HBCUs.[12]

Although she did not spend much time giving speeches to organizations—even those devoted to Catholic causes and issues—Drexel did advocate for Black Americans to be able to receive a college education. Speaking at the Catholic Students' Crusade held at the University of Notre Dame, she informed her listeners that Black leaders were desperately needed in the Catholic Church; in order for those leaders to emerge, Black people had to be granted access to higher education. Noting that in Indiana there was "no Catholic College for Negroes and in fact there are very few Catholic Colleges that admit them," Mother Katharine "pleaded with the young student body before her to interest Catholics [in admitting Black students to their colleges] so that the great opportunity which they themselves enjoyed in being educated under Catholic auspices with a Catholic environment and good Catholic teachers might be also given to their less fortunate colored brethren." The annalist reporting on the event noted that the speech was "vociferously applauded."[13]

By 1925, the SBS Council decided "after much discussion that a College was needed at New Orleans, and in September the Sisters of the Blessed Sacrament would then begin" to establish an institution of higher education. The discussion apparently centered on two issues: (1) a college would cost far more than elementary or secondary schools; and (2) the council worried about "a college conducted by women who would admit both sexes." The SBS annals note that the council agreed to found the college because "if a work were needed and there were no others to take up the work God would not fail to provide and He would also protect the Sisters in what otherwise might be a hazardous undertaking." It was clear that Black Catholics wanted the opportunity to attend college, and because Catholic colleges and universities refused to admit them, they had no choice but to "seek their higher education in Universities of Godless and sometimes of decidedly Atheistical character."[14] At the time of the university's founding, American Catholic colleges and universities were predominately single sex. Drexel, however, hoped to establish only one university, and she sought advice from Archbishop Pietro Fumasoni-Biondi, apostolic delegate to the United States, who—perhaps surprisingly—counseled her not to worry about founding a coeducational university. Pius XI, he assured her, was aware of the good work being done at Xavier and approved of her plans.[15]

Xavier University "opened its doors as an institution of higher learning of collegiate rank" in 1925 with forty-five students enrolled. The SBS were very clear that they were opening a university to prepare young adults for professional careers. An early publication of Xavier informed interested parties that "the object of the College is to offer young men and women of the Colored race an opportunity of receiving a liberal education; an education which will develop all the faculties of soul and body and find expression in clear thinking and right acting."[16] The faculty consisted of two priests, eight Sisters of the Blessed Sacrament, and three "layfolk." Rev. Edward Brunner, SSJ, was named president, and Sister Mary Frances, SBS, was appointed dean.[17] Brunner's official role as president, however, is somewhat murky in congregational history. In a letter to Mother Katharine written in 1927, Brunner informed her that he was willing to accept the position on the condition that it be "merely nominal and personal." His parish duties, the Josephite priest assured Mother Katharine, took precedence over any university tasks, and he defined those duties as only those the Sisters were not willing or able to perform. Brunner explained the word *personal* to mean that "my acceptance does not in any way bind our society [the Josephites] to replace me in the office should I be changed to a different mission." About five years later, Brunner offered his resignation to Mother Katharine—not for the first time—on the grounds that another Josephite had been appointed to the university faculty. Dr. Edward Murphy, according to Brunner, would bring more prestige to Xavier than he ever would because he held a PhD. Drexel accepted his resignation, writing somewhat tongue-in-cheek that "we feel we can no longer ask you to retain the position which you have twice resigned and therefore reluctantly accept the third resignation."[18]

The first five years of Xavier University's history demonstrate the SBS's commitment to providing Black Americans with an education that was equal to *any* college or university. At that time the university was formally founded, the College of Liberal Arts was established and the Normal School was transformed into a Teacher's College. A College of Pharmacy opened in 1927, and in 1929 the congregation purchased property to physically separate the university from Xavier University Prep. When the "new" university was dedicated in 1932, not everyone in attendance expressed enthusiasm over the new campus. A priest was heard to say, in Latin, "What a waste."[19] Mother Katharine herself attended the ceremony but was not on the dais with other dignitaries. In keeping with her desire to remain away from the limelight, and in accordance with rules governing the presence of women religious in public venues, she watched the festivities from a window, hidden from view.

Drexel clearly wanted Xavier to be able to compete with all other colleges and universities, and that goal was illustrated in the campus architecture. When Josephite Father Edward F. Murphy arrived at Xavier in 1932—the year the new campus formally opened—he wrote, "My first sight of Xavier surpassed my expectation. The handsome Indiana-limestone structure indicated that Mother Katherine [*sic*] deemed charity too beautiful a virtue to be rendered unbeautifully and that she was giving her best to a people who so often received the opposite from others." During his time at Xavier, Murphy interacted with many who did not believe Black people could or should have access to higher education. In his autobiography he described an encounter with a "sharp-faced woman." "That college called Xavier," she said, "is a shame. Higher education for Negroes! Robbing us of our servants—that's what I call it."[20]

Mother Agatha Ryan

Mother Agatha Ryan, SBS, was appointed president of Xavier University in 1932, a position she held until 1955. Ryan was well qualified for her new position. She had professed her first vows as a Sister of the Blessed Sacrament in 1900 and taught in the southwestern part of the United States from 1901 until 1914, when she was assigned to open the first Catholic school for Black children in Columbus, Ohio. In addition, she supervised the entire network of SBS schools for a number of years, traveling countless miles to observe teachers, ensuring that educational standards were upheld, and solving any problems that schools, principals, and teachers might be facing. When Mother Agatha began to lead the university community, 172 students were attending Xavier, and another 57 were enrolled in extension classes. The college was still located on the grounds of Xavier University Prep, but a new campus was in the process of being built on a site that already included a stadium. The annual cost of operating the university was estimated at $48,000. Xavier did not yet boast an endowment; in addition to tuition ($12.50 per semester), the university received funds from the Sisters of the Blessed Sacrament.[21]

By the time Mother Agatha was appointed president of Xavier, Louise Morrell was publicly extolling the university. In a radio address, Morrell told listeners that, in her opinion, three educational institutions were poised to help Black Americans overcome hardships and discrimination: Xavier University, St. Emma's Industrial and Agricultural Institute in Virginia, and Maryland's Cardinal Gibbons Institute (the latter two were heavily subsidized by Morrell). All three, she said, "stand out as beacons of hope in the Catholic field of negro education. They also serve as a compelling stimulus to a deeper and more universal interest to our Catholic laity in the great needs of the Negro race."[22]

During the early years of Mother Agatha's tenure, the sisters teaching at Xavier were very aware that their students were struggling financially as a result of the Great Depression. Students often worked all night and attended classes all day, and since many of them were living in rooming houses, they were forced to eat their meals out. This often meant they went hungry during the day, and only had a sandwich for their evening meal. When one sister was heard to comment on the fact that the football team had lost a lot of games that season, a student responded, "Sister, I think the boys are hungry, and they are working to pay their way through college, and they have not enough money to buy the food they need." In at least one instance, one of the sisters, upon learning that a student had not eaten, called him over and—being careful not to embarrass him—told him to go to the convent kitchen and make himself a sandwich. "God help the poor," the sister recounting the incident reflected. "It is when I see the hunger and poverty that I wish for riches. What a happiness to relieve the pangs of hunger."[23]

Mother Agatha Ryan, SBS, and unidentified others. Courtesy of Xavier University of Louisiana, Archives and Special Collections.

Mother Agatha and the Sisters of the Blessed Sacrament worked to ensure that Xavier University remained economically viable during this era, especially as they were seeking accreditation. In a letter to Louise Morrell written in 1933, Drexel expressed concern about the number of students owing the university money. "It amounts to $7000 or more— That is the list up to J. The list of [the] rest of [the] alphabet is not yet made out for me. M. M. Agatha is hopeful that half will pay later this term."[24] She had good reason to worry; by 1936 a financial analysis of the Drexel holdings indicated that the family had suffered considerable losses—Louise Morrell, for example, had seen some of her holdings decrease by half—and it was not clear she could continue to subsidize Xavier.[25] Later that same year, Mothers Mercedes and Mary of the Visitation met with Philadelphia Cardinal Dennis Dougherty and suggested drawing funds from Francis Drexel's estate as a way to begin an endowment for the university, which was necessary if Xavier was to receive an A rating from one of the reputable credit rating firms. Dougherty informed them that their proposal could not be implemented under the term of the will.[26]

One suggestion that emerged during the sisters' meeting with Dougherty was that the cardinal could bring the financial situation of Xavier to the attention of the American Board of Catholic Missions (ABCM), which had been founded in 1920 to consolidate missionary efforts among U.S. Catholic dioceses. When she learned that Mother Agatha was on her way to Chicago, Drexel told her to meet with Cardinal George Mundelein and "plead as well as you can, and you can do this better than anyone else, for XAVIER'S support." An additional $25,000 was needed from the ABCM for the college to receive an A bond rating, and at the same time, receive accreditation from the Southern Association. The School of Social Service, which had been established in 1934, "would have no standing" without accreditation, and it would be "useless" to continue to offer degrees in that area. Drexel directed Mother Agatha to inform Mundelein "nothing was lacking the requirements of the [accrediting] Association except the promise of a settled sum for an Annual Endowment."[27] Several years later, in 1938, Mother Agatha telegraphed her congregational leader with very good news: "Just notified tonight that the University received Class A rating and Prep accredited by Southern Association."[28]

Mother Agatha and the Xavier faculty recognized that the arts were an important component of the undergraduate experience. A music school was established in 1926, and within a few years students could join the university band or orchestra. When Sister Elise Sisson arrived at Xavier in 1934, she began to develop what would become a "world-renowned opera program." When she realized that Xavier students were unable to attend concerts at either the Municipal Auditorium or other concert venues in New Orleans, Sister Elise "determined to provide her music students with the experience on Xavier's campus that they couldn't get anywhere else." *Faust*, the first production under Sister Elise's direction, received critical acclaim and the Xavier program quickly became a favorite of opera lovers throughout the country. Sister Elise remained chair of the music department for thirty-five years and directed many operatic productions during her tenure at the university. The opera program established Xavier's reputation as top-rated music department.[29]

Responding to Racism

Although the founding of Xavier meant that Black Catholics could now access Catholic higher education, the sins related to race and racism in the United States were and are a part of the institution's story. During Mother Agatha's long tenure as president, she responded to statements and events related to race from a variety of perspectives. In December 1934, for instance, Mother Katharine directed all of the local superiors, including Mother Agatha, to send a letter to President Franklin D. Roosevelt urging the passage and enactment of the Costigan-Wagner Anti-Lynching Bill. Xavier's president tailored her letter to reflect her position as the chief administrative officer of the country's only Black Catholic college. Identifying herself as the president of Xavier University, "a Catholic College for Negro youth, with an enrollment of 539 students," she called on Roosevelt to do everything possible to ensure the passage of the bill, and referred to a "shameless abduction from one State to another" of a Black prisoner, who was subsequently lynched in Florida, calling it a "blot on the America we love and upon our common humanity."[30] Roosevelt did not publicly support the Costigan-Wagner bill, arguing that to do so would cause him to lose Southern voters essential to his reelection to a second term. Despite the letter writing campaign engineered by Drexel, Southern Senators organized a filibuster, and the bill did not pass.

Incidents directly impacting Xavier students also demanded attention from Mother Agatha. When the Xavier and Fisk University football teams met at Xavier in 1935, she described the event to Mother Mercedes, who succeeded Drexel as congregational leader. The game conveniently ended in a 6-6 tie, but the "Colored elite" representing both schools were visible that day, as well as the "old New Orleans and Straight [University] people." Following the game a dance was held at St. Joan of Arc Hall, but Mother Agatha complained that it was "impossible to engage any decent public place in the city now for dancing," and the university did not really have a site suitable for a large gathering. As a result, it was very hard to hold a dance, card party, or any other sort of event for either a social gathering or fundraising.

Mother Agatha also worried about what would happen when basketball season began. The team was quite good, she reflected, but they had no place to play. There was no easy solution to the problem; Loyola

University of New Orleans's gym was not an option. A "well-known" resident of the city had said to a priest, "[It] was a good thing that your basketball team didn't play at Loyola last year, for if they had, Loyola would have been burned to the ground." When the priest challenged his assertion, the man responded, "Well, perhaps they would not have burned it to the ground, but there would not have been a student within its walls the next day." This story, which Mother Agatha considered important enough to tell her major superior, demonstrates that even though Xavier offered a higher education to Black Catholics, the faculty, staff, and administrators could not break the barriers designed to keep Black women and men from integrating into mainstream southern culture.[31]

Other sisters assigned to New Orleans also struggled to respond to racist remarks directed to them. Sister Mary Boniface, for instance, reflected on Cardinal George Mundelein's address at Xavier in 1938 in which he noted the importance of evangelizing Black Americans. She wished, however, that Mundelein's remarks had been directed to the white audience. A white woman with whom Sister Boniface was speaking had expressed her surprise and dismay that a young Black woman had received a degree in nursing. In response, Sister Boniface told her about the Xavier students who had received college degrees, and then asked her "what she would do when she got to heaven (if she got there) and saw the Martyrs of Uganda and even some of the old humble Mammies way up high near our Lord." The woman's response was illuminating: "Oh, that will be different!...They will be white then."[32]

Black women religious were often unable to complete undergraduate and graduate degrees from Catholic institutions because of their refusal to admit students of color. Xavier University was one place where members of Black religious congregations could complete their undergraduate education and become certified as teachers. The first Sisters of the Holy Family, a congregation of Black women founded in New Orleans in 1842, began taking courses in education at Xavier in 1928. In 1943, eleven members of the congregation graduated from the university; five sisters received master's degrees.[33] During the following decades, members of the congregation enrolled at Xavier's Summer School in increasing numbers. Some took courses on campus and others were enrolled in classes taught by the Sisters of Charity from Seton Hill College in western Pennsylvania to prepare them to enter the university. All of the sisters, however, were receiving credit from Xavier for completed courses.

Preparing for Change

During the years following World War II, Xavier, like schools across the country, experienced a dramatic increase in enrollment as veterans took advantage of the G.I. Bill to receive a college education. Since a number of these students were from outside of the greater New Orleans area, including some international students from African countries, the university had to set up temporary overflow housing for men and women. More classrooms and laboratories were also needed, and in 1947, Xavier acquired a building that had been used by the Navy and converted it into a chemistry building housing four laboratories, a lecture room, offices, and a science library. In addition, the university was able to purchase huts from the War Assets Administration to use as a cafeteria annex and a music building.[34]

By 1948, Mother Agatha Ryan had become a Xavier institution. *TIME* recognized her importance to both the university and the Sisters of the Blessed Sacrament in an article describing the custom of Xavier graduates stopping by to see the president on their wedding day. "No Xavier wedding is quite complete without the blessing of Mother Agatha Ryan," the magazine reported. At that time, Mother Agatha was responsible for more than leading the nation's only Black Catholic university; she was also the "superintendent" of seventy-five grammar and secondary schools for Black and Indigenous People operated by the Sisters of the Blessed Sacrament throughout the country. The Catholic University of America recognized her accomplishments by awarding her an honorary degree in 1948. "Under her wise and competent leadership," the citation read, "Xavier University, in spite of many formidable obstacles, has become the foremost Catholic higher institution of education of Negroes in the country, and is everywhere acclaimed for its accomplishments."[35] During the decade following the *TIME*'s article, however, significant changes would impact both the university and the Sisters of the Blessed Sacrament.

Changes upon Changes

The lead headline in the March 1955 *Xavier Herald*, "Xavier Mourns Death of Beloved Foundress," signaled changes would come to the Sisters of the Blessed Sacrament and the university. Six months later, the paper—which was and still is published monthly—recognized a major administrative change at Xavier with the headline, "Sr. Josephina Appointed X.U. President. Sr. Miriam Francis Named Dean." The relatively brief story barely recognized the tenure of Mother Agatha, but focused entirely on Sister Josephina Kenny, who had been an assistant professor of education since 1949, and also served as the chair of that department.[36]

The 1950s would bring other changes to the university, specifically related to race and diversity within the student population. As early as 1952, when Mother Agatha was still the president of the university, she reported to Mother Anselm, superior general, that southern colleges and universities were beginning to desegregate. Louisiana State University, for instance, was now accepting Black students into some programs, and "by degrees they will infiltrate into the undergraduate school although there will be a hot fight against it." Loyola University in New Orleans was "finally" accepting Xavier graduates into the law school, and at least one Black student had enrolled in the graduate education program. However, Xavier had been accused of segregation and "jim crowism" because the administration had not changed the university charter, and as a result, continued to refuse to admit white students.

Founded in 1944, the United Negro College Fund (UNCF), of which Xavier was a member, believed that it would be some time before American colleges and universities were fully integrated, Ryan continued, and suggested that Black schools continue to strive to be "as fine and as good as possible." In addition, they were encouraged to "gradually welcome white students to their doors." White sisters studied at Xavier during the summer in library science classes and some white women religious and seminarians had begun taking courses in arts and sciences, but despite its all-white administration, the terms of the university's charter did not allow the school to be formally integrated. Perhaps, Mother Agatha suggested, the charter could be amended to say that Xavier was "a religious institution *primarily* [italics added] for the education of Indians and Colored People"; the university could then accept white students.[37] The congregational council did not come to a final decision on this issue, Mother Anselm stated in her reply, but the sisters saw no harm in admitting a few white students. The annals for 1955 note that two of the 1194 students enrolled at Xavier during the 1955–56 academic year were white.[38]

Xavier and the SBS assigned to work in New Orleans experienced significant changes during the 1960s and 1970s as a result of events taking place within the Catholic Church and U.S. society. University President Sister Josephina, SBS, issued a statement at the beginning of the 1960–61 academic year related to student activism during the Civil Rights Movement. Although the university did not generally approve of student protest, it agreed with the right of students to protest and would not try to interfere with those planning to participate in demonstrations or marches. This decision, however, only applied to individuals; student groups were not allowed to participate in protests or demonstrations. In addition, although no student would be penalized for their actions, they were not to consider themselves as representing the university in any way. Sister Josephina was taken to task by one critic, self-identified as "A SERIOUS CATHOLIC," who criticized the president "and her group" for not explaining to Xavier students that there were "very good reasons that Louisiana and many other States have to have laws for the separation of the races, for health purposes, as well as morals." If the students did not like the laws as currently written, they could live elsewhere.[39]

In 1961, the SBS commemorated the seventieth anniversary of their founding by issuing a "Call to Catholic New Orleans" to condemn segregation. The statement appeared in the *Times-Picayune* on February 12, 1961, and stated in part that "BOTH FROM A NATURAL AND A SUPERNATURAL POINT OF VIEW ALL MEN ARE BROTHERS....THE FUNDAMENTAL PRINCIPLES OF JUSTICE...AND THE PRIMAL OBLIGATION OF CHARITY ARE EQUALLY BINDING ON AND APPLICABLE TO ALL MEN. Forced segregation violates both Justice and Charity."[40]

Students and faculty at Xavier took part in the Civil Rights Movement in a variety of ways. As early as 1956, seventy-two students challenged the segregated transportation system in New Orleans by boarding an empty bus and sitting in seats reserved for white riders. The driver called the police, who arrested the students and charged them with disturbing the peace. The charges were later dropped.[41] A few years later, State Senator William Rainach accused both Xavier and Dillard Universities of offering classes in nonviolent resistance. Sister Josephina responded to Rainach's accusation by commenting, "We have checked our faculty and student body and find no evidence of any 'lunch counter classes'....We deplore this statement of Mr. Rainach as an attempt to involve Xavier University in that which would tend to create a racial disturbance in our community." Rainach denied Sister

Josephina's suggestion, and an editorial in the *Xavier Herald* described his accusation as "*absolutely and unequivocally false.*" The editors did, however, note that they stood "*in deepest sympathy with those persons now engaged in the passive resistance movement, for we realize that theirs is a just cause to which all people who are concerned with the future of America should rally.*"[42] In 1965, ten Xavier students chose a unique way to demonstrate their support for civil rights and equality by picketing a reception attended by Catholic bishops who were in New Orleans to celebrate John Cody's installation as archbishop. About 200 students signed a follow-up letter, describing civil rights as "a moral issue."[43]

When the Freedom Riders arrived in New Orleans on May 15, 1961, they quickly discovered that no residents of the city were willing to host the group for fear of what might happen to themselves and their property. When two Xavier students, Rudy Lombard and Vincent Roux, asked Norman Francis, who was the dean of male students at the time, to help house the Freedom Riders, Francis agreed and found beds for them on the third floor of St. Michael's dormitory. Sister Josephina permitted him to house the protestors as long as a press release was not issued. In remarks published in the New Orleans *Times Picayune* at the time of his retirement in 2015, Francis remembered the Freedom Riders emerging from cars in front of the dorm, saying, "It was a sad and triumphant sight." Although the Freedom Riders left the university the following day, it was something Francis would remember as an important moment in his career.[44]

Xavier after Drexel

Drexel's death in 1955 meant that Xavier—and other SBS institutions—began to see a significant decrease in the amount of money it received from the congregation. The SBS continued to contribute to Xavier when possible, but it was clear that a new governance and financial structure was needed if the university was to survive. In a historical sketch of the university written in 1966, Sister Mary Veronica explained that Xavier's two main sources of financial support, in addition to tuition and fees, were grants from the United Negro College Fund and an annual contribution from the American Board of Catholic Missions. Although the university boasted a small endowment, its greatest infusion of capital came from the "contributed services of the Sisters." That same year, the university was incorporated as a distinct entity as Xavier University of Louisiana, separate from the Sisters of the Blessed Sacrament for Indians and Colored People, of Louisiana, and the university and property were turned over to a board of trustees consisting primarily of laypeople with a small number of sisters representing the congregation.[45] In 1968, after a number of years of preparation, the Sisters of the Blessed Sacrament transferred the governance of the university to an independent board of trustees. Norman Francis was named the first Black, first male, and first lay president of the university, holding that position until his retirement in 2015.

During the late 1960s, Francis, along with other Xavier faculty and administrators, began to respond to issues raised by the growing number of non-Catholic students attending the university. Many of these students—along with their Catholic peers—did not think it was necessary to complete courses in philosophy and theology as part of their requirements for graduation. In 1969, students staged a sit-in to publicize their concerns. President Francis agreed to meet with the demonstrators, who demanded that the library purchase more books by Black authors, hire a Black priest to serve as chaplain, and abolish philosophy and theology requirements. During the course of their meeting the students also decried the apathy of many of their fellow students toward Black liberation. Francis responded to the students' concerns by hiring Rev. Jerome LeDoux, SVD, as university chaplain, and starting a periodical entitled *Review of Soul*, which focused on Black culture and thought.[46]

By 1978, faced with declining numbers and an aging population, the SBS were forced to begin the difficult process of withdrawing from and closing a number of ministries. The sisters living and working at Xavier insisted that a congregational presence was essential to implement Drexel's vision for the university she founded: "the development of Black Christian leaders for the Black community." The thirty sisters currently in residence were not enough, they stated, to serve approximately 1800 students. Without the SBS at Xavier, the sisters warned, "Xavier would become just another predominantly Black university." In addition, the university would suffer economically if they were withdrawn because the personnel replacing them would require higher salaries, leading to an increase in tuition and a decrease in enrollment.[47] Although SBS were withdrawn from other ministries, they remained a presence at Xavier.

The Place of the Prep

Although Xavier Prep was a separate entity from the university, the histories of the two institutions are somewhat intertwined. After its separation from the university in 1925, the size of Xavier Prep's student body grew quickly. In 1932, 325 students were enrolled; that number had increased to 500 by 1940. Unusually, the school admitted both young women and men from its founding until 1970, when it began to dedicate itself to the education of girls.[48] In 1972, the sisters at Xavier Prep reported that the staff of the school consisted of fourteen sisters and fourteen lay teachers; 375 students were enrolled. By the 1979–80 academic year, the total enrollment had increased to 523, 186 of whom were identified as non-Catholic. By the end of the 1980s, enrollment was stable; 515 students were enrolled, 262 of these students were non-Catholic.[49] In 2003, Xavier Prep added an eighth-grade class, and when Hurricane Katrina led to the closing of two archdiocesan middle schools, a seventh grade was added.

The Sisters of the Blessed Sacrament reluctantly concluded that the congregation could not sustain Xavier Prep beyond the 2012–13 academic year. The decision galvanized a small group of alumnae determined to keep the school open. The group negotiated with the SBS to purchase Xavier Prep, but the sisters stipulated that the name of the school had to change, despite the fact that "the school's mission and vision, student body and staff, would remain virtually the same." When the school reopened as an independent institution at the beginning of the 2013–14 year, it was under the new name of St. Katharine Drexel Preparatory School.[50]

The University in the Twenty-First Century

At the beginning of the twenty-first century, Xavier University could boast of a number of accomplishments. The university was ranked first in sending Black Americans to medical school, with an 80-percent acceptance rate. In addition, 25 percent of Black pharmacists received their degrees from Xavier. When Hurricane Katrina hit New Orleans in

2005—and the levees broke, flooding the city—the university had a $78 million budget and a $27 million endowment.[51]

Although Dillard and Southern Universities were largely deserted by the time Katrina made landfall just east of the city, students were still living in Xavier's dorms. The students who remained on campus, including Khalillah Hill and Clifton Holland, were eventually evacuated as a part of the "largest single displacement of Americans since the Civil War."[52] Hill remembered that when it was time to evacuate, "the trucks were there only to receive Xavier students. They wouldn't take anyone else."[53] The students sat on an interstate highway for about five hours and were then taken to Southern University in Baton Rouge—although one source notes they were evacuated to Grambling State—and from there made their way to other parts of the country.[54] The university itself sustained significant damage. Every building was flooded with four to six feet of water; estimated damage was around $100 million, which caused the university to close for a semester. The closure led to 318 employees being laid off, some of them permanently. This number included 36 percent of the faculty.[55]

Only 44 percent of Xavier's freshmen returned when the school reopened in January 2006. Among others, Hill and Holland eventually made their way back to the university. Hill went home to San Francisco, transferred to Jackson State, and then returned to Xavier. "I just decided to return," she said, "regardless of all the bad things I experienced [during the storm] at Xavier. The mass communication faculty is so great; they always try to do their best for me." Holland attended Morehouse College and converted to Islam before coming back to Xavier. He explained he "came back to Xavier so that I can get to where I'm going. The school is almost all the way back, minus a few people. But other than that, it is fully functional." His experience caused him to enroll in a number of Black studies courses because he realized that "if our people could survive what they experienced, I can survive this."[56]

Xavier faculty, students, and administrators have also played a role in the Black Lives Matter movement. In 2015, the Institute of Black Catholic Studies (IBCS) at Xavier sponsored a symposium designed to respond to the increasing number of Black Americans shot and killed by police officers and the nascent Black Lives Matter movement. Ten months later, when Bishop Edward Braxton of Belleville, Illinois, issued a pastoral letter on the subject, Xavier held a second symposium. According to Michele Peseux McCue, this meant "Black Lives Matter moved from the streets into the academy, where the potential for formulating solutions for change could be sustainable." Speaking at the first symposia, Father Maurice Nutt, who served as the director of IBCS from 2014 until 2017, said that the symposium "extended the mission of service Xavier's foundress, St. Katharine Drexel, began when the University opened in 1925. Drexel founded Xavier at a time of segregation, effectively proving that 'Black Lives Matter.'"[57]

Today, the legacy of Mother Katharine Drexel and the Sisters of the Blessed Sacrament is visible throughout Xavier's campus. Sisters remain a presence on the faculty and board of trustees. The university continues to expand. In 2012, for instance, the *Times-Picayune* reported that commuters along Interstate 10 had been watching the construction of the new Katharine Drexel Chapel, designed by award-winning architect Cesar Pelli: "The new $10 million dollar chapel juts like the Rock of Gibraltar toward the Pontchartrain Expressway."[58] But perhaps the most enduring legacy of Drexel's vision—other than the presence of the university itself—is the fact that Xavier "consistently produces more black students who apply to and then graduate from medical school than any other institution in the country," and is among the top four institutions graduating Black pharmacists.[59] As the SBS—like many other religious congregations—make very difficult decisions about the future, it is clear that Xavier University will be a legacy to the community and its founder that will last for many years to come.

Chapter Seven

WALKING IN THE FOOTSTEPS OF A SAINT

The Sisters after Drexel

On May 1, 2021, the Sisters of the Blessed Sacrament posted a Facebook video in which Sister Mary Roger Thibodeaux, a Black member of the congregation, shared some of her vocation story. Educated at Sacred Heart elementary and high schools in Lake Charles, Louisiana, Sister Mary Roger entered the congregation immediately after high school in 1958. While attending the two schools, both of which were segregated, Sister Mary Roger met the Sisters of the Blessed Sacrament, whom she remembered as "great educators." Mother Katharine Drexel was clearly committed to Sacred Heart. Funds supplied by Drexel allowed for the convent to be built and four classrooms to be added to the school. With Mother Katharine's support, the first year of high school was added to Sacred Heart grammar school in 1923, and Black students in Lake Charles were now able to receive a Catholic secondary education.[1]

So many sisters at Sacred Heart were from Ireland, Sister Mary Roger recalled, that her father told her that by third grade she had developed a "slight brogue." Although the SBS whom Thibodeaux experienced in the classroom were primarily white and Irish, she was thinking about entering the congregation by the time she entered her junior year at Sacred Heart High School. Her decision to accept her call to religious life meant that Thibodeaux relinquished her dream of attending Columbia

University (or, more likely, Barnard College). Although she spent her novitiate years in Bensalem at St. Elizabeth's, Sister Mary Roger did manage to live in New York City for several years. Her first assignment was at St. Thomas the Apostle School on 118th Street and St. Nicholas Avenue in Harlem.[2]

In 1972, Sister Mary Roger published *A Black Nun Looks at Liberation Theology*. As described by Mariam Williams, the book contains "Thibodeaux's poetic meditations about the Black Power movement she was witnessing in and outside of the church." At this time, some Black Americans believed that to embrace any form of Christianity was to participate in white supremacy, yet many Catholics were convinced that Black Power was a threat to church unity. Sister Mary Roger "challenged the church to consider Black Power as a means to make the church more just, more in step with God."[3] It is impossible to know how many SBS were supportive of Thibodeaux's decision to publish her reflection, but she thanked SBS Sister Mary Aaron, "who suggested the idea of compiling my thoughts for the public."[4]

A Black Nun Looks at Black Power offers readers some powerful ideas to ponder and demonstrates the author's connection with liberation theology. "Black Power is not foreign to Yahweh, and Yahweh is not foreign to Black Power. There is a covenant of friendship there. The cause of Justice is and always will be in strict accordance with the will of God." Other reflections are critical of the Catholic Church's response to issues regarding racial equality and Black Power. "The Catholic Church would do well to absorb some of the courage displayed during the beginning stages of the Black Power Movement. We must at times risk everything to gain a greater good." Still others reflected the frustration many Black Americans were feeling in the wake of Martin Luther King Jr.'s, assassination. "Do not say too often that some are called to spend their lives continually turning the other cheek—unless you have been appointed by God to be the perpetual striker."[5] Thibodeaux was clearly in tune with the Civil Rights Movement and its aftermath in the United States of the 1960s and 1970s.

At the same time, however, Sister Mary Roger never suggested that faith was not important in the struggle for racial justice. "God is not dead," she wrote. "And those of us who firmly give witness to the truth of that statement would caution the prejudiced minds of the subtle North and flagrant South: There will soon come a day when God will sit on his judgment seat." She also expressed a belief in the importance of serving the marginalized and dispossessed when she wrote, "To live in joy and service to others in spite of persistent oppression is the only life worth living. When we believe that we are our brothers' keepers then we must leave no stone unturned to help lead others to the path of Christ."[6] *A Black Nun Looks at Liberation Theology* was clearly written by someone who understood and had experienced racism but remained committed to the life she had chosen as a Sister of the Blessed Sacrament.

Sister Mary Roger is one example of how a member of the congregation founded by Katharine Drexel responded to the many changes impacting U.S. society and the Catholic Church during the second half of the twentieth century. In the years following the death of their beloved Mother Katharine in 1955, the SBS grappled with issues facing other American religious communities such as diminishing numbers (which resulted in withdrawal from and closing of ministries that had played a vital part in the SBS story), making congregational decisions that allowed sisters to live in small communities rather than large convents, and responding to societal struggles and changes related to the Civil Rights Movement. In addition, the SBS no longer had access to what was left of their founder's inheritance because—as stipulated by Francis Drexel's will—any remaining money was distributed among twenty-seven charities. Because the Sisters of the Blessed Sacrament were founded after the death of Francis Drexel, they were not among the beneficiaries of his vast fortune.

What Happened to the Money?

Although Katharine Drexel had been in poor health since at least 1935, her death on March 3, 1955, attracted a good deal of attention. Because many of the SBS assigned to ministries far from Philadelphia were unable to return "home" for her funeral, detailed descriptions of Drexel's last days and the events surrounding her funeral and burial were disseminated throughout the congregation. In a letter to the SBS, Mother Anselm McCann assured the sisters that those close to Drexel knew she was dying and made sure that a priest and doctor were there as she drew her last breath. Fifty members of the congregation—chosen in order of seniority—were brought to St. Elizabeth's to attend the funeral and burial, along with two Oblate Sisters of the Blessed Sacrament (from Marty, South Dakota), two Sisters of Mercy, and four Maryknoll sisters.

After the funeral Mass, which was held at the Cathedral of Saints Peter and Paul, the hearse carrying Mother Katharine Drexel's body made its way to the motherhouse in Bensalem. "By special arrangement a detour was made through the grounds of Eden Hall," an academy administered by the Society of the Sacred Heart. "The children from the grade school of St. Catherine of Siena recited the Rosary, the students from the Academy sang 'In Paradisum' and the Religious stood with lighted candles in front of the building, all paying their last tribute to our dear Reverend Mother." Mother Anselm closed her letter by encouraging the sisters to "arise and walk in the path traced out for us by our dear Reverend Mother, day by day surrendering all to God in love."[7]

Drexel had been hailed as a philanthropist and a woman of faith during her lifetime but had also been viewed through the lens of sanctity prior to her death. When Mother Mercedes O'Connor, who succeeded Drexel as the superior general of the SBS, wrote her unpublished memoir, her focus was very much on the person whom some consider the patron saint of philanthropy and racial justice. Mother Mercedes remembered that Drexel "practiced mortification in [sic] a heroic degree." She knew this because as a young novice charged with cleaning Mother Katharine's office and cell, she had found a "heavy discipline all blood stained." Mother Mercedes also remembered that Drexel "practiced kneeling on her fingertips behind the main altar after night prayers from 15 to 20 minutes at a time, also with arms outstretched in the form of a cross for like or longer periods." In addition, Mother Mercedes described Drexel as "most abstemious." Mother Katharine rarely ate dessert, she recounted, and when a particular "dish was presented to her it was noticed that she always took the toughest and worst portion of meat, saying that she liked that the best." Even when traveling with other sisters, Drexel did her best to make herself uncomfortable, "carrying the heaviest bag or suitcase, and never unless absolutely under obedience to do so would she travel in any but the cheapest way, saying that she preferred the day coaches and those that were crowded to their utmost capacity."[8] The memoirs of Mother Mercedes supported the image of Katharine Drexel as one who gave up her status as one of the richest women in the United States to serve God and those who were marginalized and oppressed. This idea was engrained in the consciousness of American Catholics—and some non-Catholics—before her death and continued to gain momentum until her canonization in 2000.

In what has been described as his "funeral oration," Auxiliary Bishop Joseph McShea admitted that the Catholic Church did not usually allow priests to offer "discourses of lavish praise and idle panegyric" at funerals. The remarks he offered on Mother Katharine would be an exception to this rule, McShea explained, because she was truly exceptional. After offering a brief biographical sketch of the future saint, McShea suggested that "the world has perhaps paused for a few moments of astonished surprise on reading the obituaries of this marvelous woman." Even the most "callous observer," he claimed, would be surprised to learn all that Drexel had given up in order to serve Black and Indigenous People. But it was her love of God, the bishop reminded his listeners, that led Drexel to devote her life and fortune to the work embraced by the Sisters of the Blessed Sacrament. Although she certainly provided a good deal of material assistance to those in need, it was the reason behind her actions that was important; hers "was simply a problem of neglected souls."[9]

At the end of his eulogy, McShea addressed what can best be described as the elephant in the room. "Not the least among [the] difficulties" the congregation was now facing, he told the SBS present at the Mass, "will be the cessation of the great personal income of Mother Katharine which for so many years has been expended in its entirety for the maintenance of your apostolic enterprises." They should not worry about this loss of support, however, because "Catholic generosity will not fail you." Bishops, priests, and laity would make sure that the congregation and its ministries remained financially viable.[10]

McShea's assurance that American Catholics would support the SBS was certainly not based in any kind of factual evidence. U.S. Catholics seemed convinced that Drexel remained wealthy despite losses suffered during the Great Depression, but Katharine Drexel and the Sisters of the Blessed Sacrament—there were 501 at the time of her death—knew that all income from her father's trust would cease upon her death. Sister Consuela Duffy, SBS, suggests that had Francis Drexel known his daughter would found a congregation of women religious, the terms of the will would have been very different. According to Duffy, Drexel never had any plans or desire to contest her father's will even though she fully understood that schools she had founded would suffer financially after her death. "But she also felt," Duffy writes, "that Catholic Americans could and should rally to the upkeep of various works supported for so long a period by her father's wealth. She gave it all while she lived. She counted on the generosity of Americans to give after her death."[11]

Drexel's death meant, of course, that a number of other charities were about to receive money that could be used to support their own ministries. On April 16, 1956, the NCWC issued a bulletin related to the Drexel fortune, but this time it was to announce that President Judge Charles Klein of the Orphans Court in Philadelphia had ruled that $14 million—the amount of Francis Drexel's fortune—could now be distributed to twenty-seven Catholic institutions named in his will. Beneficiaries included St. Charles Borromeo Seminary, St. Joseph's College (University), St. Mary's Hospital, St. John's Orphan Asylum, Sisters of St. Francis of Philadelphia, La Salle College (University), House of the Good Shepherd, and St. Mary Magdalen de Pazzi Asylum for Italian Orphan Girls.[12]

Philadelphia Archbishop John O'Hara—he was named a cardinal in 1958—was very aware that the Sisters of the Blessed Sacrament would be seriously impacted by Drexel's death and the distribution of the trust. In an attempt to counteract this situation, O'Hara took a series of rather complicated steps to ensure that the congregation would remain financially viable. First, he asked Pope Pius XII for permission to "turn over to the mission works of these Sisters such funds as are not needed by these parishes and institutions." In other words, if one of the beneficiaries named in Francis Drexel's will did not need the money, the funds would be given to the SBS. The next step involved applying this plan to the "Catherine and Louise Drexel Trust," which had been set up from the sale of real estate and was treated as part of Francis Drexel's estate. After recommending that beneficiaries turn over money received from this trust to the SBS, fourteen charitable institutions contributed between $4,500 and $16,400 to the congregation for a total of $165,000.[13]

One example of how this distribution worked can be seen in the way the Sisters of St. Francis of Philadelphia (SOSF) handled the situation. The congregation informed O'Hara that they had decided to "relinquish in favor of the Sisters of the Blessed Sacrament the share of our Community and that of St. Mary's Hospital in the Deed of Trust."[14] A check for $32,852.16 was then sent to the Sisters of the Blessed Sacrament. The congregation's decision to turn over their share of the money to the SBS was gratefully acknowledged by Mother M. Anselm McCann a couple of months later. Writing to Mother Mary Leandro, Mother Anselm expressed her "profound and prayerful gratitude for your magnanimous charity toward the Sisters of the Blessed Sacrament in relinquishing in our favor the allocation for St. Mary's Hospital and the Sisters of St. Francis of Glen Riddle under the deed of Trust established by our Mother Foundress and Mrs. Morrell."[15]

The SBS managed to keep a number of their ministries afloat by soliciting funds from some of the very agencies that had once depended on the largesse of Katharine Drexel and Louise Morrell. In 1969, for instance, Rev. J. B. Tennelly, secretary for the Commission for the Catholic Missions among the Colored People and Indians, sent Mother Mary David Young, superior general, a check for $95,000. It was "the amount of the grant which the Board of Directors authorized me to send you for the work of your Congregation among the Negroes and Indians." Tennelly was sorry that the commission could not provide more funds for the work of the SBS, but the annual collection for work among Black and Native Americans had decreased from the previous year, and all of the associations in need of funds were receiving less money.[16]

As time passed, it became more difficult for the SBS to depend on the American bishops for funding. When David Byers of the American Board of Catholic Missions notified Sister Juliana Haynes, the congregation's president, that the SBS would receive $60,000 to subsidize their work at St. Catherine's in Santa Fe and Arizona's St. Michael Indian School in 1986, she thanked them for the money but reminded the bishops that the grant represented only 40 percent of the request. This was worrisome, Sister Juliana explained in a letter of Palm Beach Bishop Thomas V. Daily, because the SBS thought they might have to reduce their financial commitment to those schools. "At this time in the history of the congregation," she wrote, "our financial needs for retirement are increasing *significantly*, as I am sure you are aware....[W]e know we will not be able to continue to subsidize our apostolic works to the extent we have in the past." She hoped the board would reconsider their decision and increase their allotment to the SBS. The problem was, Byers explained in this reply, every congregation was facing financial issues related to aging sisters and their retirement needs. The grant would not be increased.[17]

Changes in Religious Life

Religious congregations of women and men underwent a number of changes as a result of the work of the Second Vatican Council (1962–65) and the societal and cultural changes of the sixties. Convened by Pope John XXIII, the council promulgated several documents that were especially relevant for the lives and ministries of women religious. *Lumen Gentium* (1964) and *Gaudium et Spes* (1965) encouraged sisters to work with the laity and clergy to provide material and spiritual sustenance to the poor, and *Perfectae Caritatis*, issued in 1965, called sisters to return to their roots and examine the reasons they were founded in light of their contemporary ministries. When coupled with the changes and upheavals of the sixties, congregations of women religious, including the Sisters of the Blessed Sacrament, responded to changes taking place in their church and society in a variety of ways.[18] Some changes impacted individual sisters or small groups while others focused on the congregation as a whole. A number of SBS sisters, for instance, began to ask for and receive more choices related to living arrangements. In one case, SBS assigned to Xavier University in New Orleans chose to move out of the convent—located on the campus—and begin an experiment in small group living. The new DAWN Community was composed of six sisters who moved onto the third floor of the House of Studies—once designated for junior sisters studying and continuing their formation at Xavier—on September 8, 1972. The official apostolate of DAWN was to "develop unity through participating more often with students in liturgy and prayer, meals, recreation and reflection."[19] After only four months, the sisters living in this "experimental house" realized it was too early "for a real evaluation of a small community attempting to live an apostolic, Eucharistic life in the spirit of the gospel in an institutional setting," but nonetheless believed they were making progress.[20]

The sisters gathered together for supper and ate breakfast and lunch in a campus cafeteria. When Mass was celebrated in the space reserved for the community, students were invited to participate. Overall, the evaluations offered by the sisters living in DAWN were positive, and perhaps even enhanced their work at the university. One wrote that "DAWN has meant NEW LIFE to me in this my 25th year of profession.... The freedom to pray spontaneously morning and night is a joy." This anonymous sister especially enjoyed the opportunity to eat in the cafeteria with students and faculty. "Many students are of other faiths, many having never known either white people or sisters. Mealtime is a time when they can learn of our lifestyle and we can learn of theirs." DAWN ended in 1992, when the sisters were informed that the university needed the space. "The demise of our community," a member noted, was "not due to a lessening of the attractive power of Xavier University."[21]

By the seventies, sisters assigned to a particular ministry felt free to articulate their disagreements with decisions made by congregational leaders related to the school with which they were involved. The sisters at New Orleans's Xavier Prep expressed their dissatisfaction with the way the SBS leaders had handled the principal's decision to leave in 1979. Writing to Sister Mary Elizabeth and the councilors, they informed them of their hope that future decisions would reflect "the wisdom of utilizing lay leadership and of offering remuneration that is at least commensurate with the Archdiocesan scale."[22]

Other changes experienced by the congregation were the result of the Sisters of the Blessed Sacrament adjusting to the new reality of religious life that involved decreasing numbers and resources. As sisters either left the congregation or retired to the motherhouse, the SBS were faced with a number of difficult decisions. A declining number of available sister teachers, for instance, meant that SBS schools were becoming staffed and administered by laywomen and men. In 1987, Sister Juliana Haynes informed the faculty and staff at Xavier Prep that the congregation had developed a set of responsibilities for the school's principal and president. The principal—lay or religious—was given responsibility related to day-to-day operations "of all academic programs and related faculty and student matters." The president, who reported to the board of directors, was "ultimately accountable to the SBS President and Council." In addition, Sister Juliana explained, the president "is responsible for fostering, articulating, and implementing the overall vision of Xavier Prep, as well as the school's specific goals and purposes." Policy statements such as this demonstrated that the SBS recognized that they were no longer the sole leaders of the schools they had founded, but still wanted to ensure that ministries such as Xavier Prep remained faithful to the SBS mission, vision, and values.[23]

Individual members of the congregation sometimes requested to work in a ministry that was outside of those supported by the SBS. From 1994 to 1996, Sister Patricia Rogan lived and worked in West Palm

Beach, Florida, in order to care for her elderly mother. During the time that she lived in that area, Sister Patricia served as the volunteer coordinator at Camillus House, a ministry operated by the Little Brothers of the Good Shepherd that offers the poor and homeless a "system of care" that includes providing shelter, clothing, and meals to those who are homeless and indigent.[24]

SBS sisters sometimes welcomed members of other congregations of religious women and men as they sought new ministerial experiences for a variety of personal and vocational reasons. Writing to her community—the Sparkill Dominicans—in 1991, Sister Sandra Magnini recounted her experiences at St. Michael Indian School in Arizona. She wrote that she "was living with twenty-two SBS along with eight other women religious representing six different congregations." Sister Sandra was assigned to the third grade, and all but two of her students were Navajo. Since she started, Sister Sandra told her community, her students "have changed from being very shy, quite children to lively, chatty kids."[25] Sister Sandra's experience at St. Michael's and her interactions with the Sisters of the Blessed Sacrament were clearly proving to be a positive experience in a ministry that went beyond the boundaries of her own congregation's work.

Downsizing

Many American congregations of women religious, including the SBS, found themselves faced with issues related to declining numbers and aging members during the closing decades of the twentieth century. As the number of women religious began to drop from 179,954 in 1965 to 41,357 in 2020, sisters were forced to make difficult decisions regarding closing or withdrawing from ministries.[26] The SBS were particularly impacted by these declining numbers because they had not experienced the growth other congregations had enjoyed during the forties and fifties. In addition, because their ministry was limited to Black and Indigenous People—unlike other congregations who staffed hundreds of parochial elementary and secondary schools—the SBS did not have many feeder schools from which to draw new members. Women who joined the SBS were called not just to religious life, but also to a certain kind of ministry. The congregation's numbers were never large when compared to larger communities, such as the Sisters of St. Joseph or the

Sisters of Mercy, but they were still impacted by women leaving religious life at the same time that the numbers of new women entering declined dramatically.[27]

Decisions concerning closing ministries were not made lightly and often caused great sorrow among members whose work had been closely connected to a particular ministry. Many revolved around parish schools—elementary and secondary—that had been staffed by the SBS for many years throughout the United States. Sister Mary Elizabeth Fitzpatrick informed Father E. G. Gehlen, SVD, pastor of St. Anselm's parish in Chicago, that the number of sisters assigned to the school would be decreased by one in 1976. If the congregation was going to remain present in many of their schools, she explained, the number of teaching sisters would have to be reduced. Five years later, Sister Jane O'Donnell informed the pastor that she could not honor the request for additional sisters for the 1981–82 school year. The two sisters assigned to St. Anselm's could remain at the school through 1982–83, after which the SBS would not commit any sisters to the school. The reason for this decision, Sister Jane explained, was a "lack of available personnel." Over 60 percent of SBS working in schools were over fifty years old. In 2006, the SBS ceased ministering in the Archdiocese of Chicago when the last sisters left St. Elizabeth's parish.[28] As the SBS withdrew from elementary and secondary schools, they reflected a larger national trend, which saw the number of Catholic elementary schools decrease from 9,366 in 1970 to 4,903 in 2020.[29]

The SBS had lived and worked among Louisiana's Black Catholics since the late nineteenth century, and when the congregation made the decision to withdraw from schools in the Archdiocese of New Orleans, Archbishop Philip Hannan asked if they could delay making the announcement for several months in hopes that the state legislature would pass "some measures which will be helpful to parochial schools." Sister Mary Elizabeth Fitzpatrick, president, believed this plan was not feasible because many already knew about the sisters' decision; sisters and pastors associated with the schools, for instance, had been informed.[30]

Because the SBS were committed exclusively to ministries involving Black and Indigenous People, closing ministries often hit members of a parish and the local ordinary particularly hard. When the sisters announced their withdrawal from Atlanta's Our Lady of Lourdes parish in 1972, for instance, Archbishop Thomas Donnellan wrote a heartfelt

letter to Mother Elizabeth expressing his concern over the congregation's decision. Although Donnellan could not help but note that he
should have been consulted about any decisions made to withdraw sisters in his archdiocese, his main concern was the effect this decision
would have on Atlanta's Black Catholics. Our Lady of Lourdes was one
of only two institutions serving that community, the archbishop told
Mother Elizabeth, and their work had impacted both Black and white
Catholics.

Donnellan clearly had great respect and admiration for the Sisters
of the Blessed Sacrament. He admired the fact that they "lived with the
poor and like the poor," and remembered the first time he had visited
their convent when he was "shocked at the conditions which they bore
cheerfully and without complaint." The Church's already limited witness
to Black Catholics would suffer when the congregation was no longer
a presence at Our Lady of Lourdes. "In other large cities," Donnellan
wrote, "the Sisters' withdrawal would effect one parish. Here it deals a
major blow to the Church's witness among the Blacks."[31]

The archbishop of Atlanta's appeal appeared to have worked, at
least temporarily. Mother Elizabeth solicited advice from a number of
sisters who had been associated with Our Lady of Lourdes, including
one member of the congregation who had taught there for two years
beginning in 1914. Her final conclusion was that it was simply not feasible for the SBS to maintain a presence at the school. In 1970, Mother
Elizabeth told Donnellan, 265 students were enrolled in the school; that
number had dropped to 187 in 1973. The community would withdraw
from Our Lady of Lourdes at the end of the 1973–74 academic year.[32]

Decisions related to downsizing ministries founded and funded
by the Sisters of the Blessed Sacrament were especially difficult. When
the place of the SBS at Xavier University was scrutinized, the sisters
advocated for a strong congregational presence at the university. In
a 1978 document, the sisters at Xavier reminded community leaders
that there were about 1,800 students enrolled at Xavier and only thirty
SBS. The placement of sisters in critical positions was as important as
the numbers, however, and the congregation was urged to make sure
those assigned to the university were qualified and prepared to assume
responsibilities in academic administration, student life, and campus
ministry, as well as serving on the faculty. The SBS at Xavier realized
that one option was to withdraw the congregation from the university. If

that were to happen, "Xavier would become just another predominately Black university....With the Sisters of the Blessed Sacrament comes the presence of the Eucharist which is not only the vital core of Catholic spiritual life, but also one of the great factors in interracial growth and understanding." In addition, if the sisters were "withdrawn," those hired to replace them would command higher salaries, which would cause tuition to increase—a problem occurring across the country as laypeople involved in education at all levels required better pay and medical benefits for their families. In turn, rising costs associated with increased tuition and fees to meet the needs of lay faculty would have a negative impact on students' financial resources. Members of the congregation decided to continue a presence at the university.[33]

"Our Boys" and Sister Louis Mark (Bernadette Stack), Our Lady of Lourdes School, Atlanta, Georgia. Courtesy of SBS Archives, CHRC, Archdiocese of Philadelphia.

The decision to close St. Catherine Indian School in Santa Fe may have been the most difficult decision made by the SBS. The school, after all, had been founded and funded by Mother Katharine Drexel herself and had been a congregational ministry since 1894. Issues concerning the ability of the SBS to manage the school surfaced as early as 1969, when several sisters assigned to the school wrote to Mother David Young detailing the "lack of adequate and qualified personnel" at St. Catherine's. There were a number of lay teachers at the school, but some were new teachers and unqualified to take on any additional duties. In addition, they were assigned to monitor extracurricular activities and needed evenings to prepare their classes for the following day. The sisters explained that they were worried about their students. Some of the boys, for instance, clearly needed "a fully qualified male counselor to guide them in handling problems of sex, alcohol, and drugs." They closed their letter by inviting Mother David to visit the school so that she could see for herself the issues the SBS at Catherine's were facing.[34]

Brian Collier, who has written about St. Catherine's, argues that Katharine Drexel never planned to establish schools for Native Americans on a permanent basis; her hope was that they would eventually become self-sufficient. During the 1980s, as the SBS continually reassessed their work, Joseph Abeyto, Sr., a longtime employee of St. Catherine's, visited the motherhouse in Bensalem to deliver a message. Abeyto told the sisters that Drexel had founded St. Catherine's—and other schools—"with an understanding that Indian people would do it for themselves. We are at that point now."[35] Determining what role the SBS and Native American educators and tribal leaders would play in taking the school into the future was easier said than done.

Despite the community's financial and spiritual commitment, the school continued to struggle. Recognizing that it was becoming difficult to continue their support, the SBS leased St. Kate's, as it was affectionately known, to an independent board that included Indigenous and Latinx members. Both parties agreed that at the end of ten years the school would be closed or permanently turned over to the board. The transition was "painful." A 1994 headline in the *Santa Fe Reporter* claimed that there were "dark clouds" hanging over St. Catherine's. Written by Anne Constable, the article reported that "at least a dozen members of the St. Catherine faculty have quit or been fired since the beginning of the school year." Members of the board claimed low salaries as the reason for the rapid turnover, but teachers argued that many students were "unmanageable."

Faculty and staff also complained about the way St. Catherine's was being administered. "There is little recognition of the special learning styles of Native Americans—or, indeed, of contemporary teenagers." Others complained that the "unrealistic" grading system—any grade below a 70 was a failure—meant that students did not qualify for certain scholarships. The article went on to discuss the lack of activities for students, poor living conditions, and a lack of respect for Native cultures. The article ended with an unnamed teacher speculating that the school "was going to die."[36]

Despite the appointment of a new president and serious efforts to balance the budget, St. Catherine's was unable to survive. An editorial in *The Santa Fe New Mexican* claimed, "St. Kate's too good to end," and called for philanthropic individuals and organizations "to supply a reliable amount of money to match the sisters' contribution and keep the worthy tradition of St. Kate's alive."[37] Even though supporters of the school raised over $100,000, an effort that was happening across the country when alumni rallied—not always successfully—to save their particular alma mater, it was not enough to sustain St. Kate's. In 1998, *The Santa Fe New Mexican* reported that St. Catherine's would permanently close in May of that year.[38] On March 3, 2006, the Feast of St. Katharine Drexel, former students, teachers, Sisters of the Blessed Sacrament, and friends of St. Kate's participated in a farewell blessing for the former school. At the conclusion of the service, those in attendance remembered the fifteen members of the congregation buried at St. Catherine's.[39]

The Civil Rights Movement

The struggle for civil rights was important to the Sisters of the Blessed Sacrament and their ministries to the Black community. The legacy of the SBS as it relates to race is somewhat complicated and has been discussed in several other chapters throughout this volume. In this section, we turn our attention to the sisters' role in actions considered part of the history of the Civil Rights Movement of the second half of the twentieth century, as well as how some contemporary historians are interpreting their work and history.

The sisters assigned to Our Mother of Mercy in Church Point, Louisiana, were clearly very interested in developments related to civil rights and remarked on them in their convent annals. When President Lyndon B. Johnson signed the 1964 Civil Rights Act into law on July 2, 1964, for instance, the community's annals remarked on the fact that the following day a Black parishioner entered a local restaurant and ordered lunch. Although his actions passed without incident, local whites were ready for future actions related to the integration of public places. "The parents of one of our high school students, whose daughter tried several times to enter this same restaurant, were warned that they would lose their jobs if the girl continued her attempts to integrate," the annalist explained.[40]

Like members of other religious congregations, Sisters of the Blessed Sacrament participated in some components of the movement. Sometimes they acted as individuals determined to assist in dismantling segregation. In 1958, for instance, Mother John Vianney took a group of children to a beach near Gulfport, Mississippi. Although the beach was designated as federal property, the police ordered the group to leave. One year later, Sister Consuela Duffy accompanied the Xavier University History Club on a visit to the home of Jefferson Davis. When they stopped to eat lunch on the beach between Gulfport and Biloxi, they encountered a similar problem and were not allowed to remain. The incidents were reported to the U.S. Civil Rights Commission and a lawsuit ensued. Both sisters testified, and the court determined that the beach should be integrated.[41]

In other instances, members of the congregation challenged segregation in a larger venue. In the early twentieth century, Drexel provided funds to build the church and school of Our Lady of Lourdes parish in Atlanta. The parish is located very close to Ebenezer Baptist Church, where Martin Luther King, Jr., worshiped and served as assistant pastor. In 1963, seven sisters assigned to Our Lady of Lourdes marched to Atlanta's federal courthouse along with King and other movement leaders. They also participated in demonstrations designed to push businesses and stores to commit to hiring Black employees.[42] After King's assassination on April 4, 1968, four SBS attended his funeral, along with forty students representing Xavier University. The following month, three sisters marched in a demonstration in Atlanta supporting the Poor People's Campaign.[43]

Mother Mary David Young, superior general from 1964 until 1970, allowed members of the community to participate in demonstrations and marches *if* the activity was nonviolent and if they were invited by the local bishop. Marches, she believed, were a way to demonstrate one's belief. In a 1965 letter to the congregation, Mother David reminded sisters that many of them had "visited [marginalized Black Americans] in their homes, witnessed their poverty, sickness, misery; tried to understand their problems...not for the past decade, as a donated service,... but as a lifelong dedication, a gift of self...until death. All know where we stand and have stood, practically alone, for decades."[44] The SBS ministering at St. John the Baptist parish in Selma in that same year, however, were not permitted to march for voting rights because Archbishop Thomas J. Toolen refused to allow any sisters or priests in his diocese to participate in civil rights demonstrations. The SBS, however, did their best to support the marchers. The night before the march, they housed young northern women in the school cafeteria. But in order to remain in Selma, they had no choice but to follow Toolen's directive.[45]

The SBS leadership expressed empathy when young Black Catholics grew frustrated with their church during this era. When a group of Black activists under the leadership of H. Rap Brown "stormed" St. Francis de Sales Church in New Orleans because they were not permitted to meet in the parish's main building, Mother David Young did not condemn the protestors. Indeed, neither she nor the SBS as a congregation condemned the Black Power movement. Instead, she said, "We must be very conscious of the changing thought patterns and attitudes of our people; we must learn to appreciate them; know how to accept them; help those who are struggling for personal identity in this time of crisis."[46]

As we have seen, Katharine Drexel founded schools for Black Americans throughout the South because she believed they both deserved and required an education. Legalized educational segregation meant that Black Southerners were often denied the opportunity to go to school; a small town might have only one school and it was designated for white children only. In 1954, *Brown v. Board of Education* declared that the doctrine known as "separate but equal" had no place in American education; this decision would have a great impact on many of the schools that had been founded and funded by Drexel and the SBS.

Southern Catholic bishops slowly began to desegregate Catholic elementary and secondary schools within their respective dioceses. When Atlanta Archbishop Paul Hallinan announced that Catholic schools would be integrated in the upcoming academic year, the annalist for Our Lady of Lourdes wrote that the announcement "must have been received with great relief by many of our parents, both Catholic and non-Catholic, who had been upholding the Church in the face of sharp criticism from co-workers."[47] Shortly after the beginning of the new school year, Sister Mary Ruth informed Mother Gonzaga Welsh that "integration here is going very smoothly and the white people seem as delighted as the colored."[48]

Integration of parochial schools did not necessarily mean educational equity. When a Black Catholic school was merged with the white parish school, the new reality was that Black students were often assigned to a new school where neither they nor their parents had a voice that was equal to the white students and parents. In addition, desegregation was sometimes implemented for financial reasons rather than a commitment to social justice because Catholic dioceses stood to benefit financially from a bishop's decision to integrate schools. When Nashville Bishop William Adrian decided to integrate diocesan schools in 1954, for instance, it meant that Immaculate Mother Academy—administered and staffed by the SBS—would close, along with Holy Family parish and Holy Family High School (see chapter 2). As Mark Newman, author of *Desegregating Dixie*, explains, "Adrian was not motivated by a desire to promote integration but by the need to find alternative Catholic education for their students because the schools were expensive to run, and had a combined enrollment of 172 students, only 60 of them Catholic." The bishop believed he was obligated to offer the affected students a Catholic education, even if meant admitting them to all-white schools. A day after the closings were announced, two girls' schools administered and staffed by the Dominican Sisters announced that they would accept "qualified" Black Catholic students that fall.[49]

Desegregation of southern parochial schools continued through the sixties and seventies. The SBS assigned to Our Mother of Mercy in Church Point—located in central Louisiana—appear to have been deeply involved in the desegregation of public *and* parochial schools in their area. By 1964, the sisters were trying to find an integrated high school that the graduates of their elementary school could attend. When the pastor of the parish, Father John Tyne, SSJ, suggested that the town's high school be integrated, Mayor Theodore Roosevelt Daigle became upset. When the mayor then told Tyne that he planned to advocate that a bond be issued to build a new segregated high school, the pastor argued against it. The bond was—to no one's surprise—approved; only property owners were allowed to vote and most of the area's Black residents were sharecroppers. Black students attended school in the town of Sunset; the sisters accepted this temporary solution because the school was accredited and offered a college prep curriculum.[50]

Integrating the Black and white parochial schools in Church Point also constituted a struggle in which the SBS were involved. In 1969, Mother David Young and Sister Cleophas arrived in Church Point to participate in discussions on integration. The arguments focused on how integration would be implemented and focused on two models. The first model was known as pairing and utilized all of the schools in a district, black and white. The school a student attended was determined by the grade in which he or she was enrolled. Consolidation, the second model, meant that only some schools would remain open. The white Catholic elementary school, for instance, would become the parish elementary school. After a good deal of discussion—some of it heated—it was decided that integration would take place using the pairing model. Shortly after this decision was made, it was reversed; there were simply not enough children enrolled in parochial schools to warrant the use of two buildings. This situation was exacerbated by the fact that black students were transferring from parochial to public schools for a number of reasons, and the white community was opposed to pairing because it might mean their children would attend a school formerly designated for Black children. Since there were so few Black students enrolled in parochial schools, the SBS decided the congregation would no longer staff the school, and concentrated their efforts on religious education classes. The new school was known as Our Mother of Peace.[51]

The way in which local bishops handled the integration of churches and schools often caused concern on the part of sisters assigned to Black schools. A member of the congregation working in Church Point resigned from her job when the bishop decided to close the Black parochial school and send its students to a white school, claiming that "the act of consolidating schools does not contribute to the dignity and brotherhood of man." Bishops, the anonymous sister continued, did not take into account "the hard earned efforts of the black people building their own institution," and—perhaps more importantly—they did not consult with those who would be most impacted by their decision. When Black students enrolled in the formerly all-white school, the sister concluded,

"It is reasonable to believe that the patterns of the past will be perpetuated in an institution controlled by whites and owned by them."[52]

As we have seen, several scholars writing in the late twentieth and
early twenty-first centuries have suggested that the schools founded by
Katharine Drexel and the Sisters of the Blessed Sacrament perpetuated
segregation. Mark Newman, for instance, claims, "Although the S.B.S.
fulfilled an educational need by providing a better education than the
segregated public school system and, like the Josephites [an order of
priests dedicated to ministry among Black Americans], did not advocate
segregation, the order's schools and support for black churches contributed to the growth of Catholic segregation."[53] Newman acknowledges
that the SBS, along with other religious congregations, were "sincerely
dedicated to blacks," but their work made it possible for the U.S. bishops
to create a segregated church.[54] Although it is clear, as Newman notes,
that the work of religious communities like the Sisters of the Blessed
Sacrament allowed members of the hierarchy and other congregations
to ignore the spiritual and educational needs of Blacks (and Indigenous
People, in the case of the SBS), at least some sisters understood the negative effect closing schools could have on the Black Catholic community.

In some cases, Sisters of the Blessed Sacrament informed those in
authority that diocesan policies and mandates concerning the desegregation of churches and schools were not being enforced. A sister
working in the Diocese of Lafayette in 1969 informed Bishop Maurice
Schexnayder that Black Catholics were still facing discrimination in
white churches. Recounting what she had observed in her own parish, she told Schexnayder that Black parishioners entered through their
own door and received the Eucharist separately from the whites in
the congregation. Explaining that letters issued by the local ordinary
on the subject of race relations and integration were not enough, she
strongly protested the situation. "The very existence of such a horror—
the very presence of a Catholic priest presiding over such a scandal with
the apparent approval of his bishop speaks to the people of the diocese
much more loudly and clearly than the six letters you referred to in your
latest communication with us."[55]

Schexnayder—at least at times—worried that the Sisters of the
Blessed Sacrament living and working in the Diocese of Lafayette were
acting in ways that suggested they were engaged with more radical components of the Civil Rights Movement. Less than a month after receiving a letter from a sister criticizing a local pastor for allowing segregated

practices at a local parish to continue, he complained to Mother David Young that the sisters at St. Lawrence parish in Mowata had "incited the people to riot." Although the pastor knew that Black parishioners were now able to sit in the main part of the church's sanctuary, the sisters had chosen to remind them that inequalities remained. The pastor had complained to Schexnayder that the SBS "sow the seeds of distrust among the colored people and go so far as to say that something is going to happen to the church, that it could be bombed." Some of the people with whom they spoke were "so frightened" that they did not return to the church. The sisters would be more productive, Schexnayder concluded, if "they attended to their own duties in their respective parishes." Mother David Young, responding from the motherhouse in Bensalem, informed the bishop that the account reported by her sisters was very different from that of the bishop and pastor. "Their story was quite different from what you had been told," she wrote.[56]

The Sisters of the Blessed Sacrament also looked within their own congregation to confront issues related to race and civil rights. In her history of the congregation, Sister Patricia Lynch claims that Mother David Young was enthusiastic about the first National Black Sisters' Conference that was held in Pittsburgh in 1968. Fourteen Black members of the congregation expressed an interest in attending, and their names were sent to Sister Martin de Porres Grey, the conference organizer and founder. Mother David, along with four other white sisters, attended the sessions of the 1969 meeting that were open to them. In order to assist the Conference financially, the SBS contributed $5000 to help organize and establish a national office.[57]

The congregation did not ignore its history of refusing to admit Black members until the 1950s and the issues those women faced as they struggled to find their place in the SBS. A 1976 document entitled "Program for On-Going Education on Black and Indian Concerns," grappled with the fact that the SBS had not accepted Black women into the community until 1952 but had encouraged them to join one of the three Black congregations of women religious. When "women of African descent" began to enter the SBS, the authors explained, they were diverse in terms of socioeconomic background and educational levels but shared a characteristic in common: they were Black women entering an all-white congregation. The congregation during these years reflected white America's response to civil rights; progress was "very slow, and in some sections, non-existent." The "racial attitudes and characteristics which were then, and are still now, prevalent in the United States were and are prevalent in white religious congregations, ours included." For Black sisters in the SBS, "just getting through each day, could easily be termed, *survival!*"

The writers of the document recognized that vocations to religious life were declining throughout the United States, but also pointed out that the number of Black women entering the Sisters of the Blessed Sacrament had always been low. The question, they asked, was, why? After all, they noted, the SBS had been a viable presence in New Orleans, a center of Black Catholicism, for many years. "Have we individually as well as collectively invited young black women to join us in our consecrated celibacy for the kingdom of God?" The suggested answer was no. Only once, one author noted, had she heard a congregational "authority figure" publicly invite SBS high school students—women of color, all—to enter the community. In addition, the SBS did not seem willing to own their history. The 1976 Xavier Prep yearbook, for instance, celebrated Black achievements but did not mention that Sister Norbert Maline was the school's first graduate to enter the community.

The document concluded by offering concrete suggestions related to Black women and the Sisters of the Blessed Sacrament. Recommendations included ensuring that black candidates were given the opportunity to network with other Black SBS sisters, as well as those in other congregations; supporting the National Black Sisters' Conference; making an effort to eliminate racism from the SBS; and maintaining strong relationships with Black communities, including the Holy Family Sisters, Oblate Sisters of Providence, and the Franciscan Handmaids of Mary, "so that we may more effectively share in the complete liberation of black people."[58] Almost fifty years after this document was produced, the congregation continues to work to eliminate racism within the SBS as well as in the United States.

About eight years after this document was disseminated, Sister Juliana Haynes became president of the Sisters of the Blessed Sacrament, the first Black sister to hold this position. Entering the congregation in 1952, Sister Juliana made her first vows the day after the death of Mother Katharine Drexel. She served in a number of ministries before becoming one of the congregation's leaders, including Xavier University and St. Peter Claver parish in Philadelphia. At the 1980 General Assembly, she was elected vice president, and when illness forced the resignation of Sister Mary Jane O'Donnell, she became president. She was elected to her own five-year term as president in 1985.[59]

One Hundred Years and Counting

In 1991, the Sisters of the Blessed Sacrament celebrated their one-hundredth anniversary as a religious congregation devoted to the service of Indigenous People and Black Americans. Celebrated from February 11, 1990, to February 10, 1991, the theme for the centennial year was "Sharing the Bread in Service, SBS 1891–1991." Opening with an internal celebration at the motherhouse in Bensalem, Sister Juliana Haynes proclaimed that the centennial was "a year for us to affirm loudly and clearly the validity of the charism of Blessed Katharine, the Spirit-filled vision of a Eucharistic society in which all peoples of all races are invited and welcomed at the banquet table—that vision which has not yet become a reality."[60]

During their centennial year, the SBS celebrated in a variety of ways, including a fundraising concert at Drexel University—founded by Mother Katharine's uncle—that included a performance by the Xavier University Choir and Jazz Ensemble. Many smaller events were held at SBS missions throughout the country, but—as Sister Patricia Lynch wrote—the "heart of the year" was a reunion at the motherhouse that included SBS, alumni/ae, and friends from all over the United States. One part of the reunion weekend was devoted to a gathering of former members of the congregation who were able to reconnect with current sisters. When Sister Juliana Haynes welcomed the former sisters back to St. Elizabeth's, she "expressed sorrow, in the name of the congregation, for any hurt or injustice done in the past." It was, Sister Patricia explained, "a moment of peaceful healing."[61]

Although the Sisters of the Blessed Sacrament had closed or withdrawn from a number of ministries by 1990, they were not averse to opening new missions—albeit smaller than those sponsored by Mother Katharine Drexel—if sisters were willing to serve. Their numbers had decreased from 551 sisters in 1964 to only 309 professed sisters in 1991, but they still opened forty-one new ministries during these years.[62] Many of these missions did not involve staffing schools, but they did focus on working with those marginalized by society. In 1990, the congregation opened its first international mission when Sisters Patricia Downs and

Donna Breslin began work in Ferrier, Haiti, where the congregation served from that year until 2001, and again from 2005 to 2007. In the same year that the ministry to Haiti opened, the community approved opening a House of Prayer in Atlanta. Proposed and founded by Sister Loretta McCarthy, the house "would be especially devoted to intercessory prayers for the city in which it was located." Sister LaSalette Ouelett joined Sister Loretta at this ministry, which they named Maisha House, after the Swahili word for life. The sisters living at Maisha House, which was located in Our Lady of Lourdes parish, participated in the prayer life of the surrounding community, who were invited to attend a weekly liturgy and scheduled days of prayer. In addition, the sisters worked with the parish's RCIA program and became involved in the life of the area's Black community.[63] When Sister Loretta's election to the SBS leadership team in 2006 meant that she would have to relocate to the motherhouse, she had no choice but to close Maisha House. After sixteen years, the house of prayer came to an end. She told the congregation, "It took another month of packing, distributing and cleaning with help from faithful friends of Maisha before the sign came off the door and all was left in readiness for the new owners."[64]

During the first three decades of the twenty-first century, the Sisters of the Blessed Sacrament continued to support a variety of ministries. In 2018, the SBS numbered approximately one hundred; about one-half of the congregation's members were retired. As their website explains, although those sisters still work "primarily among Black and Native American peoples," they do not minister exclusively to those two groups. In addition to Xavier University and St. Michael Indian School, the SBS serve in Boston, Philadelphia, Florida, Georgia, Louisiana, Tennessee, Virginia, Arizona, and New Mexico. The current mission statement for the SBS serves as a reminder of the work they were originally called to do by St. Katharine Drexel and reflects the importance of anti-racism in both the congregation and the larger society: "Guided by the spirit of Katharine Drexel, we are called to share the gospel message with the poor, especially among the Black and Native American peoples, and to challenge all forms of racism as well as the other deeply rooted injustices in the world."[65]

Epilogue

THE JOURNEY CONTINUES

"*R*emains of Saint Katharine Drexel to be moved to the Cathedral this summer," read the headline of *The Philadelphia Inquirer* on July 18, 2018. The Sisters of the Blessed Sacrament were selling the 144-acre property on which the congregation's motherhouse, a shrine dedicated to the saint from Philadelphia—including her burial crypt—and a residence for elderly and ailing sisters were located. The property, the congregation explained, was simply too expensive to maintain.

Officials of the Archdiocese of Philadelphia were clearly pleased that the second American-born saint would be moving to the Cathedral of Saints Peter and Paul. Ken Gavin, spokesperson for the archdiocese, commented that moving St. Katharine's body was a "very involved process," and noted, "it is a rare occurrence for something like this to take place." Sheila King, speaking on behalf of the SBS, said that the move would give Drexel a "more prominent and public shrine....It will be right there in the Cathedral, so a lot more people will know about her and the order and her work."[1]

Several months later—on October 30—the *Inquirer*'s readers learned that Drexel's tomb at the cathedral had been officially unveiled. Open to the public, the tomb is located toward the rear of the building, "next to an altar dedicated to the Drexel family." Katharine Drexel had, Rev. Dennis Gill, rector of the cathedral commented, come home to a place that was important to her and the Drexel family. Sister Donna Breslin, president of the community reflected, "The fact that she is no longer at the motherhouse is a loss for me," but went on to say she believed "many people will come to know about her in her new home. Most important, they will know about the mission that God entrusted to her and her community."[2]

Several weeks after Drexel's body was relocated to the cathedral, Archbishop Charles Chaput presided over a liturgy to mark the solemn celebration of the installation of the tomb. Attended by members of the congregation, Black Americans, and Indigenous People representing missions that had been established and supported by Drexel and the Sisters of the Blessed Sacrament, and students from Xavier University in Louisiana, Drexel was remembered as a woman who had given up a life of wealth and privilege to focus on two of the most marginalized groups in American society. Despite the celebratory tone to the event, it was somewhat bittersweet. "It's an honor to be here but it is a little bit of a heartbreak," said Bensalem mayor, Joseph DiGirolamo. "I graduated from St. Charles School (across from St. Elizabeth Convent) in 1957. In my eyes she will always be there."[3]

The Sisters of the Blessed Sacrament were not financially able to support the removal of Drexel's body from the motherhouse to the cathedral. They were assisted in this endeavor by financial assistance from the Connelly Foundation, a Philadelphia-based philanthropic organization. The sale of the motherhouse property, however, would provide a significant infusion of money into the congregation. The sisters planned to use the money to "fund international charitable initiatives and care for the order's aging nuns." In 2018, there were eighty-seven Sisters of the Blessed Sacrament, most of them living in a local retirement community.[4]

One of the messages that ran throughout the process of transferring Drexel's body to the cathedral was that Drexel was not just an important figure to the Sisters of the Blessed Sacrament; she was a saint for everyone. Chaput, for instance, remarked that Katharine Drexel had founded the SBS when she was still a relatively young woman—actually she was in her early thirties—and should serve as a role model for today's young adults. "Would that young women of the twenty-first century had hearts like her," he said. Drexel is still, however, the cornerstone of the history of the SBS; without her, there would be no congregation. The SBS in the third decade of the twenty-first century remain committed to the work for which they were founded, even as most of them are no longer able to engage actively in those ministries.

Further Research

Katharine Drexel and the Sisters of the Blessed Sacrament

Although some Catholics refer to St. Katharine Drexel as the patron saint of philanthropists and racial justice, much work remains to be done on the congregation's work with Black and Indigenous People. When over 1,300 unmarked graves were unearthed at the sites of four former residential schools in western Canada, historians and archaeologists knew—intellectually and emotionally—that more graves would be found in that country, as well as in the United States. Although apologists for residential schools dedicated to the education of Indigenous People have argued that most of the children died "of diseases like tuberculosis," a "cursory reading of the historical literature on residential schools shows just how wrong this line of thinking is." The real issue, *Scientific American* reports, was the condition of the schools in which thousands of children were forced to live.[5] As the story unfolds and the history of residential schools is examined in light of recent discoveries, the schools founded and funded by the Sisters of the Blessed Sacrament—for better or worse—will have to be studied and placed within the story.

The sisters were involved with several residential schools during their 130-year history, including St. Catherine's in New Mexico; St. Paul's (now the Marty Indian School) in South Dakota; and St. Michael Indian School in Arizona. Lawsuits have been filed related to issues of abuse at all three schools.[6] Because records are sealed and often involved out-of-court settlements, it is difficult to know whether the SBS admitted—or had reason to admit—wrongdoing. The focus of the lawsuits seems to be priests connected with the schools, but the SBS are often named as well. The question is: What did the SBS know—if they did—and when did they know it?

In addition to issues related to residential schools for Indigenous Peoples and the way in which the children attending them were treated, Catholics in the United States and throughout the world have been struggling with the sexual abuse crisis since at least 2002, when the *Boston Globe*'s Spotlight Team began reporting on the way in which hundreds of priests involved in the sexual abuse of minors were protected by those in the upper echelons of church administration. Boston, of course, was not the only diocese to shield priest abusers; virtually every American diocese has been faced with lawsuits related to priests who preyed on children. At some point in the not-too-distant future, U.S. Catholics will be forced to wrestle with the aftermath of the sexual abuse crisis *and* face their own reality related to residential schools for Indigenous People.

Historians and others working in the field of Catholic studies are trying to determine the best way to write about sexual abuse within the context of larger issues, including the general area of Catholicism in the United States. As Catherine R. Osborne writes in her introduction to a roundtable on this subject held in 2016, "This kind of event and the Church's treatment of them [victims and their abusers], are anything but irrelevant to our understanding of mid-twentieth-century Catholicism.... We must," Osborne continues, "re-evaluate the events of recent decades and the actions and characters of historical figures ranging from well-known bishops [and saints] to obscure laymen and [lay] women."[7] To do otherwise, is to discount the lives, stories, and trauma of the victims. Their stories, too, are part of the history of the Catholic Church in the United States.

Because the Sisters of the Blessed Sacrament were founded to minister to Indigenous People and Black Americans, they—as well as other congregations of women religious—will certainly be a part of future studies of American Catholics, sexual abuse, and race. According to historian Matthew J. Cressler, "Given the profound entanglements between white Catholics and American racism and colonialism, we can infer that there are many Black, Latinx, and Native American survivors [of sexual abuse] in the United States. (*How many? I won't pretend to know.*)"[8] It is not my intention to accuse the congregation of any wrongdoing; I simply note that historians are struggling to document the history of child sexual abuse in the Catholic Church, and the SBS—along with other congregations of women religious—will be a part of future histories on this topic.

Because there are no documents related to either accusations of abuse or lawsuits stemming from the victims and their families found in the SBS archives—at least in the ones to which I have had access—it is hard to know if there is extant material related to issues of abuse of any kind within the context of Native and Black Catholics. (This may be true for the archives of many other congregations of women religious, as well.) But any further study of St. Katharine Drexel and the Sisters of the Blessed Sacrament may have to grapple with this issue.

Keeping the Mission Alive

As the congregation continues to decrease in numbers, it is important that the work and legacy of the SBS be remembered and continued in some way. Sister Donna Gould, SBS, associate professor of English at Xavier University, helps undergraduates understand and appreciate the mission of the Sisters of the Blessed Sacrament through her course entitled Foundation of Native American Literature, which "studies literature by Native Americans who bridge oral cultures (which preserve knowledge through rituals, ceremonies, song, chants, drumming, pottery, weaving) with cultures that understand the world through written language." Developing this course, she wrote in an article published by *Global Sisters Report*, meant that two of Mother Katharine Drexel's missions "met and embraced: from the university she founded to her first mission in the Southwest."[9]

Students enrolled in the course participated in a traditional classroom component but then traveled together to New Mexico to "share an experience with the Pueblo people." At Laguna Pueblo, they were hosted by two members of the congregation, Sisters Consolata and Rosita. They then visited the Jemez and Santo Domingo Pueblos and were able to meet and talk with Sister Patrick Marie, SBS, who has been ministering in the Southwest for over fifty years. Under Sister Patrick Marie's tutelage, they were able to experience "ancient sacred corn dances" and visit with a number of families in their homes. The students "observed what St. Katharine Drexel must have experienced at these dances over 125 years ago—watching these Pueblo dancers painted in blue, green, red, and orange clay, it seemed as if the earth stood up to dance." In addition, they seemed to agree, wrote Sister Donna, that "Sr. Patrick Marie— watching the dances, standing silently and reverently for a long period of time in the unrelenting sun—seemed to be part of the ceremony."[10]

The Pueblos treated the Xavier students as if they were family members, related through Katharine Drexel. "At each greeting, there were questions and stories about other Sisters of the Blessed Sacrament who had made a difference in their lives." Sister Donna concludes by reflecting,

I am sure Mother Katharine is smiling in love at her Sisters of the Blessed Sacrament who followed her and created the pathway from the Pueblos of New Mexico to Xavier University of Louisiana—and at the alumni, students, and the generations of Pueblo people who still speak her name with respect and honor her passion for justice.[11]

Faculty, staff, and SBS recognize the importance of students at schools connected with the Sisters of the Blessed Sacrament—Xavier University and St. Michael Indian School—understanding their connection with Katharine Drexel and the SBS so that the congregation's legacy will continue even when there are no sisters engaged in active ministry with Black and Indigenous People.[12] As Xavier University recognized and celebrated the anniversary of the day the school's campus was dedicated in 1932, they reminded the students attending the university in 1921 of their responsibility to continuing the mission, "St. Katharine Drexel and the Sisters of the Blessed Sacrament opened the doors of this campus knowing that you would one day arrive to continue the legacy of creating a more just and humane society."[13]

NOTES

Introduction

1. See David O'Reilly, "Decreed a Saint. Phila's Katharine Drexel Canonized," *The Philadelphia Inquirer*, October 2, 2000, A1, A9.

2. Whenever possible, I have used *Black* as an adjective modifying a noun throughout this book (Black people, Black Catholics, etc.). I capitalize *Black* because the term refers to people who have been categorized a certain way based on race, as well as a distinct culture. I am grateful to Maureen H. O'Connell for her help sorting out this very important issue. See Maureen H. O'Connell, *Undoing the Knots: Five Generations of American Catholic Anti-blackness* (Boston: Beacon Press, 2021), 230n1.

3. See, for example, Cheryl C. D. Hughes, *Katharine Drexel: The Riches-to-Rags Story of an American Catholic Saint* (Grand Rapids: William B. Eerdmans, 2014).

4. See Katherine Burton, *The Golden Door: The Life of Katharine Drexel* (New York: P.J. Kenedy & Sons, 1957); Kathleen Sprows Cummings, *A Saint of Our Own: How the Quest for a Holy Hero Helped Catholics Become American* (Chapel Hill: University of North Carolina Press, 2019), 186–87.

5. Cummings, *A Saint of Our Own*, 187.

6. Cummings, *A Saint of Our Own*, 186.

7. Cummings, *A Saint of Our Own*, 205.

8. Cummings, *A Saint of Our Own*, 207–8.

9. Quoted in Cummings, *A Saint of Our Own*, 216.

10. Clyde Haberman, "Pope Beatifies Philadelphia Nun Who Educated Blacks and Indians," *New York Times*, November 21, 1988, p. 14;

https://www.nytimes.com/1988/11/21/us/pope-beatifies-philadelphia-nun-who-educated-blacks-and-indians.html.

11. Quoted in Lou Baldwin, "Ceremony to Be Held Nov. 20 in Rome, Archbishop Says," *Catholic Standard and Times,* 28 July 1988, p. 1.

12. "St. Katharine's Journey to Canonization," accessed June 1, 2021, http://www.katharinedrexel.org/wp-content/uploads/2014/09/Journey-to-Canonization.pdf.

13. James F. Garneau, "Saint Katharine Drexel in Light of the New Evangelization," *Josephinum Journal of Theology* 10 (2003): 131.

14. Lou Baldwin, *Saint Katharine Drexel: Apostle to the Oppressed* (Philadelphia: The Catholic Standard and Times, 2000), 196.

15. [Petition], [1927], H40 B5 Interracial Movement, Box 1, folder 5, Sisters of the Blessed Sacrament Archives, Catholic Historical Research Center of the Archdiocese of Philadelphia (hereafter SBS Archives, CHRC).

16. St. Joseph's Hospital, Board of Managers to Mother Katharine and Mrs. Morrell, March 30, 1927, H40 B5 Interracial Movement, Box 1, folder 5, SBS Archives, CHRC.

17. See, for example, James B. Bennett, *Religion and the Rise of Jim Crow in New Orleans* (Princeton, NJ: Princeton University Press, 2005).

18. Raymond Pace Alexander, "A Tribute to Mother Katharine Drexel," *Negro History Bulletin* 29 (Fall 1966): 181, 191.

19. Cummings, *A Saint of Our Own,* 208.

20. See Ibram X. Kendi, *How to Be an Antiracist* (New York: One World, 2019), 1, 20.

21. Drexel has not been officially named the patron saint of either racial justice or philanthropy.

22. See "Our Ministries," Sisters of the Blessed Sacrament, accessed October 14, 2021, katharinedrexel.org/sisters-of-the-blessed-sacrament/sbs-ministries.

Chapter One

1. Cordelia Frances Biddle, *Saint Katharine: The Life of Katharine Drexel* (Yardley, PA: Westholme Publishing, 2014), 40. See Martha Hodes, *Mourning Lincoln* (New Haven, CT: Yale University Press, 2015), 144–49, for a full account of Lincoln's public funeral.

2. Biddle, *Saint Katharine,* 40–41.

3. Dan Rottenberg, *The Man Who Made Wall Street: Anthony J. Drexel and the Rise of Modern Finance* (Philadelphia: University of Pennsylvania Press, 2001), 18.

4. Boise Penrose, "The Early Life of F. M. Drexel, 1792–1837: The Peregrinations of a Philadelphia Painter-Banker," *Pennsylvania Magazine of History and Biography* 60 (October 1936): 342–43.

5. Lou Baldwin, *Saint Katharine Drexel: Apostle to the Oppressed* (Philadelphia: The Catholic Standard and Times, 2000), 3–4.

6. Penrose, "The Early Life," 345–57.

7. Rottenberg, *The Man Who Made Wall Street*, 27.

8. Rottenberg, *The Man Who Made Wall Street*, 37.

9. Rottenberg, *The Man Who Made Wall Street*, 39–40, 48.

10. Rottenberg, *The Man Who Made Wall Street*, 67.

11. See Sister Consuela Mary Duffy, SBS, *Katharine Drexel: A Biography* (Philadelphia: Peter Reilly Company, 1965), 22; Rottenberg, *The Man Who Made Wall Street*, 60–79, provides an in-depth discussion of the growth of the Drexel fortune during these years.

12. Baldwin, *St. Katharine Drexel*, 5–6.

13. Baldwin, *St. Katharine Drexel*, 8. Drexel was baptized Catherine Marie and usually signed legal documents as Catherine or Catharine. When she entered religious life, she became Katharine. For the sake of consistency, I spell her name as Katharine Drexel throughout this book unless a direct quote is involved.

14. Burton, *The Golden Door*, 4–5.

15. Baldwin, *St. Katharine Drexel*, 9.

16. Biddle, *Saint Katharine*, 28–30.

17. Rottenberg, *The Man Who Made Wall Street*, 43.

18. Duffy, *Katharine Drexel*, 36; Biddle, *Saint Katharine*, 47; Rottenberg, *The Man Who Made Wall Street*, 53.

19. Duffy, *Katharine Drexel*, 36.

20. See Duffy, *Katharine Drexel*, 41–42; Baldwin, *St. Katharine Drexel*, 23–24 (quote, 24).

21. See Mary J. Oates, *The Catholic Philanthropic Tradition in America* (Bloomington: Indiana University Press, 1995), 126; Baldwin, *St. Katharine Drexel*, 18.

22. Oates, *The Catholic Philanthropic Tradition*, 126.

23. Quoted in Oates, *The Catholic Philanthropic Tradition*, 126.

24. Baldwin, *St. Katharine Drexel*, 15.

25. Quoted in Oates, *The Catholic Philanthropic Tradition*, 126.

26. Benjamin Knute Haavik, "Eden Hall: A Cultural Historic Landscape," (MS thesis, University of Pennsylvania, 1998), 43–45.

27. Baldwin, *St. Katharine Drexel*, 25–26; quoted in Duffy, *Katharine Drexel*, 45.

28. Rottenberg, *The Man Who Made Wall Street*, 101; Baldwin, *St. Katharine Drexel*, 27.

29. Baldwin, *St. Katharine Drexel*, 29–30. Baldwin notes that Sister Consuela Duffy, SBS, suggested that the young man in question was Walter George Smith, who later married Elizabeth Drexel.

30. Biddle, *Saint Katharine*, 73–74.

31. Duffy, *Katharine Drexel*, 71.

32. Biddle, *Saint Katharine*, 76.

33. Baldwin, *St. Katharine Drexel*, 49–50.

34. Baldwin, *St. Katharine Drexel*, 52; Rottenberg, *The Man Who Made Wall Street*, 150.

35. Duffy, *Katharine Drexel*, 95; Cheryl C. D. Hughes, *Katharine Drexel: The Riches-to-Rags Story of an American Catholic Saint* (Grand Rapids: Eerdmans, 2014), 49; Biddle, *Saint Katharine*, 80.

36. See Duffy, *Katharine Drexel*, 100–101.

37. Biddle, *Saint Katharine*, 89; Duffy, *Katharine Drexel*, 101.

38. Many sources report this story, but one source is Margaret M. McGuinness, *Called to Serve: A History of Nuns in America* (New York: New York University Press, 2013), 99–100.

39. See Kathleen Sprows Cummings, *A Saint of Our Own: How the Quest for a Holy Hero Helped Catholics Become American* (Chapel Hill: University of North Carolina Press, 2019), 95–98, for a purported account of Cabrini's meeting with Leo XIII.

40. See *The Catholic University of America Yearbook 1914–1915* (Washington, DC: The Catholic University of America, 1914), 49.

41. Duffy, *Katharine Drexel*, 78–79.

42. See Baldwin, *St. Katharine Drexel*, 55–56; Duffy, *Katharine Drexel*, 202.

43. Anne M. Butler, *Across God's Frontiers: Catholic Sisters and the American West, 1850–1920* (Chapel Hill: University of North Carolina Press, 2012), 194.

44. Butler, *Across God's Frontiers*, 195.

45. Drexel to O'Connor, November 13, 1872, H10 B MMK Correspondence, Box 42, folder 1, Sisters of the Blessed Sacrament Archives, Catholic Historical Research Center of the Archdiocese of Philadelphia (hereafter SBS Archives, CHRC).

46. Quoted in SBS Original Annals 1876–1884, H40 A1 Box 1, folder 2, SBS Archives, CHRC.

47. Quoted in Hughes, *Katharine Drexel: The Riches-to-Rags Story*, 46–47.

48. See "Louise Bouvier," Find a Grave, accessed February 9, 2021, https://www.findagrave.com/memorial/150389481/louise-bouvier.

49. Quoted in Duffy, *Katharine Drexel*, 126.

50. O'Connor to Drexel, August 29, 1885, H10 A1 MMK Writings, Box 41, folder 4, SBS Archives, CHRC.

51. O'Connor to Drexel, March 5, 1887, H10 B MMK Correspondence, Box 41, folder 7, SBS Archives, CHRC.

52. O'Connor to Drexel, March 5, 1887, H10 B MMK Correspondence, Box 41, folder 7, SBS Archives, CHRC.

53. Butler, *Across God's Frontiers*, 205.

54. Drexel to O'Connor, November 26, 1888, H10 A1 MMK Writings, Box 6, folder 11, SBS Archives, CHRC.

55. Quoted in Duffy, *Katharine Drexel*, 130.

56. Duffy, *Katharine Drexel*, 130.

57. O'Connor to Drexel, December 21, 1888, H10 B MMK Correspondence, Box 41, folder 11, SBS Archives, CHRC.

58. Drexel to O'Connor, February 24, 1889, H10 A1 MMK Writings, Box 32, folder 11, SBS Archives, CHRC.

59. See Baldwin, *St. Katharine Drexel*, 70–71.

60. Baldwin, *St. Katharine Drexel*, 71–72.

61. Quoted in Baldwin, *St. Katharine Drexel*, 75.

62. Duffy, *Katharine Drexel*, 138.

63. Butler, *Across God's Frontiers*, 208.

64. Sister M. Delores [Letterhouse], *The Francis A. Drexel Family* (Cornwall Heights, PA: Sisters of the Blessed Sacrament, 1939), 359.

65. Butler, *Across God's Frontiers*, 208–9.

66. Letterhouse, *The Francis A. Drexel Family*, 414; Baldwin, *St. Katharine Drexel*, 92.

67. Butler, *Across God's Frontiers*, 210.

Chapter Two

1. See Donna Patricia Peterson, "Conflict, Tension, Strength: The History of St. Paul's Mission, St. Labre Indian School, and St. Stephen's Indian School, 1884–Present" (PhD diss., University of New Mexico, 2015), 89–91, for a brief history of the early history of St. Stephen's. Peterson describes the congregation that finally assumed responsibility for the school as the Sisters of St. Francis, Pendleton, Oregon. The correct title of the community is the Sisters of St. Francis of Philadelphia.

2. See Sister Consuela Mary Duffy, SBS, *Katharine Drexel: A Biography* (Philadelphia: Peter Reilly Company, 1965), 173–77; and Lou Baldwin, *Saint Katharine Drexel: Apostle to the Oppressed* (Philadelphia: The Catholic Standard and Times, 2000), 98–99.

3. Sister Emily Ann Herbes, OSFS, "Histories of the Sisters of St. Francis of Philadelphia in Wyoming since 1892," accessed September 5, 2022, https://dcwy.org/documents/2020/6/SistersofStFrancis.pdf. Note that the "Foundation Book" identifies the archbishop as James Wood. In fact, it was Patrick Ryan.

4. Duffy, *Katharine Drexel*, 177.

5. Baldwin, *Saint Katharine Drexel*, 99; quoted in Duffy, *Katharine Drexel*, 177.

6. According to Sister Patricia Lynch, SBS, Archbishop Ryan "preferred" the term *mother superior*. When the SBS Constitutions were approved by Rome in 1907, she became superior general and was addressed as Reverend Mother. Sister Patricia Lynch, SBS, *Sharing the Bread in Service: Sisters of the Blessed Sacrament, 1891–1991* (Bensalem, PA: Sisters of the Blessed Sacrament, 1998), 48.

7. See Lynch, *Sharing the Bread in Service*, 48.

8. Sister Frances never had the "privilege" of working with Indigenous People. SBS Oral History Projects, H30 H Questionnaires, Books of Anecdotes, Box 1, folder 8, SBS Archives, CHRC; Baldwin, *Saint Katharine Drexel*, 100.

9. McGuinness, *Called to Serve*, 30; Lynch, *Sharing the Bread in Service*, 50.

10. Gus Puleo, "A Holy Encounter," *American Catholic Studies* 129 (Spring 2018): 91–101.

11. See Baldwin, *Saint Katharine Drexel*, 30; Puleo, "A Holy Encounter," 92.

12. Duffy, *Katharine Drexel*, 278.

13. Baldwin, *Saint Katharine Drexel*, 130.

14. Puleo, "A Holy Encounter," 94; Baldwin, *Saint Katharine Drexel*, 131; Duffy, *Katharine Drexel*, 281–82.

15. SBS Original Annals 1915, H40 A1 Box 3, folder 6, SBS Archives, CHRC.

16. SBS Original Annals, 1916 H40 A1, Box 3, folder 7, SBS Archives, CHRC.

17. Patricia Lynch, SBS, "Collective Biography: Founding Women of the Sisters of the Blessed Sacrament," *U.S. Catholic Historian* 10 (1991/1992): 102.

18. Edmund Gibbons to Drexel, February 1, 1938, SBS Original Annals, Jan.-August 1932, Box 6, folder 1, SBS Archives, CHRC.

19. SBS Original Annals, 1913, H40 A1 Box 3, folder 4, SBS Archives, CHRC.

20. Sr. M. Francis Xavier to Drexel, June 28, 1931, in SBS Original Annals 1931 [May–Dec.], H40 A1 Box 5, folder 7, SBS Archives, CHRC.

21. S. M. Mercedes to Drexel, June 2, 1931, in SBS Original Annals 1931 [May–Dec.], H40 A1 Box 5, folder 7, SBS Archives, CHRC.

22. "Draft of Paper," undated, H30 C Sisters' Collections Mother Mercedes O'Connor, Box 1, folder 8, SBS Archives, CHRC.

23. Suellen Hoy, "Ministering Hope to Chicago," *Chicago History* 31 (Fall 2002): 8.

24. "Donations to Indian Missions by Reverend Mother M. Katharine," [1904], H 10 I MMK Stewardship Benefactions 1889–1929, Box 2, folder 6, SBS Archives, CHRC.

25. Duffy, *Katharine Drexel*, 89; Amanda Bresie, "By Prayer and Petition: The Sister of the Blessed Sacrament's Mission of Evangelization and Americanization, 1891–1935" (PhD diss., Texas Christian University, 2014), 82–83.

26. Drexel to William Ketcham, July 9, 1909, H10 A 1MMK Writings A-BCIM (1911), Box 17, folder 13, SBS Archives, CHRC.

27. Drexel to Reverend Mother, undated, the Records of the Mission Helpers of the Sacred Heart, Archives of the Catholic University of America (hereafter ACUA), Washington, DC.

28. Douglas Slawson, CM, "Segregated Catholicism: The Origins of St. Katharine's Parish, New Orleans," *Vincentian Heritage Journal* 17 (Fall 1996): 149–58.

29. Slawson, "Segregated Catholicism," 160.

30. Slawson, "Segregated Catholicism," 161.

31. See Bresie, "By Prayer and Petition," 92, 95.

32. See, for example, Drexel to Reverend Mother M. Veronica, September 3, 1937, H10 A MMK Writings, Box 26B, folder 2, SBS Archives, CHRC; and Mother M. Nothburga to Rev. Mother M. Katharine, April 12, 1931, H10 A MMK Writings Box 26 B, folder 2, SBS Archives, CHRC. The Franciscan Sisters returned to the school after the Sisters of Loretto departed.

33. SBS Original Annals, 1892–1893, H40 A1 Box 1, folder 10, SBS Archives, CHRC. For information on this native sisterhood, see Thomas W. Foley, "Father Francis M. Craft and the Indian Sisters," *US Catholic Historian* 16 (Spring 1998): 41–55. I am grateful to Stephanie Morris for her help sorting out the story of Sister Mary Elizabeth Burton.

34. Shannen Dee Williams, "Forgotten Habits, Lost Vocations: Black Nuns, Contested Memories, and the 19th Century Struggle to Desegregate U.S. Catholic Religious Life," *Journal of American History* 101 (Summer 2016): 248.

35. SBS Original Annals, 1892–1893, H40 A1 Box 1, folder 10, SBS Archives, CHRC; the second quote is found in Gary Wray McDonogh, *Black and Catholic in Savannah, Georgia* (Knoxville: University of Tennessee Press, 1993), 214.

36. SBS Original Annals, 1892–1893, H40 A1 Box 1, folder 10, SBS Archives, CHRC.

37. SBS Original Annals, 1892–1893, H40 A1 Box 1, folder 10, SBS Archives, CHRC; Agreement, Drexel to Mother Mathilda Beasley, July 26, 1910, H10 B MMK In-Coming Correspondence, Box 3, folder 11, SBS Archives, CHRC; Shannen Dee Williams, "Black Nuns and the Struggle to Desegregate Catholic America after World War I" (PhD diss., Rutgers University, 2013), 105; SBS Original Annals, 1946, H40 A1 Box 13, folder 2, SBS Archives, CHRC; Hughes, 107.

38. Lynch, *Sharing the Bread*, 407. Lynch bases her information on a statement by Sister Consuela Marie Duffy, SBS, located in the Duffy Papers in the SBS Archives.

39. Williams, "Black Nuns," 107–8. A good deal more work needs to be done on Mother Mathilda Beasley.

40. J. R. Slattery, Memoranda, November 22, 1898, H10 B MMK Correspondence, Box 51, folder 11, SBS Archives, CHRC. The memoranda indicates that the Mission Helpers of the Sacred Heart had imple-

mented Slattery's ideas about Black women serving as "Aids," but after several years "arranged for the number on hand (seven in all) to be received by the Sisters of the Holy Family."

41. Drexel to Slattery, December 12, 1898, H10 B MMK Writings, Box 26B, folder 6, SBS Archives, CHRC.

42. See SBS Original Annals, 1924, H40 A1 Box 4, folder 6; and folder labeled "Educational," "Material for Mother Agatha's Book about Xavier," Archives, Xavier University of Louisiana (hereafter XULA).

43. See Susan Alice Kennedy, "'You Have Made No Mistake in Seeking to Save Souls among Us': Catholic Evangelization among Black Nashvillians, 1898–1908" (PhD diss., University of Tennessee, Knoxville, 2019), 101–4.

44. Quoted in Kennedy, "You Have Made No Mistake," 110–11.

45. Kennedy, "You Have Made No Mistake," 112.

46. Kennedy, "You Have Made No Mistake," 123.

47. Kennedy, "You Have Made No Mistake," 140–41, 146.

48. Kennedy, "You Have Made No Mistake," 160.

49. See SBS Original Annals, 1904, cont'd. –1905, H40 A1 Box 2, folder 5, SBS Archives, CHRC.

50. Kennedy, "You Have Made No Mistake," 161.

51. Quoted in SBS Original Annals, 1904, cont'd. –1905, H40 A1 Box 2, folder 5, SBS Archives, CHRC.

52. Quoted in Kennedy, "You Have Made No Mistake," 169.

53. Lynch, *Sharing the Bread*, 133.

54. Quoted in SBS Original Annals, 1904, cont'd. –1905, H40 A1 Box 2, folder 5, SBS Archives, CHRC.

55. Quoted in SBS Original Annals, 1904, cont'd. –1905, H40 A1 Box 2, folder 5, SBS Archives, CHRC.

56. Kennedy, "You Have Made No Mistake," 174–76.

57. Kennedy, "You Have Made No Mistake," 182–83.

58. Lynch, *Sharing the Bread*, 133–34.

59. SBS Original Annals, 1904, cont'd. –1905, H40 A1 Box 2, folder 5, SBS Archives, CHRC.

60. Kennedy, "You Have Made No Mistake," 242.

61. Kennedy, "You Have Made No Mistake," 262–74.

62. See Lynch, *Sharing the Bread*, 252–55; "Philadelphia Nun's Charity Gift Opened Tax Loophole for Wealthy," unidentified clipping, [1969], H 10 I "MMK Stewardship Benefactions, 1889–1929," Box 2, folder 22, SBS Archives, CHRC.

63. SBS Original Annals, 1930, H40 A1 Box 5, folder 5, SBS Archives, CHRC.

64. Sister Mary Grace to Mother M. Mercedes, Easter 1929 and April 13, 1929, in SBS Original Annals, 1929, H40 A1 Box 5, folder 4, SBS Archives, CHRC.

65. Excerpt from the *Franciscan Herald*, [1936], H 10 1 MMK Stewardship Benefactions 1889–1929, Box 2, folder 8.

66. Drexel to Very Reverend William Slattery, May 10, 1937, and Gerard Murphy to Very Rev. William Slattery, June 21, 1937, H10 Archives A MMK Writings, Box 26B, folder 7, SBS Archives, CHRC.

67. See "Survey of Indian and Colored Expenses from January 1928—December 1940," [1941], H10 I MMK Stewardship Benefactions 1889–1929, Box 2, folder 15, SBS Archives, CHRC; and "Donations Made in 1936 to Colored Schools Outside the Congregation of the Sisters of the Blessed Sacrament," [1936], H 10 1 MMK Stewardship Benefactions 1889–1929, Box 2, folder 14, SBS Archives, CHRC.

68. Drexel to Msgr. Joseph M. Corrigan, October 22, 1939, in SBS Original Annals, H40 A1 Box 8, folder 7, SBS Archives, CHRC.

Chapter Three

1. SBS Original Annals 1936, Aug.–Dec., H40 A1 Box 7, folder 6, SBS Archives, CHRC.

2. Anne M. Butler, *Across God's Frontiers: Catholic Sisters and the American West, 1850–1920* (Chapel Hill: University of North Carolina Press, 2012), 192.

3. Sister Albertine only served in the SBS ministries in Philadelphia for part of her sixty-one years as a Sister of the Blessed Sacrament. She spent forty-two years in New Iberia, Louisiana.

4. Gary B. Nash, *First City: Philadelphia and the Forging of Historical Memory* (Philadelphia: University of Pennsylvania Press, 2002), 147; See Margaret Mary Markmann, "Katharine Drexel of Philadelphia: Educational Reformer and Institution Builder" (PhD diss., Temple University, 2012), 5. Markmann notes that Drexel, who grew up at 1503 Walnut Street, lived within walking distance of this neighborhood as a child and young adult.

5. Nash, *First City*, 180–81.

6. W. E. B. Du Bois, *The Philadelphia Negro: A Social Study* (1899; repr., New York: Oxford University Press, 2007), 142–47.

7. Du Bois, *The Philadelphia Negro*, 147, 154.

8. Stephanie Morris, "St. Peter Claver Church and School, Philadelphia, PA: A Collaborative Effort," *American Catholic Studies* 128 (Spring 2017): 101.

9. M. Reginald Gerdes, "To Educate and Evangelize: Black Catholic Schools of the Oblate Sisters of Providence, 1828–1880," *U.S. Catholic Historian* 7 (Spring-Summer 1988): 192.

10. Morris, "St. Peter Claver Church and School," 102; Gerdes, "To Educate and Evangelize," 190.

11. Quoted in Morris, "St. Peter Claver Church and School," 102.

12. Gerdes, "To Educate and Evangelize," 193.

13. See Morris, "St. Peter Claver Church and School," for a discussion of the early years.

14. Markmann, "Katharine Drexel of Philadelphia," 97.

15. SBS Original Annals, 1892–1893, H40 A1 Box 1, folder 10, SBS Archives, CHRC.

16. SBS Original Annals, 1892–1893, H40 A1, Box 1, folder 10, SBS Archives, CHRC.

17. Markmann, "Katharine Drexel of Philadelphia," 121.

18. SBS Original Annals, 1894, H40 A1 Box 1, folder 11, SBS Archives, CHRC.

19. SBS Original Annals, 1914, H40 A10 Box 3, folder 5, SBS Archives, CHRC.

20. Markmann, "Katharine Drexel of Philadelphia," 121.

21. "Holy Providence History 1839–1919 Research Notes," H40 B2 PA: Motherhouse Holy Providence—History, News Items, etc. 1931–1972, Box 1, folder 28, SBS Archives, CHRC, SBS Archives, CHRC.

22. SBS Original Annals, 1907, H40 A1 Box 1, folder 7, SBS Archives, CHRC.

23. SBS Original Annals, 1907, H40 A1 Box 1, folder 7, SBS Archives, CHRC.

24. See A. J. Emerick, "The Colored Mission of Our Lady of the Blessed Sacrament, Philadelphia, PA," *The Woodstock Letters: A Record* 42 (1913): 70–74.

25. A. J. Emerick, "The Colored Mission of Our Lady of the Blessed Sacrament, Philadelphia, PA. (Continued)," *The Woodstock Letters: A Record* 42 (1913): 180.

26. Emerick, "The Colored Mission of Our Lady of the Blessed Sacrament, Philadelphia, PA. (Continued, 1913)," 180. (SBS annals do not indicate that Lewis was any sort of problem to Drexel or the founding of OLBS.)

27. Emerick, "The Colored Mission of Our Lady of the Blessed Sacrament, Philadelphia, PA. (Continued, 1913)," 182.

28. Emerick, "The Colored Mission of Our Lady of the Blessed Sacrament, Philadelphia, PA. (Continued, 1913)," 183.

29. Emerick, "The Colored Mission of Our Lady of the Blessed Sacrament, Philadelphia, PA. (Continued, 1913)," 185.

30. Emerick, "The Colored Mission of Our Lady of the Blessed Sacrament, Philadelphia, PA. (Continued, 1913)," 186–87.

31. A. J. Emerick, "The Colored Mission of Our Lady of the Blessed Sacrament, Philadelphia, PA (Continued)," *Woodstock Letters* 42 (1913): 354.

32. A. J. Emerick, "The Colored Mission of Our Lady of the Blessed Sacrament, Philadelphia, PA (Continued)," *Woodstock Letters* 43 (1914): 22.

33. Emerick, "The Colored Mission of Our Lady of the Blessed Sacrament, Philadelphia, PA. (Continued, 1914)," 23.

34. Emerick, "The Colored Mission of Our Lady of the Blessed Sacrament, Philadelphia, PA. (Continued)," *The Woodstock Letters: A Record* 43 (1914), 194.

35. See "Summary of Annals 1877–1967," H40 B2 PA: Philadelphia, Our Lady of the Blessed Sacrament, Box 1, folder 4, SBS Archives, CHRC.

36. Christine Lyons Medlin, "Catholic Sister Educators in Germantown's Parochial, Academy and Mission Schools," *Germantown Crier* 65 (Spring 2015): 12.

37. Sister Patricia Lynch, SBS, *Sharing the Bread in Service: Sisters of the Blessed Sacrament, 1891–1991* (Bensalem, PA: Sisters of the Blessed Sacrament, 1998), 273.

38. See "St. Catherine's Convent, Germantown, Philadelphia, Pennsylvania, From Foundation to the Jubilee Year, 1941," H40 B2 PA: Philadelphia, Germantown, St. Catherine of Siena, Box 1, folder 3, SBS Archives CHRC, for quote; also "St. Catherine of Siena School," H40 B2 PA: Philadelphia, Germantown, St. Catherine of Siena," Box 1, folder 4, SBS Archives, CHRC.

39. Dever to Dougherty, March 27, 1923. Dougherty Papers, 80.4643, CHRC.

40. Reverend Vincent Dever to Cardinal Dennis Dougherty, May 19, 1923, 80.4643, Dougherty Papers, CHRC.

41. "The Parish Monthly Calendar," 80.4643, Dougherty Papers, CHRC.

42. "St. Ignatius Annals to 1934–1935," H40 B2 PA: St. Ignatius, Box 1, folder 1, SBS Archives, CHRC.

43. "St. Ignatius, Philadelphia, PA," "Historical Background 1924–2007," H40 B1 PA: St. Ignatius, Philadelphia, Box 6, folder 1, SBS Archives, CHRC.

44. SBS Original Annals, 1936, Aug.–Dec., H40 A1 Box 7, folder 6, SBS Archives, CHRC.

45. SBS Original Annals, 1936, Aug.–Dec., H40 A1 Box 7, folder 6, SBS Archives, CHRC.

46. "Annals, 1955–1972," H40 B2 PA: Philadelphia, Germantown, St. Catherine of Siena, Box 1, folder 2, SBS Archives, CHRC.

47. "Annals 1915–1972 (typed)," H40 B2 PA: Philadelphia: St. Catherine of Siena, Box 1, folder 3, SBS Archives, CHRC.

48. "Annals 1915–1972 (typed)," H40 B2 PA: Philadelphia: St. Catherine of Siena, Box 1, folder 3, SBS Archives, CHRC.

49. See "Summary of Annals, 1877–1967," H40 B2 PA: Philadelphia, Our Lady of the Blessed Sacrament, Box 1, folder, 4, SBS Archives, CHRC.

50. "Our Lady of the Blessed Sacrament Annals, 1941–1962," (1933–1934) H40 B2 PA: Philadelphia, Our Lady of the Blessed Sacrament, Box 1, folder 2, SBS Archives, CHRC.

51. "Summary of Annals, 1877–1967," H40 B2 PA: Philadelphia, Our Lady of the Blessed Sacrament, Box 1, folder 4, SBS Archives, CHRC.

52. "St. Ignatius Annals, 1949–1956," H40 B2 PA: St. Ignatius, Box 1, folder 4, SBS Archives, CHRC.

53. "Annals—Our Lady of the Blessed Sacrament, Phila., January thro' December 1961," "Summary of Annals, 1877–1967," H40 B2 PA: Philadelphia, Our Lady of the Blessed Sacrament, Box 1, folder 4, SBS Archives, CHRC; "Annals for 1962 Our Lady of the Blessed Sacrament Convent, Philadelphia," H40 B2 PA: Philadelphia, Our Lady of the Blessed Sacrament, Box 1, folder 3, SBS Archives, CHRC.

54. Sisters at OLBS to Drexel, December 16, 1953, H40 B2 PA: Philadelphia, Our Lady of the Blessed Sacrament, Box 1, folder 17, SBS Archives, CHRC.

55. "Our Lady of the Blessed Sacrament, Annals 1915–1927," H40 B2 PA: Philadelphia, Our Lady of the Blessed Sacrament, Box 1, folder 1, SBS Archives, CHRC.

56. "Our Lady of the Blessed Sacrament Convent, Phila. Pa., Jan. through Dec., 1951," "OLBS Summary of Annals, 1877–1967," H40 B2 PA: Philadelphia, Our Lady of the Blessed Sacrament, Box 1, folder 4, SBS Archives, CHRC.

57. "Visitations, 1938," H40 B2 PA: Philadelphia, Our Lady of the Blessed Sacrament, Box 2, folder 4, SBS Archives, CHRC; "Visitations, 1939," H40 B2, PA: Philadelphia, Our Lady of the Blessed Sacrament, Box 2, folder 4, SBS Archives, CHRC.

58. Quoted in Morris, "St. Peter Claver Church and School," 109.

59. SBS Original Annals, 1918, H40 A1 Box 3, folder 9, SBS Archives, CHRC.

60. "OLBS Annals 1915–1927," October 11, 1915, H40 B2 PA: Philadelphia, Our Lady of the Blessed Sacrament, Box 1, folder 1, SBS Archives, CHRC.

61. *Souvenir Volume for the Golden Jubilee 1891–1941* (Sisters of the Blessed Sacrament for Indians and Colored People, [1941]), 102.

62. See "Visitations, 1937," H40 B2 PA: Philadelphia, Our Lady of the Blessed Sacrament, Box 2, folder 3, SBS Archives, CHRC.

63. "Annals, 1915–1927," H40 B2 PA: Philadelphia, Our Lady of the Blessed Sacrament, Box 1, folder 1, SBS Archives, CHRC.

64. Sister M. Vincentia to Dever, undated, Dougherty Correspondence, 80.4643, CHRC.

65. Dougherty to Dever, March 5, 1927, Dougherty Correspondence, 80.4673, CHRC.

66. "Holy Providence Carries on Mission," *Philadelphia Inquirer*, November 16, 1969. Clipping found in "Holy Providence—History, News Items, etc. 1931–1972," H40 B2 PA: Motherhouse, Box 1, folder 27, SBS Archives, CHRC.

67. Memorandum, John J. Krol to Reverend Arthur J. Nace, March 28, 1967, Our Lady of the Blessed Sacrament, Chancery File, CHRC; "Summary of Local House Annals of Our Lady of the Blessed Sacrament Convent, Philadelphia," H40 B2 PA: Philadelphia Our Lady of the Blessed Sacrament, Box 1, folder 4, SBS Archives, CHRC.

68. "Two Parish Schools to Close," *Catholic Standard and Times*, August 11, 1967, clipping found in H40 B2 PA: Philadelphia Our Lady of the Blessed Sacrament, Box 1, folder 12, SBS Archives, CHRC.

69. "Black Catholics Knock Plans to Close Parish," *Catholic Free Press*, [June 9, 1972], clipping found in H40 B2 PA: Philadelphia Our Lady of the Blessed Sacrament, Box 1, folder 12, SBS Archives, CHRC.

70. "Summary of Annals, 1877–1967," August 10, 1967, H40 B2 PA: Philadelphia, Our Lady of the Blessed Sacrament, Box 1, folder 4, SBS Archives, CHRC.

71. Mother Mary of the Visitation to Cardinal John Krol, April 6, 1948, St. Catherine of Siena (Germantown), Chancery Files, CHRC.

72. "Annals, 1955–1972," H40 B2 PA: Philadelphia, Germantown, St. Catherine, Box 1, folder 2, SBS Archives, CHRC.

73. Mother Mary Elizabeth to John Cardinal Krol, February 4, 1972, St. Peter Claver, Chancery Files, CHRC.

74. "St. Catherine of Siena, Provincial Council Minutes. 1960–1996," Germantown Parishes, Box 8, 10T.1, Ducournau Archives of the Eastern Province of the Congregation of the Mission, Philadelphia, PA.

75. Cardinal John Krol to the Faithful of St. Catherine of Siena Parish, May 15, 1972, H40 B2 PA: Philadelphia, [St. Catherine], Box 1, folder 10, SBS Archives, CHRC.

76. Morris, "St. Peter Claver Church and School," 110; Mother Mary Elizabeth to the Parents of the Students of St. Peter Claver School, January, 1972, St. Peter Claver, Chancery Files, CHRC.

77. "St. Ignatius School [Feasibility Study]," H40 B2 PA: St. Ignatius, Box 1, folder 7, SBS Archives, CHRC.

78. Sister Caritas to Sister Alma, December 27, 1975, H40 B2 PA: St Ignatius, Box 4, folder 1, SBS Archives, CHRC.

79. "St. Ignatius, Annals 1986–1987," H40 B2 PA: St. Ignatius, Box 1, folder 14, SBS Archives, CHRC.

80. "St. Ignatius School, Imani Center," H40 B2 PA: St. Ignatius, Box 5, folder 15, SBS Archives, CHRC.

Chapter Four

1. SBS Original Annals, 1894, H40 A1 Box 2, folder 11, SBS Archives, CHRC.

2. M. M. Katharine, "The Sisters of the Blessed Sacrament," copy of Report sent to ABCM, in SBS Original Annals 1934, Jan.–July, H 10 A1 Box 6, folder 5, SBS Archives, CHRC; SBS Original Annals, 1894, H40 A1 Box 2, folder 11, SBS Archives CHRC.

3. SBS Original Annals, 1894, H40 A1, Box 2, folder 11, SBS Archives, CHRC.

4. M. M. Katharine, "The Sisters of the Blessed Sacrament," SBS Original Annals 1934, Jan.–July, H40 A1 Box 6, folder 5, SBS Archives, CHRC. Earlier, Drexel credited visits from Bishop Martin Marty with her interest in Indigenous missions, and believed Catholics had a responsibility to evangelize Indians. This thought came "from the grace of God." Drexel to Rev. Behrman, July 22, 1922, H10 A MMK Writings, Box 17, folder 5, SBS Archives, CHRC.

5. Lou Baldwin, *Saint Katharine Drexel: Apostle to the Oppressed* (Philadelphia: The Catholic Standard and Times, 2000), 56–57; Sister Patricia Lynch, SBS, *Sharing the Bread in Service: Sisters of the Blessed Sacrament, 1891–1991* (Bensalem, PA: Sisters of the Blessed Sacrament, 1998), 22–23.

6. SBS Original Annals, 1946, H40 A1 Box 13, folder 8, SBS Archives, CHRC.

7. SBS Original Annals, 1942, H40 A1 Box 11, folder 4, SBS Archives, CHRC.

8. See Francis Paul Prucha, *The Churches and the Indian Schools, 1888–1912* (Lincoln: University of Nebraska Press, 1979), 1.

9. See Amanda Bresie, "Mother Katharine's Benevolent Empire: The Bureau of Catholic Indian Missions and the Education of Native Americans, 1885–1935," *U.S. Catholic Historian* 32 (Summer 2014): 5–6.

10. Bresie, "Mother Katharine's Benevolent Empire," 8–9.

11. Bresie, "Mother Katharine's Benevolent Empire," 10.

12. Bresie, "Mother Katharine's Benevolent Empire," 12.

13. See Sister Georgina Rockwell, History, H 40 B2 PA: Carlisle St. Katherine's Hall, Carlisle, History by Sister Georgina Rockwell, pp. i-ix, 1–78, Box 1, folder 1, SBS Archives, CHRC.

14. See Sister Georgina Rockwell, History, 40, 46, 47–48, Box 1, folder 1, SBS Archives, CHRC.

15. Negotiations over repatriation of the bodies of the children who died at the Carlisle were still taking place in 2021. See Jeff Gam-

mage, "Finally, Going Home," *Philadelphia Inquirer*, June 27, 2021, A1, A10-A11.

16. See Robert A. Trennert, "From Carlisle to Phoenix: The Rise and Fall of the Indian Outing System, 1878-1930," *Pacific Historical Review* 52 (August 1983): 267-91; Sister Georgina Rockwell History, 55-57, Box 2, folder 2, SBS Archives, CHRC.

17. Sister Georgina Rockwell History, 44-45, Box 1, folder 1, SBS Archives, CHRC; Sister Georgina Rockwell History, 119-120, Box 1, folder 2, SBS Archives, CHRC.

18. Sister Georgina Rockwell History, 145-47, Box 2, folder 2, SBS Archives, CHRC.

19. Kimberly E. Armstrong, "A Failed Uncle Tom's Cabin for the Indian: Helen Hunt Jackson's Ramona and the Power of Paratext," *Western American Literature* 52 (Summer 2017): 129-56; see also Rosemary Whitaker, "Helen Hunt Jackson (1830-1885)," *Legacy* 3 (Spring 1986): 58-59.

20. Bresie, "Mother Katharine's Benevolent Empire," 13.

21. Amanda Bresie, "By Prayer and Petition: The Sister of the Blessed Sacrament's Mission of Evangelization and Americanization, 1891-1935" (PhD diss., Texas Christian University, 2014), 88-89.

22. See, for example, Margaret M. McGuinness, "Why Relationships Matter: Sisters, Bishops, and the History of Catholicism in the United States," *Catholic Historical Review* 100 (Spring 2014): 219-42.

23. Sister Mary Ruth to Katharine Drexel, October 8, 1892, H30 C Sisters Collections Mother Agatha Ryan, Box 1, folder 1, SBS Archives, CHRC; SBS Original Annals 1902, H40 A1 Box 2, folder 3, SBS Archives, CHRC.

24. Carol K. Coburn and Martha Smith, *Spirited Lives: How Nuns Shaped Catholic Culture and American Life, 1836-1920* (Chapel Hill: University of North Carolina Press, 1999), 94.

25. Stephan to Drexel, September 29, 1899, in SBS Original Annals 1898-1899, H40 A1 Box 2, folder 1, SBS Archives, CHRC.

26. Suellen Hoy, *Good Hearts: Catholic Sisters in Chicago's Past* (Urbana: University of Illinois Press, 2006), 87-88.

27. Quoted in Anne M. Butler, *Across God's Frontiers: Catholic Sisters and the American West, 1850-1920* (Chapel Hill: University of North Carolina Press, 2012), 197.

28. M. M. Katharine to Sister Macaria, March 12, 1934, H10 A MMK Writings, Box 22, folder 7, SBS Archives, CHRC; Monsignor William

Hughes to Drexel, January 11, 1934, H10 B MMK Correspondence, Box 10, folder 11, SBS Archives, CHRC; Monsignor William Hughes to Drexel, January 30, 1935, H10 B MMK Correspondence, Box 10, folder 13, SBS Archives, CHRC.

29. See, for example, Denise K. Lajimodiere, *Stringing Rosaries: The History, the Unforgivable, and the Healing of Northern Plains American Indian Boarding School Survivors* (Fargo: North Dakota State University Press, 2019).

30. Collin Gortner, "Reconciliation and Cultural Empowerment of American Indian Catholic Schools," *Journal of the West* 59 (Summer 2020): 27–28.

31. Brian S. Collier, Collin Gortner, and Will Newkirk, "Introduction: Finding Sovereignty—Native American Catholic Schools and the American West," *Journal of the West* 59 (Summer 2020): 11.

32. See Brian S. Collier, "Saint Catherine Indian School, Santa Fe, 1887–2006" (PhD diss., Arizona State University, 2006), 78–95.

33. SBS Original Annals, 1894, H40 A1 Box 1, folder 11, SBS Archives, CHRC.

34. Lynch, *Sharing the Bread*, 83: Baldwin, *Saint Katharine Drexel*, 111.

35. SBS Original Annals, 1903–June 1904, H40 A1 Box 2, folder 4, SBS Archives, CHRC.

36. SBS Original Annals, 1918, H40 A1 Box 3, folder 9, SBS Archives, CHRC.

37. See Connie P. Sze, "Gone but Not Forgotten: St. Catherine's Industrial Indian School," *Bulletin of the Historic Santa Fe Foundation* 30 (Summer 2003): 14–18.

38. Sister Tarcisius to Mother M. Mercedes, December 13, 1937, H40 B2 NM: Santa Fe St. Catherine Indian School SBS, Box 2, folder 10 SBS Archives, CHRC.

39. Collier, "St. Catherine Indian School," 131.

40. Collier, "St. Catherine Indian School," 143, 153.

41. SBS Original Annals, 1911, H40 A1 Box 3, folders 1–2, SBS Archives, CHRC.

42. Bresie, "By Prayer and Petition," 140–41.

43. Connie P. Sze, "'Roots That Are Very Deep': Excerpts from an Interview with Patrick Toya," *Bulletin of the Historic Santa Fe Foundation* 30 (Summer 2003): 27.

44. "St. Catherine Indian School, Inc. Santa Fe, New Mexico 1887–1994," H40 B2 NM: Santa Fe St. Catherine Indian School History, Box SCIS 9, folder 10, SBS Archives, CHRC.

45. The events leading up to the closing of St. Catherine's will be discussed further in chapter 7.

46. Bresie, "By Prayer and Petition," 130.

47. Collier, Gortner, and Newkirk, "Introduction," 11–12.

48. Sze, "Roots That Are Very Deep," 26, 29; Collier, "Saint Catherine Indian School," 156–59. Toya left St. Catherine's before finishing and attended the government school.

49. The story of residential schools for Indigenous Peoples is larger than the United States. See, for example, Ian Mosby, "Canada's Residential Schools Were a Horror," *Scientific American*, August 1, 2021, https://www.scientificamerican.com/article/canadas-residential-schools-were-a-horror/.

50. See Mary Eisenman Carson, *Blackrobe for the Yankton Sioux: Fr. Sylvester Eisenman, O.S.B. (1891–1941)* (Chamberlain, SD: Tipi Press, 1989), 103, for a discussion of the founding of St. Paul's. Bresie, "By Prayer and Petition," 116.

51. "Early History of St. Paul's," H40 B2 SD: Marty St. Paul Indian School, Box 1, folder 1, SBS Archives, CHRC; "Visitation," H40 B2 SD: Marty St. Paul Indian School, Box 1, folder 5, SBS Archives, CHRC.

52. See Thomas W. Foley, *Father Francis M. Craft: Missionary to the Sioux* (Lincoln: University of Nebraska Press, 2002), 148–49.

53. SBS Oral History Projects Questionnaires Books of Anecdotes, H30 H, Box 1, folder 8, SBS Archives, CHRC.

54. SBS Oral History Projects Questionnaires Books of Anecdotes, H30 H, Box 1, folder 8, SBS Archives, CHRC.

55. Eisenman to Mother Katharine, March 5, 1935, H10 B MMK Correspondence, Box 20, folder 14, SBS Archives, CHRC; Drexel to Father Sylvester, OSB, March 2, 1935, H40 B2, SD: Marty St. Paul Indian School, Box 1, folder 7, SBS Archives, CHRC.

56. "Oblates' Beginning," H40 B2 SD: Marty St. Paul Indian School, Box 2x, folder 13, SBS Archives, CHRC.

57. "What Shall Be the Aim That the Oblate Sisters Shall Attain?" H 10 B MMK Correspondence, Box 20, folder 14, SBS Archives, CHRC; Sister Mary of Lourdes to Reverend Mother, SBS Original Annals, 1937, July–Dec., H40 A1 Box 7, folder 8, SBS Archives, CHRC.

58. SBS Original Annals, 1938 April–June, H40 A1 Box 8, folder 2, SBS Archives, CHRC; SBS Original Annals 1949, Jan.–June, H40 A1 Box 13, folder 8, SBS Archives, CHRC; SBS Original Annals 1951, H40 A1 Box 14, folder 4, SBS Archives, CHRC.

59. "1970–71" and "1971–1972 Marty Indian Mission," H40 B2 SD: Marty 1964–1981 Box 2x, folder 15, SBS Archives, CHRC.

60. Sr. Marjorie Everett, "Recollections of St. Paul School, Marty, South Dakota," H40 B2, St. Paul's Indian Mission School Marty, SD, Box 1, folder 5, SBS Archives, CHRC. See chapter 7 for a fuller discussion of the Second Vatican Council and the Sisters of the Blessed Sacrament.

61. "Annals Blessed Sacrament Convent, Marty, South Dakota 1980," H40 B2 SD: Marty 1964–1981 Annals, Box 2x, folder 15, SBS Archives, CHRC.

62. See Robert L. Wilken, *Anselm Weber, O.F.M.: Missionary to the Navajo 1898–1926* (Milwaukee: Bruce Publishing, 1955), 36–37; Kristie Lee Butler, "Along the Padres' Trail: the History of St. Michael's Mission to the Navajo" (MA thesis, Arizona State University, 1991), 36.

63. Butler, "Along the Padres' Trail," 68–70; Wilken, 83; Sally J. Southwick, "Educating the Mind, Enlightening the Soul: Mission Schools as a Means of Transforming the Navajo, 1898–1928," *Journal of Arizona History* 37 (Spring 1996): 51–52.

64. Southwick, "Educating the Mind, Enlightening the Soul," 53.

65. Southwick, "Educating the Mind, Enlightening the Soul," 53–55.

66. SBS Original Annals, 1904 cont'd –1905, H40 A1 Box 2, folder 5, SBS Archives, CHRC; Sister Evangelist is quoted in Southwick, "Educating the Mind, Enlightening the Soul," 53–54.

67. SBS Original Annals, 1911, H40 A1 Box 3, folders 1–2, SBS Archives, CHRC.

68. See Benjamin R. Brady and Howard M. Bahr, "The Influenza Epidemic of 1918–1920 among the Navajos: Marginality, Mortality, and the Implications of Some Neglected Eyewitness Accounts," *American Indian Quarterly* 38 (Fall 2014): 470–72 for a discussion of Weber and his decision to quarantine those associated with St. Michael's.

69. Mother Mary of the Visitation, SBS, to Rev. Edwin V. Byrne, [March 1946], in SBS Original Annals 1946, H40 A1 Box 3, folder 3, SBS Archives, CHRC.

70. "The Sisters of the Blessed Sacrament for Indians and Colored People," *Indian Sentinel* 6 (1907): 4–19.

71. Mother M. Katharine, "Sisters Visit Indian Homes," *Indian Sentinel* 4 (April 1924): 66.

72. Sister M. Stanislaus, "Visiting the Indian Pueblos," *Indian Sentinel* 4 (October 1924): 71–72.

73. Sister M. Philip Neri, "The Medicine Dance," *Indian Sentinel* 5 (October 1925): 157–158.

74. Sister Francis Mary Riggs, SBS, "Attitudes of Missionary Sisters toward American Indian Acculturation" (PhD diss., Catholic University of America, 1967), 7, 47.

75. Riggs, "Attitudes of Missionary Sisters," 86.

76. Riggs, "Attitudes of Missionary Sisters," 142, 144.

77. Riggs, "Attitudes of Missionary Sisters," 223, 256.

78. Riggs, "Attitudes of Missionary Sisters," 285–87.

79. Kathleen Holscher, "Children's Graves in Canada Reflect Catholic Logic of Indigenous Vanishment," *National Catholic Reporter*, June 22, 2021, https://www.ncronline.org/news/accountability/canadian-native-childrens-graves-reflect-history-indigenous-vanishment.

80. "About," St. Michael Indian School, accessed July 1, 2021, https://stmichaelindianschool.org/about/.

81. Nora McGreevy, "Calling Home," *Notre Dame Magazine*, Spring 2020, https://magazine.nd.edu/stories/calling-home-2/.

Chapter Five

1. Sr. M. Benedicta to Reverend Mother M. Katharine, September 8, 1937, H40 A1 SBS Original Annals 1936, Aug.–Dec., Box 7, folder 6 SBS Archives, CHRC.

2. Quoted in James B. Bennett, *Religion and the Rise of Jim Crow in New Orleans* (Princeton, NJ: Princeton University Press, 2005), 146.

3. Bennett, *Religion*, 146; Nicole Farmer Hurd, "The Master Art of a Saint: Katharine Drexel and Her Theology of Education (Ph.D. diss., University of Virginia, 2002), 17.

4. Bennett, *Religion*, 163.

5. Hurd, "The Master Art of a Saint," 20.

6. [Katharine Drexel], "This Race Problem," *Mission Fields at Home* (September–October 1940), 7.

7. Suellen Hoy, "Lives on the Color Line: Catholic Sisters and African Americans in Chicago, 1890s–1960s," *U.S. Catholic Historian* 22 (Winter 2004): 74.

8. Katharine Drexel to Rev. Joseph M. Coulombe, April 24, 1933, H10 Archives A MMK Writings, Box 20, folder 7, SBS Archives, CHRC.

9. Cordelia Frances Biddle, *Saint Katharine: The Life of Katharine Drexel* (Yardley, PA: Westholme Publishing, 2014), 218.

10. Sister Patricia Marshall, "Katharine Drexel on Racial Justice," H40 B4 Interracial Movement MMK Nat. Fed. Col. Cath, Box 1, folder 5, SBS Archives, CHRC.

11. Marshall, "Katharine Drexel on Racial Justice."

12. Emanuel Friedman to George K. Hunton, November 12, 1946, H40 B5 Interracial Movement, Box 2, folder 5, SBS Archives, CHRC.

13. [Radio Address], December 19, 1933, and March 17, 1937, H40 B5 Interracial Movement, Box 2, folder 1, SBS Archives, CHRC.

14. Bennett, *Religion*, 158.

15. Bennett, *Religion*, 200.

16. Bennett, *Religion*, 174.

17. Bennett, *Religion*, 200.

18. Colette Madeleine Bloom, "A Catholic Negro Child in the Segregated South of the 1950s and 1960s: A Postmodern Retrospective on St. Katharine Drexel's Mission in New Orleans," *Catholic Southwest: A Journal of History and Culture* 21 (2010): 31.

19. Sister Patricia Lynch, *Sharing the Bread in Service: Sisters of the Blessed Sacrament, 1891–1991* (Bensalem, PA: Sisters of the Blessed Sacrament, 1998), 66.

20. Lynch, *Sharing the Bread*, 90; Gerald P. Fogarty, SJ, *Commonwealth Catholicism: A History of the Catholic Church in Virginia* (Notre Dame, IN: University of Notre Dame Press, 2001), 324.

21. Quoted in Lynch, *Sharing the Bread*, 91.

22. Quoted in Sister Marie Barat Smith, SBS, "A History of St. Emma's Military Academy and St. Francis de Sales High School" (MA thesis, Catholic University of America, 1949), 7.

23. Smith, "A History of St. Emma's Military Academy," 7.

24. Smith, "A History of St. Emma's Military Academy," 11–16.

25. Smith, "A History of St. Emma's Military Academy," 17–19. It is not clear how the decision was made to have white faculty responsible for academic subjects while Black teachers handled industrial and vocational courses.

26. Smith, "A History of St. Emma's Military Academy," 10; "Taps at St. Emma's Academy," *Richmond News Leader*, July 17, 1982, clipping found in H40 B2 VA: Rock Castle St. Francis de Sales Post-Closure Uses, Box RC-36, folder 3, SBS Archives, CHRC; Michael Alexander Smith, "St. Bootstraps," *Washington Post*, January 9, 1993, clipping found in H40 B2 VA: Rock Castle St. Francis de Sales Post-Closure Uses, Box RC-36, folder 3, SBS Archives, CHRC. Although there were—and are—historically Black boarding schools, St. Emma's has been called "A school unlike any other in America," and "the nation's only military academy for African-American males." See Greg McQuade, "Former Cadets Push to Save Old African-American Military Academy," WTVR-TV, June 19, 2020, https://www.wtvr.com/i-have-a-story/former-cadets-push-to-save-old-african-american-military-academy.

27. SBS Original Annals, 1898–1899, H10 A 1 Box 2, folder 1, SBS Archives, CHRC; Lynch, *Sharing the Bread in Service*, 66, 93.

28. Lynch, *Sharing the Bread in Service*, 97–99.

29. SBS Original Annals, 1900–1901, H40 A1, Box 2, folder 2, SBS Archives, CHRC.

30. Ellen Tarry, *The Third Door: The Autobiography of a Negro Woman* (Tuscaloosa: University of Alabama Press, 2014, originally published 1956), 28.

31. Tarry, *The Third Door*, 48.

32. Hurd, "The Master Art of a Saint," 159.

33. Lynch, *Sharing the Bread in Service*, 201.

34. P.O. Le Beau, to Mother Katherine [*sic*], November 21, 1911, and P.O. Le Beau to Mother Katherine [*sic*], January 22, 2012, Copies: Letters, etc. Early Days, X.U. 1900–1917, Archives and Special Collections, Xavier University of Louisiana (hereafter AXUL).

35. See Amanda Bresie, "'To Make All Your People Saints:' Mother Katharine's Schools in Rural Louisiana," *Catholic Southwest* 24 (2013): 32.

36. Bresie, "To Make All Your People Saints," 33. In 1980, the Diocese of Lake Charles was divided from the Diocese of Lafayette. Figaro is referred to in various sources as Eleanor or Eleanora.

37. Lynch, *Sharing the Bread in Service*, 225.

38. See Lynch, *Sharing the Bread in Service*, 223–32 (quote, 232).

39. Drexel to SBS [May 13, 1921], H40 B3a SBS Ministries Rural Schools Correspondence, Teachers, Reports Abbeville-Eunice, Box 1, folder 1, SBS Archives, CHRC.

40. See Richard Fossey and Nancy Austin, "'Every Day Is a New Beginning:' Lela Gordon Mouton and St. Katharine Drexel's Rural School in Prairie Basse, Louisiana," *Catholic Southwest* 24 (2013): 49–50.

41. Claude Oubre, *A History of the Diocese of Lafayette* (Strasbourg, France: Editions du Signe, 2001), 89; ["History..."], [1970], 3, H40 B2 LA: Latwell, Mallet St. Ann 1970–1991, Box 1, folder 3, SBS Archives, CHRC.

42. Agnes G. Lagarde to Sister Georgiana, March 30, 1982, and Mrs. Roland Lagarde, "Story of St. Ann Mission, in Mallet, Louisiana," Summer 1981, H40 B2 LA: Latwell, Mallet St. Ann 1970–1991, Box 1, folder 4, SBS Archives, CHRC.

43. M.M. Katharine to Jules B. Jeanmard, July 14, 1923, H40 B3a SBS Ministries Rural Schools Correspondence, Teachers, Reports Abbeville-Eunice, Box 1, folder 2, SBS Archives, CHRC.

44. [Drexel] to Mother Eucharia, [August 6, 1923], H40 B3a SBS Ministries Rural Schools Correspondence, Teachers, Reports Abbeville-Eunice, Box 1, folder 7, SBS Archives, CHRC.

45. Fossey and Austin, "Every Day Is a New Beginning," 50–53.

46. "History of St. Martin's School, St. Martinville, La.," "Material for Mother Agatha's Book about Xavier," AXUL. In this document, the date given for the opening of the school is incorrectly noted as 1936.

47. This information was found in the front matter of H40 B1 Closed Houses LA—St. Martinville, Box 1, SBS Archives, CHRC. The SBS remained in St. Martinville until 2002.

48. Sister Gabriella to Mother Katharine, February 22, 1939, SBS Original Annals 1932 Jan.–August, H40 A10 Box 6, folder 1, SBS Archives, CHRC.

49. Katharine Drexel to Jules Jeanmard, April 29, 1937, H10 Archives A MMK Writings, Box 24, folder 4, SBS Archives, CHRC.

50. SBS Original Annals, 1943, Jan.–Feb., H40 A10 Box 12, folder 1, SBS Archives, CHRC.

51. Hoy, *Good Hearts*, 88.

52. Timothy B. Neary, *Crossing Parish Boundaries: Race, Sports, and Catholic Youth in Chicago, 1914–1954* (Chicago: University of Chicago Press, 2016), 31, 47; "The Beginning of an Era," "St. Elizabeth's Church," May 25, 1952, H40 B2 IL: Chicago St. Monica's, Box 1x, folder 5, SBS Archives, CHRC; Hoy, *Good Hearts*, 88–89.

53. Lynch, *Sharing the Bread in Service*, 162–63.

54. ST. MONICA SCHOOL, Chicago, Excerpt, H40 B2 IL; Chicago St. Monica's St. Monica Parish Church Chicago, Illinois, Articles, Box 1x, folder 4, SBS Archives, CHRC.

55. Neary, *Crossing Parish Boundaries*, 23.

56. Neary, *Crossing Parish Boundaries*, 24–25.

57. Timothy B. Neary, "Black-Belt Catholic Space: African-American Parishes in Interwar Chicago," *U.S. Catholic Historian* 18 (Fall 2000): 87.

58. Mother Katharine Drexel to Most Reverend George Mundelein, May 13, 1922, A10 Archives A MMK Writings, Box 25, folder 11, SBS Archives, CHRC.

59. Lynch, *Sharing the Bread in Service*, 297–99.

60. Sister M. John Vianney to Reverend Mother, September 6, 1936, and Sister Alma to Reverend Mother, September 2, 1936, SBS Original Annals, 1936, Aug.–Dec., H40 A1 Box 7, folder 6, SBS Archives, CHRC.

61. SBS Original Annals 1937, Jan.–June, H40 A1 Box 7, folder 7, SBS Archives, CHRC.

62. Neary, *Crossing Parish Boundaries*, 49–50.

63. Neary, *Crossing Parish Boundaries*, 52.

64. St. Anselm's P.T.A. to Reverend Mother M. David, February 27, 1968, and Mother David to St. Anselm's P.T.A., March 21, 1968, H40 B2 IL: Chicago St. Anselm Correspondence 1960–1969, Box 1, folder 14, SBS Archives, CHRC.

65. SBS Original Annals, 1912, H40 A1 Box 3, folder 3, SBS Archives, CHRC.

66. SBS Original Annals, 1912, H40 A1 Box 3, folder 3, SBS Archives, CHRC.

67. Cecilia A. Moore, "Keeping Harlem Catholic: African-American Catholics and Harlem, 1920–1960," *U.S. Catholic Historian* 114 (Fall 2003): 6.

68. Lawrence Lucas, *Black Priest/White Church: Catholics and Racism* (New York: Random House, 1970), 19.

69. Lucas, *Black Priest/White Church*, 23, 30.

70. I am grateful to Cecilia A. Moore for providing me with this story about Diane Nash and the SBS. This material is part of a new chapter on Black Catholics and civil rights that will appear in a revised edition of Cyprian Davis's *Black Catholics in the United States*.

71. SBS Original Annals, 1914, H40 A1 Box 3, folder 5; William C. Leonard, "A Parish for the Black Catholics of Boston," *Catholic Historical Review* 83 (January 1997): 45–46.

72. "St. Bootstrap;" "Belmead," H40 B2 VA: Rock Castle St. Francis de Sales Post-Closure Uses, Box RC-36, folder 3, SBS Archives, CHRC.

73. DeNeen L. Brown, "Nuns Move Out of Belmead on the James after Former Plantation in Virginia is Put Up for Sale," *Washington Post*, February 8, 2017, https://www.washingtonpost.com/news/local/wp/2017/02/08/nuns-move-out-of-belmead-on-the-james-after-former-plantation-in-virginia-is-put-up-for-sale/.

74. Mother Elizabeth to Dear Sisters, October 16, 1970, H40 B2 Closed Houses LA—Church Point Our Mother of Mercy 1944–2000, Box 2, folder 1, SBS Archives, CHRC.

75. "June 1979," H40 B2 Closed Houses LA—Church Point Our Mother of Mercy 1944–2000, Box 1, folder 4, SBS Archives, CHRC.

76. Mother M. David to Albert Cardinal Meyer, December 4, 1965, H40 B2 IL: Chicago St. Elizabeth High School Corres. re SBS withdrawal, 1964–1965, Box 1, folder 2, SBS Archives, CHRC.

77. "St. Elizabeth School," May 1971, H40 B2 IL: Chicago St. Elizabeth's Apostolic Profiles, 1970–1980, Box 4, folder 2, SBS Archives, CHRC; Francis Cardinal George to Sister Patricia Suchalski, SBS, July 21, 2006, H40 B2 IL: Chicago St. Elizabeth 2006—SBS Departues, Box 4, folder 3, SBS Archives, CHRC; Thomas Lester to author, email December 3, 2020. I am grateful to Mr. Lester, director, Archive and Library, Archdiocese of Boston, for researching the closing of Blessed Sacrament Mission Center and providing me with the correct information. Also, Sister Mary Jane O'Donnell to Msgr. Joseph O'Keefe, March 14, 1981, H40 B2 NY: New York St. Mark's, Box 2, folder 3, SBS Archives, CHRC.

Chapter Six

1. See "Xavier University Annals, 2000–2005," AXUL.

2. See R. Bentley Anderson, *Black, White, and Catholic: New Orleans Interracialism, 1947–1956* (Nashville: Vanderbilt University Press, 2005), 7; SBS Original Annals, 1915, H40 A1, Box 3, folder 6, SBS Archives, CHRC.

3. SBS Original Annals, 1915, H40 A1 Box 3, folder 6, SBS Archives, CHRC.

4. Mother Mercedes O'Connor to Sisters, 1915, "Copies: Letters, etc. Early Days of X.U. 1900–1917," AXUL.

5. "Copy of St. Francis Xavier Annals 1915–1945," LA: New Orleans Xavier University Convent, AXUL.

6. Sister Mary Paul of the Cross to Reverend Mother, [September 1915], "Copies—Letters, etc. Early Days, X.U. 1900–1917," AXUL.

7. See Amanda Bresie, "By Prayer and Petition: The Sisters of the Blessed Sacrament's Mission of Evangelization and Americanization, 1891–1935" (PhD diss., Texas Christian University, 2014), 215; Sr. Mary Frances to My very dear Mother, September 24, 1915, "Copies: Letters, etc. Early Days, X.U. 1900–1917," AXUL.

8. Amanda Bresie, "'You Are As Good as Anyone That Walks God's Earth, and Never Forget It!' The SBS Create the 'Negro Notre Dame' in Jim Crow Louisiana," *Catholic Southwest* 25 (2014): 46.

9. SBS Original Annals, 1915, H40 A 1 Box 3, folder 6, SBS Archives, CHRC.

10. SBS Original Annals, 1916, H40 A 1 Box 3, folder 7, SBS Archives, CHRC.

11. Walter R. Allen, Joseph O. Jewell, Kimberly A. Griffin, De'Sha S. Wolf, "Historically Black Colleges and Universities: Honoring the Past, Engaging the Present, Touching the Future," *Journal of Negro Education* 76 (Summer 2007): 267.

12. Allen et al., "Historically Black Colleges and Universities," 269.

13. SBS Original Annals, 1923, H40 A1 Box 4, folder 4, SBS Archives, CHRC.

14. SBS Original Annals, 1925, H40 A1 Box 4, folder 7, SBS Archives, CHRC.

15. Sister Patricia Lynch, *Sharing the Bread in Service: Sisters of the Blessed Sacrament, 1891–1991* (Bensalem, PA: Sisters of the Blessed Sacrament, 1998), 208.

16. Quoted in Bresie, "By Prayer and Petition," 221–22.

17. "Xavier University of Louisiana—MMA's material for Xavier Book," "Material for Mother Agatha's Book about Xavier," AXUL.

18. Edward G. Brunner, SSJ, to Mother Katharine Drexel, September 15, 1937, and August 6, 1932, "Xavier History," AXUL; Drexel to Brunner, August 12, 1932, H10 A MMK Writings, Box 19, folder 9, SBS Archives, CHRC.

19. Quoted in Patricia Marshall, SBS, "Sister Mary Frances Buttell (1884–1977): Visionary for Xavier University," in *Religious Pioneers:*

Building the Faith in the Archdiocese of New Orleans, ed. Dorothy Dawes and Charles Nolan (New Orleans: Archdiocese of New Orleans, 2004), 292.

20. Edward F. Murphy, *Yankee Priest: An Autobiographical Journey, with Certain Detours, from Salem to New Orleans* (Garden City, NY: Doubleday, 1952), 191, 196.

21. SBS Original Annals, 1932, Jan.–August, H40 A1 Box 6, folder 1, SBS Archives, CHRC.

22. [Radio Address, 1933/1937], H40 B5 Social Justice: Interracial Movement, Box 2, folder 1, SBS Archives, CHRC.

23. SBS Original Annals, 1931—May–Dec., Box 5, folder 7, SBS Archives, CHRC.

24. Mother Katharine Drexel to Louise Morrell, March 15, 1933, MMK Writings, Box 25, folder 8, SBS Archives, CHRC.

25. Mother Katharine Drexel to Mother Agatha, March 29, 1936, H30 C2 Sisters' Collections, Mother Agatha Ryan, Box 1, folder 13, SBS Archives, CHRC.

26. SBS Original Annals, 1936, Aug.–Dec., Box 7, folder 6, SBS Archives, CHRC.

27. Mother Katharine Drexel to Mother M. Agatha, September 9, 1935, H30 C2 Sisters' Collections Mother M. Agatha (Halpin) Ryan, Box 1, folder 12, SBS Archives, CHRC.

28. Sister M. Agatha to Mother Katharine Drexel (telegram), March 29, 1938, H30 C2 Sisters' Collections Mother M. Agatha (Halpin) Ryan, Box 1, folder 4, SBS Archives, CHRC.

29. Bresie, "By Prayer and Petition," 100; website for the Creole Genealogical and Historical Association, Inc., accessed January 20, 2022, www.creolegen.org/2018/04/05/opera/.

30. Mother Agatha to Franklin D. Roosevelt, December 24, 1934, H10 A MMK Writings, Box 26A, folder 11, SBS Archives, CHRC.

31. Mother Agatha Ryan to Mother Mercedes O'Connor, October 17, 1935, H30 C2 Sisters' Collections Mother Agatha (Halpin) Ryan, Box 1, folder 9, SBS Archives, CHRC.

32. Sister Mary Boniface to [Mother Katharine Drexel], December 1938, H40 B2 LA: New Orleans Xavier Univ. Prep. Correspondence 1915–2011, Box 5, folder 2, SBS Archives, CHRC.

33. [SBS Annals, 1943], "Material for Mother Agatha's Book about Xavier," AXUL.

34. "Xavier University, Annals, 1941–1959," AXUL.

35. "The Red & the Black," *TIME*, August 30, 1948, 56; "Xavier University Annals 1941–1959," AXUL.

36. *Xavier Herald*, March 1955, 1, and October 1955, 1.

37. Mother Agatha to Mother Anselm, October 30, 1952, "MM Anselm Business 1952–1953," AXUL.

38. Mother Anselm to Mother Agatha, December 4, 1952; and Mother Agatha to Mother Anselm, December 21, 1952, "MM Anselm Business 1952–1955," AXUL; "Xavier University Annals, Jan.–Dec. 1955," AXUL. Xavier joined the United Negro College Fund in 1946.

39. Justin D. Poché, "Religion, Race, and Rights in Catholic Louisiana, 1938–1970" (PhD diss., University of Notre Dame, 2007), 231; Statement by Sister M. Josephina, "Policies of XU Spring 1960–Summer 1965," "MM Anselm Business 1952–1955," AXUL; A Serious Catholic to Sister Josephine, undated, "MM Anselm Business 1952–1955," AXUL.

40. A copy of this statement can be found in H40 B 5 MMK Nat. Fed. Col. Cath., Interracial Movement, Box 1, folder 5, SBS Archives, CHRC.

41. Adam Fairclough, *Race & Democracy: The Civil Rights Struggle in Louisiana, 1915–1972* (Athens: University of Georgia, 1995), 212.

42. Quoted in Poché, "Religion, Race, and Rights," 229–30; "A Student Manifesto," *Xavier Herald*, March 1960, 1.

43. Mark Newman, *Desegregating Dixie: The Catholic Church in the South and Desegregation, 1945–1992* (Jackson: University of Mississippi Press, 2018), 193.

44. Jed Lipinski, "On His Last Day at Xavier, Norman Francis Is Remembered for Providing Refuge to Freedom Riders," nola.com, June 30, 2015, https://www.nola.com/news/education/article_373b537b-cac 7-5094-b6b4-0caf77694840.html.

45. Sister Veronica, "Xavier University of Louisiana: A Historical Sketch," [Fall 1966], AXUL. Xavier's decision was part of a much larger movement among U.S. Catholic colleges and universities to transition to boards composed primarily of laypeople.

46. See Poché, "Religion, Race, and Rights," 338–39.

47. "Xavier University—New Orleans, Louisiana," "Local Apostolate Profile 1978," AXUL.

48. "Historical Overview Xavier Prep School," H40 B2 LA: New Orleans Xavier Univ. Prep History, Box 13, folder 1, SBS Archives, CHRC.

49. "S.B.S. Apostolic Profile," H40 B2 LA: New Orleans Xavier Univ. Prep, Box 1, folder 12, SBS Archives, CHRC; "Principal's Statistical Report, 1979–1980," H40 B2 LA: New Orleans Xavier Prep, Box 7, folder 5, SBS Archives, CHRC; "Principal's Statistical Report, 1989–1990," H40 B2 LA: New Orleans: Xavier Univ. Prep., Box 7, folder 6, SBS Archives, CHRC.

50. "Our History and Philosophy," Saint Katharine Drexel Preparatory School, accessed July 23, 2019, https://drexelprep.com/history.

51. Bobby L. Lovett, *America's Historically Black Colleges & Universities: A Narrative History from the Nineteenth Century into the Twenty-first Century* (Macon, GA: Mercer University Press, 2011), 272.

52. Clyde C. Robertson, "Hurricane Katrina through the Eyes of African American College Students: The Making of a Documentary," *Journal of African American History* 93 (Summer 2008): 393.

53. Robertson, "Hurricane Katrina," 398.

54. See "Hurricane Katrina's Devastating Effect on African-American Higher Education," *Journal of Blacks in Higher Education* 49 (Autumn 2005): 58, for Xavier students taken to Grambling State. It is, of course, possible that students were evacuated to both schools.

55. "Hurricane Katrina's Devastating Effect on African-American Higher Education," 59–60.

56. Robertson, "Hurricane Katrina," 398–400. Quotes are found on 400.

57. Michele Peseux McCue. "Tapping a Treasure: The Impact of the Institute for Black Catholic Studies on Black Catholicism and the American Catholic Church" (ThD diss., La Salle University, 2017), 272–73, https://digitalcommons.lasalle.edu/religion_thd/3.

58. Doug MacCash, "Xavier University's New St. Katharine Chapel Designed with Mystery in Mind," *Times-Picayune*, October 1, 2012, https://www.nola.com/entertainment_life/arts/article_45e6e726-16e1-5e34-8256-c8f519445123.html.

59. Nikole Hannah-Jones, "A Prescription for More Black Doctors," *New York Times Magazine*, September 9, 2015, https://www.nytimes.com/2015/09/13/magazine/a-prescription-for-more-black-doctors.html.

Chapter Seven

1. Sister Mary Roger Thibodeaux, Sisters of the Blessed Sacrament, Facebook, May 1, 2021; "Sacred Heart High School, Lake Charles, Louisiana," accessed August 9, 2021, https://africanamericanhighschoolsinlouisianabefore1970.com/sacred-heart-high-school-lake-charles-louisiana/.

2. Thibodeaux, Facebook.

3. Mariam Williams, "A Black Nun and a Black Writer Look at Black Power," *National Catholic Reporter*, February 27, 2018, https://www.ncronline.org/news/opinion/intersection/black-nun-and-black-writer-look-black-power.

4. Sister Mary Roger Thibodeaux, *A Black Nun Looks at Black Power* (New York: Sheed & Ward, 1972), x.

5. Thibodeaux, *A Black Nun Looks at Black Power*, 5, 7, 11.

6. Thibodeaux, *A Black Nun Looks at Black Power*, 17, 35.

7. Mother Anselm to My Dear Mother and Sisters, March 13, 1955, H40 B1 PA: St. Ignatius, Box 3, folder 9, SBS Archives, CHRC.

8. "Memoir of Sr. M. Mercedes," H30 C2 Sisters' Collections Mother Mercedes O'Connor, Box 1, folder 1, SBS Archives, CHRC.

9. Joseph McShea, "Funeral Oration for Mother Mary Katharine Drexel," *Records of the American Catholic Historical Society of Philadelphia* 66 (June 1955): 95, 97, 98, 99.

10. McShea, "Funeral Oration," 100.

11. Sister Consuela Marie Duffy, SBS, *Katharine Drexel: A Biography* (Philadelphia: The Peter Reilly Co., 1966), 75.

12. NCWC News Service, "WAY CLEAR FOR DISTRIBUTION OF $14 MILLION TO 27 CATHOLIC INSTITUTIONS UNDER DREXEL WILL," April 16, 1956, H40 B5 Interracial Movement, Box 3, folder 1, SBS Archives, CHRC.

13. See Sister Patricia Lynch, *Sharing the Bread in Service: Sisters of the Blessed Sacrament, 1891–1991* (Bensalem, PA: Sisters of the Blessed Sacrament, 1998), 426; Kathleen Sprows Cummings, *A Saint of Our Own: How the Quest for a Holy Hero Helped Catholics Become American* (Chapel Hill: University of North Carolina Press, 2019), 187.

14. Mother Mary Leandro to Cardinal John F. O'Hara, CSC, June 29, 1955, Legal Matters Mother Katharine Drexel Life and Legacy, Blessed Sacrament Sisters Mother Katharine Drexel Correspondence, 1888–1998, Box 3, folder 5, Sisters of Saint Francis of Philadelphia Archives (hereafter SOSF Archives).

15. Mother M. Anselm to Mother Mary Leandro, September 19, 1955, Legal Matters Mother Katharine Drexel Life and Legacy, Blessed Sacrament Sisters Mother Katharine Drexel Correspondence, 1888–1998, Box 3, folder 5, SOSF Archives.

16. Rev. J.B. Tennelly to Mother Mary David, December 1, 1969, H10 B MMK Correspondence, Box 58, folder 5, SBS Archives, CHRC.

17. David M. Byers to Sr. M. Juliana Hayes, October 20, 1985; Sister M. Juliana Haynes to Most Reverend Thomas V. Dailey, November 27, 1985; David M. Byers to Sr. M. Sister Juliana Haynes, January 9, 1986; H10 B MMK Correspondence, Box 58, folder 7, SBS Archives, CHRC.

18. Margaret M. McGuinness, *Called to Serve: A History of Nuns in America* (New York: New York University Press, 2013), 162.

19. Lynch, *Sharing the Bread in Service*, 539.

20. "Dawn Community, Xavier University," H40 B2 LA: New Orleans Experimental Houses, Box 1, folder 2, SBS Archives, CHRC.

21. [DAWN community], undated, H40 B2 LA: New Orleans Experimental Houses, Box 1, folder 1, SBS Archives, CHRC; "Dawn Community, Xavier University."

22. Sister Marie de Montfort et al. to Sister Mary Elizabeth and Councilors, April 18, 1979, H40 B2 LA: New Orleans Xavier Univ. Prep Correspondence 1915–2011, Box 5, folder 5, SBS Archives, CHRC.

23. Sr. M. Juliana Haynes to the Xavier Prep School Community, [1987], H40 B2 LA: New Orleans Xavier Univ. Prep Board of Directors Annual Report, SACS," Box 7, folder 1, SBS Archives, CHRC.

24. See the finding aid for H40 B2 FL: Miami Camillus House, 1994–1996, SBS Archives, CHRC; see www.camillus.org for information on Camillus House (accessed September 21, 2021). I am grateful to Stephanie Morris, former SBS archivist, for producing such a complete set of detailed finding aids.

25. Sister Sandra Magnini to Sparkill Dominicans, March 1991. I am grateful to Sister Mary Dunning, OP, for providing me with a copy of the letter.

26. See "Frequently Requested Church Statistics," accessed October 19, 2021, cara.georgetown.edu/frequently-requested-church -statistics/.

27. Cheryl C.D. Hughes, *Katharine Drexel: The Riches-to-Rags Story of an American Catholic Saint* (Grand Rapids: Eerdmans, 2014), 139.

28. Sister Mary Elizabeth to Reverend E. G. Gehlen, SVD, January 30, 1976; Sister Jane O'Donnell, SBS to Reverend Melvin James, SVD, March 4, 1983; Sister Jane O'Donnell, SBS to Reverend Melvin James, SVD, January 14, 1984, H40 B2 IL: Chicago St. Anselm Correspondence, 1970–1984, Box 1, folder 15, SBS Archives, CHRC; Francis Cardinal George to Sister Patricia Suchalski, SBS, July 21, 2006, H40 B2 IL: Chicago St. Elizabeth 2006-SBS Departures, Box 4, folder 3, SBS Archives, CHRC.

29. See "Frequently Requested Church Statistics."

30. Mother Mary Elizabeth to Sister M. Sheila, February 10, 1972, H40 B2 LA: New Orleans Xavier Univ. Prep Correspondence 1915–2011, Box 5, folder 5, SBS Archives, CHRC.

31. Archbishop Thomas A. Donnellan to Mother Mary Elizabeth, February 9, 1972, Our Lady of Lourdes School Collection. Office of Archives and Records, Roman Catholic Archdiocese of Atlanta, Georgia.

32. Mother Elizabeth to Most Rev. Thomas Donnellan, October 12, 1973, H40 B2 GA: Atlanta Our Lady of Lourdes, Box 1, folder 11, SBS Archives, CHRC.

33. "Local Apostolate Profile 1978," AXUL.

34. The Councilors at St. Catherine's to Mother M. David, November 3, 1969, H40 B2 NM: Santa Fe St. Catherine Indian School SBS Correspondence, Box SCIS 2, folder 15, SBS Archives, CHRC.

35. Quoted in Brian S. Collier, "St. Catherine Indian School, Santa Fe, 1887–2006" (PhD diss., Arizona State University, 2006), 214.

36. Clipping, Anne Constable, "Dark Clouds over St. Kate's," *Santa Fe Reporter*, March 30–April 5, 1994, 15–16, H40 B2 NM: Santa Fe St. Catherine Indian School SBS Correspondence, Box SCIS-2, folder 16, SBS Archives, CHRC.

37. Clipping, "'St. Kate's' Tradition Too Good to End," *Santa Fe New Mexican*, April 9, 1998," H40 B2 NM: Santa Fe St. Catherine Indian School SBS Correspondence, Box SCIS-3, folder 5, SBS Archives, CHRC.

38. Clipping, Richard Change, "Sisters Seal Fate of School," *The New Mexican*, May 14, 1998, H40 B2 NM: Santa Fe St. Catherine Indian

School SBS Correspondence, Box SCIS-3, folder 5, SBS Archives, CHRC.

39. Sr. Marjorie Everett, SBS and Sr. Carole Eden, SBS, "Final Blessing at St. Catherine Indian School," *SBS Connections*, April 2008, H40 B2 NM: Santa Fe St. Catherine Indian School History, Box SCIS-10, folder 15, SBS Archives, CHRC.

40. "Annals, 1964," H40 B2 Closed Houses LA Church Point Our Mother of Mercy 1944–2000, Box 1, folder 2, SBS Archives, CHRC.

41. Lynch, *Sharing the Bread in Service*, 458.

42. Mark Newman, *Desegregating Dixie: The Catholic Church in the South and Desegregation, 1945–1992* (Jackson: University Press of Mississippi, 2019), 38; "Our Lady of Lourdes Catholic Church: Atlanta's First African-American Catholic Church," accessed September 10, 2021, https://georgiahistory.com/ghmi_marker_updated/our-lady -of-lourdes-catholic-church-atlantas-first-african-american-catholic -church/; Andrew S. Moore, "Black and Catholic in Atlanta: Challenge and Hope," in *Catholics in the Vatican Era: Local Histories of a Global Event*, ed. Kathleen Sprows Cummings, Timothy Matovina, and Robert Orsi (Cambridge: Cambridge University Press, 2018), 139.

43. Annals, April 1968, May 1968, H40 B2 GA: Atlanta Our Lady of Lourdes, Box 1, folder 5, SBS Archives, CHRC.

44. Quoted in Lynch, *Sharing the Bread in Service*, 459.

45. Lynch, *Sharing the Bread in Service*, 460.

46. Quoted in Justin D. Poché, "Religion, Race, and Rights in Catholic Louisiana, 1938–1970" (PhD diss., University of Notre Dame, 2007), 322.

47. Annals, June 10, 1962, H40 B2 GA: Atlanta Our Lady of Lourdes, Box 2, folder 5, SBS Archives, CHRC.

48. Sister M. Ruth to Mother Gonzaga, September 14, 1962, H40 B2 GA: Atlanta Our Lady of Lourdes, Box 2, folder 5, SBS Archives, CHRC.

49. Newman, *Desegregating Dixie*, 144–45.

50. Annals 1964, H40 B2 Closed Houses LA—Church Point Our Mother of Mercy 1944–2000, Box 1, folder 2, SBS Archives, CHRC.

51. "Annals of Our Mother of Mercy Convent Church Point, Louisiana—1969," "Annals of Our Mother of Mercy Convent Church Point, La., Sept. 1970–May 1971," "Annals of Our Mother of Mercy Convent Church Point La., Jan. 1971–Dec. 1971," H40 B2 Closed Houses LA—

Church Point Our Mother of Mercy 1944–2000," Box 1, folder 3, SBS Archives, CHRC.

52. Quoted in Poché, "Religion, Race, and Rights," 290. The sister's name was withheld.

53. Newman, *Desegregating Dixie*, 8.

54. Newman, *Desegregating Dixie*, 9.

55. Quoted in Poché, "Religion, Race, and Rights," 325.

56. Quoted in Poché, "Religion, Race, and Rights," 345.

57. Lynch, *Sharing the Bread in Service*, 462.

58. "PROGRAM FOR ON-GOING EDUCATION ON BLACK AND INDIAN CONCERNS," 1976, H40 B2 IL: Chicago "Black (and Indian) Curriculum-Educational Concerns," Box 4, folder 8, SBS Archives, CHRC.

59. Lynch, *Sharing the Bread in Service*, 575–76.

60. Quoted in Lynch, *Sharing the Bread in Service*, 603.

61. Lynch, *Sharing the Bread in Service*, 603–4.

62. Hughes, 141–43. Hughes states there were 309 professed sisters in 1990, but later gives the total number of SBS at this time as 328.

63. Lynch, *Sharing the Bread in Service*, 607–8.

64. "Claver House Taking Root after Maisha House Closes," *Georgia Bulletin*, January 11, 2007, https://georgiabulletin.org/news/2007/01/claver-house-taking-root-maisha-house-closes/.

65. See the website for the Sisters of the Blessed Sacrament, accessed September 23, 2021, https://www.katharinedrexel.org/.

Epilogue

1. Julia Terruso, "Remains of Saint Katharine Drexel to Be Moved to the Cathedral This Summer," *Philadelphia Inquirer*, July 18, 2018, https://www.inquirer.com/philly/news/st-katharine-drexel-remains-basilica-sisters-blessed-sacrament-20180724.html.

2. Kristen E. Holmes, "Moved from Bensalem, St. Katharine's Drexel Tomb Unveiled at Cathedral," *Philadelphia Inquirer*, October 30, 2018, https://www.inquirer.com/philly/news/saint-katharine-drexel-tomb-moved-bensalem-philadelphia-archdiocese-cathedral-peter-paul-sisters-blessed-sacrament-20181030.html.

3. Lou Baldwin, "St. Katharine Drexel's Tomb Blessed at New Home in Cathedral," catholicphilly.com, November 20, 2018, https://

catholicphilly.com/2018/11/news/local-news/st-katharine-drexels
-tomb-blessed-at-new-home-in-cathedral/ (accessed September 5, 2022).

4. Holmes, "Moved from Bensalem."

5. Ian Mosby and Erin Millions, "Canada's Residential Schools Were a Horror," *Scientific American*, August 1, 2021, https://www.scientificamerican.com/article/canadas-residential-schools-were-a-horror/.

6. See, for example, "Editorial: Hard Lessons, Truth for Sisters of the Blessed Sacrament," *Gallup Independent*, November 2, 2017, https://www.bishop-accountability.org/news66/2017_11_02_Editorial_Hard_lessons.htm; Alaina Beautiful Bald Eagle, "Charbonneau Sisters Address Sex Abuse at Boarding Schools," *Native Sun News Today*, February 4, 2021, https://www.nativesunnews.today/articles/charbonneau-sisters-address-sex-abuse-at-boarding-schools/; and Susan Montoya Bryan, "Lawsuit Claims Sexual Abuse at St. Catherine's Indian School," *Santa Fe New Mexican*, March 29, 2019, https://www.santafenewmexican.com/news/local_news/lawsuit-claims-sexual-abuse-at-st-catherine-s-indian-school/article_aa75f260-251e-5665-a9f8-1d112ea852b5.html.

7. Catherine R. Osborne, "Introduction: Writing Catholic History after the Sex Abuse Crisis," *American Catholic Studies* 127 (Summer 2016): 1.

8. Matthew J. Cressler, "Introduction: Forum: Catholic Sex Abuse and the Study or Religion," *American Catholic Studies* 130 (Summer 2019): 1.

9. Donna Marie Gould, "Sharing the Culture of the Pueblos People," *Global Sisters Report*, November 12, 2018, https://www.globalsistersreport.org/column/ministry/sharing-culture-pueblos-people-55602.

10. Gould, "Sharing the Culture of the Pueblos People."

11. Gould, "Sharing the Culture of the Pueblos People."

12. Gould, "Sharing the Culture of the Pueblos People."

13. Xavier University of Louisiana, "On this day in 1932, Xavier held a dedication ceremony for the opening of our current campus! St. Katharine Drexel & the Sisters of the Blessed Sacrament opened the doors of this campus knowing you would one day arrive to continue the legacy of creating a more just and humane society," Facebook, October 12, 2021, https://www.facebook.com/XULA1925.

BIBLIOGRAPHY

Archives

Archives of the Archdiocese of Atlanta, Georgia

Archives of the Catholic University of America, Washington, DC

Archives of the Diocese of Harrisburg, Pennsylvania

Archives of the Diocese of Lafayette, Louisiana

Archives of the Sisters of St. Francis of Philadelphia, Aston, Pennsylvania

Archives of the Sisters of the Blessed Sacrament, Philadelphia, Pennsylvania

Archives of Xavier University, New Orleans, Louisiana

Catholic Historical Research Center of the Archdiocese of Philadelphia

Charles L. Blockson Afro-American Collection, Temple University, Philadelphia, Pennsylvania

Ducournau Archives of the Eastern Province of the Congregation of the Mission (Vincentians), Philadelphia, Pennsylvania

Bibliography

Alberts, John B. "Black Catholic Schools: The Josephite Parishes during the Jim Crow Era." *U.S. Catholic Historian* 12 (Winter 1994): 77–98.

——. "Origins of Black Catholic Parishes in the Archdiocese of New Orleans, 1718–1920." PhD diss., Louisiana State University, 1999.

Alexander, Raymond Pace. "A Tribute to Mother Katharine Drexel." *Negro History Bulletin* 29 (Fall 1966): 181–82, 189, 191–92.

Allen, Walter R., Joseph O. Jewell, Kimberly A. Griffin, and De'Sha S. Wolf. "Historically Black Colleges and Universities: Honoring the Past, Engaging the Present, Touching the Future." *Journal of Negro Education* 76 (Summer 2007): 263–80.

Anderson, R. Bentley. *Black, White, and Catholic: New Orleans Interracialism, 1947–1956.* Nashville: Vanderbilt University Press, 2005.

Armstrong, Kimberly E. "A Failed *Uncle Tom's Cabin* for the Indian: Helen Hunt Jackson's *Ramona* and the Power of Paratext." *Western American Literature* 52 (Summer 2017): 129–56.

Bahr, Howard M., ed. *The Navajo as Seen by the Franciscans, 1898–1921.* Lanham, MD: Scarecrow, 2004.

Baldwin, Lou. "Ceremony to Be Held Nov. 20 in Rome, Archbishop Says." *The Catholic Standard and Times*, July 28, 1988.

———. "A Home on the Hill: Memories of St. Vincent's Home, Drexel Hill, PA." *American Catholic Studies* 126 (Spring 2015): 91–101.

———. "Katharine Drexel: The Formation of a Saint." *American Catholic Studies* 121 (Fall 2010): 115–21.

———. *Saint Katharine Drexel: Apostle to the Oppressed.* Philadelphia: Catholic Standard and Times, 2000.

———. "St. Katharine Drexel's Tomb Blessed at New Home in Cathedral." November 20, 2018. https://catholicphilly.com/2018/11/news/local-news/st-katharine-drexels-tomb-blessed-at-new-home-in-cathedral/.

Barozza, Vincent S. and Janet Fiegel. "Saving the Black Catholic Experience of Xavier University of Louisiana." XULA Digital Commons, Fall 2020. Accessed May 13, 2021. https://digitalcommons.xula.edu/fac_pub/261.

Beautiful Bald Eagle, Alaina. "Charbonneau Sisters Address Sex Abuse at Boarding Schools." *Native Sun News Today*, February 4, 2021. https://www.nativesunnews.today/articles/charbonneau-sisters-address-sex-abuse-at-boarding-schools/.

Becker, J. W., and William S. Porter. "The Lincoln Funeral Train." *Journal of the Illinois State Historical Society* 9 (October 1916): 315–19.

Bennett, James B. *Religion and the Rise of Jim Crow in New Orleans.* Princeton, NJ: Princeton University Press, 2005.

Berg, Carol J. "Agents of Cultural Change: The Benedictines at White Earth." *Minnesota History* 48 (Winter 1982): 158–70.

Bernard, Raymond, SJ. "Some Anthropological Implications of the Racial Admission Policy of the U.S. Sisterhoods." *American Catholic Sociological Review* 19 (June 1958): 124–33.

Biddle, Cordelia Frances. *Saint Katharine: The Life of Katharine Drexel.* Yardley, PA: Westholme Publishing, 2014.

"Black Higher Education in New Orleans Three Years after Hurricane Katrina." *Journal of Blacks in Higher Education* 61 (Autumn 2008): 79–81.

Blatt, Genevieve. "Katherine Mary Drexel of Philadelphia." In *Quest for Faith, Quest for Freedom: Aspect of Pennsylvania's Religious Experience*, edited by Otto Reimherr. Selinsgrove, PA: Susquehanna University Press, 1987.

Bloom, Colette Madeleine. "A Catholic Negro Child in the Segregated South of the 1950s and 1960s: A Postmodern Retrospective on St. Katharine Drexel's Mission in New Orleans." *Catholic Southwest: A Journal of History and Culture* 21 (2010): 23–33.

Bodo, Murray, ed. *Tales of an Endishodi: Father Bernard Haile and the Navajos, 1900–1961.* Albuquerque: University of New Mexico Press, 1998.

Bonner, Thomas Jr. "Facing the Flood: The English Department as a High Axle Vehicle." *South Central Review* 24 (Fall 2007): 55–60.

Brady, Benjamin R., Howard M. Bahr, "The Influenza Epidemic of 1918–1920: Marginality, Mortality, and the Implications of Some Neglected Eyewitness Accounts," *American Indian Quarterly* 38 (Fall 2014): 459–91.

Brandewie, Ernest. *In the Light of the World: Divine Word Missionaries of North America.* Maryknoll, NY: Orbis Books, 2000.

Bresie, Amanda. "By Prayer and Petition: The Sisters of the Blessed Sacrament's Mission of Evangelization and Americanization, 1891–1935." PhD diss., Texas Christian University, 2014.

———. "Mother Katharine Drexel's Benevolent Empire: The Bureau of Catholic Indian Missions and the Education of Native Americans, 1885–1935." *U.S. Catholic Historian* 32 (Summer 2014): 1–24.

———. "One Bread, One Body: The Sisters of the Blessed Sacrament in Southeast Texas." *Catholic Southwest* 22 (2011): 21–38.

———. "'To Make All Your People Saints:' Mother Katharine's Schools in Rural Louisiana." *Catholic Southwest* 24 (2013): 30–47.

————. "'You Are as Good as Anyone That Walks God's Earth, and Never Forget It!' The SBS Create the 'Negro Notre Dame' in Jim Crow Louisiana." *Catholic Southwest* 25 (2014): 44–59.

Brinkley, Douglas. *The Great Deluge: Hurricane Katrina, New Orleans, and the Mississippi Gulf Coast.* New York: Harper Collins, 2006.

Brown, DeNeen L. "Nuns Move Out pf Belmead on the James after Former Plantation in Virginia Is Put Up for Sale." *Washington Post,* February 8, 2017. https://www.washingtonpost.com/news/local/wp/2017/02/08/nuns-move-out-of-belmead-on-the-james-after-former-plantation-in-virginia-is-put-up-for-sale/.

Brown, Stephanie. "Bourgeois Blackness and Autobiographical Authenticity in Ellen Tarry's *The Third Door.*" *African American Review* 41 (Fall 2007): 537–70.

Bryan, Susan Montoya. "Lawsuit Claims Sexual Abuse at St. Catherine's Indian School." *Santa Fe New Mexican*, March 29, 2019. https://www.santafenewmexican.com/news/local_news/lawsuit-claims-sexual-abuse-at-st-catherine-s-indian-school/article_aa75f260-251e-5665-a9f8-1d112ea852b5.html.

Burton, Katherine. *The Golden Door: The Life of Katharine Drexel.* New York: P. J. Kenedy & Sons, 1957.

Butler, Anne M. *Across God's Frontiers: Catholic Sisters in the American West, 1850–1920.* Chapel Hill: University of North Carolina Press, 2012.

————. "There Are Exceptions to Every Rule: Adjusting the Boundaries—Catholic Sisters and the American West." *American Catholic Studies* 116 (Fall 2005): 1–22.

————. "Western Spaces, Catholic Places." *U.S. Catholic Historian* 18 (Fall 2000): 25–39.

Butler, Kristie Lee. "Along the Padres' Trail: The History of St. Michael's Mission to the Navajo." MA thesis, Arizona State University, 1991.

Carroll, James T. *Seeds of Faith: Catholic Indian Boarding Schools.* New York: Garland Publishing, 2000.

————. "Self-Direction, Activity, and Syncretism: Catholic Indian Boarding Schools on the Northern Great Plains in Contact." *U.S. Catholic Historian* 16 (Spring 1998): 78–89.

————. "Watchmen and Gatekeepers: Native American Catholicism in the 20th Century." *American Catholic Studies Newsletter* (Spring 2010): 13–15.

Bibliography

Carson, Mary Eisenman. *Blackrobe for the Yankton Sioux: Father Sylvester Eisenman, O.S.B.* Chamberlain, SD: Tipi Press, 1989.

The Catholic University of America Yearbook 1914–1915. Washington, DC: The Catholic University of America, 1914.

"The Centenary of Eden Hall, 1847–1947." *Records of the American Catholic Historical Society of Philadelphia* 57 (September 1946): 145–59.

Clark, Dennis. "Urban Blacks and Irishmen: Brothers in Prejudice." In *Black Politics In Philadelphia*, edited by Miriam Ershkowitz and Joseph Zikmund. New York: Basic Books, 1973, 15–30.

Clatterbuck, Mark. *Demons, Saints, & Patriots: Catholic Visions of Native America Through The Indian Sentinel.* Milwaukee: Marquette University Press, 2009.

Coburn, Carol K. and Martha Smith, *Spirited Lives: How Nuns Shaped Catholic Culture and American Life, 1836–1920.* Chapel Hill: University of North Carolina Press, 1999.

Collier, Brian S. "St. Catherine Indian School, Santa Fe, 1887–2006." PhD diss., Arizona State University, 2006.

Collier, Brian S., Collin Gortner, and Will Newkirk. "Introduction: Finding Sovereignty—Native American Catholic Schools and the American West." *Journal of the West* 59 (Summer 2020): 11–15.

Collopy, William. "Welfare and Conversion: The Catholic Church in African American Communities in the U.S. South, 1884–1939." PhD diss., Texas A & M University, 2011.

Copeland, M. Shawn. "Another of the Best Kept Secrets of the Catholic Church in the United States: Xavier University of Louisiana's Institute for Black Catholic Studies." Online Supplement, a *Jesuit Journal of the Social Apostolate* (Winter 2004). http://www.jesuit.org/jesuits/wp-content/uploads/IATBlack-and-Catholic-Supplement-Winter-04.pdf.

Cressler, Matthew J. ed. "Forum: Race, White Supremacy, and the Making of American Catholicism." *American Catholic Studies* 127 (Fall 2016): 1–37.

———. "Introduction: Forum: Catholic Sex Abuse and the Study or Religion." *American Catholic Studies* 130 (Summer 2019): 1–3.

Cummings, Kathleen Sprows. *A Saint of Our Own: How the Quest for a Holy Hero Helped Catholics Become American.* Chapel Hill: University of North Carolina Press, 2019.

Downey, Jack and Kathleen Holscher. "What the U.S. Catholic Church Gets Wrong about Native Dispossession." *Religion and Politics*, January 29, 2019. https://religionandpolitics.org/2019/01/29/covington-what-the-u-s-catholic-church-gets-wrong-about-native-dispossession/.

Drewry, Henry N., and Humphrey Doermann in collaboration with Susan H. Anderson. *Stand and Prosper: Private Black Colleges and Their Students*. Princeton, NJ: Princeton University Press, 2001.

[Drexel, Katharine]. "This Race Problem." *Mission Fields at Home*, September–October 1940.

Du Bois, W. E. B. *The Black North: A Social Study*. New York: Arno Press and *The New York Times*, 1969.

―――. *The Philadelphia Negro: A Social Study*. Reprint, New York: Oxford University Press, 2007.

Duffy, Sister Consuela Marie, SBS. *Katharine Drexel: A Biography*. Philadelphia: The Peter Reilly Co., 1966.

―――. "Mrs. Louise Drexel Morrell." *Records of the American Catholic Historical Society of Philadelphia* 56 (December 1945): 331–37.

Duncan, Patricia. "Our Lady of the Assumption School." *Louisiana History: The Journal of the Louisiana Historical Association* 47 (Winter 2006): 100.

Dunne, William. "The Roman Catholic Church: The Rationale and Policies Underlying the Maintenance of Higher Institutions for Negroes." *Journal of Negro Education* 29 (Summer 1960): 307–14.

"Editorial: Hard Lessons, Truth for Sisters of the Blessed Sacrament." *Gallup Independent*, November 2, 2017. https://www.bishop-accountability.org/news66/2017_11_02_Editorial_Hard_lessons.htm.

Emerick, A. J. "The Colored Mission of Our Lady of the Blessed Sacrament, Philadelphia, PA." *The Woodstock Letters: A Record* 42 (1913): 69–82, 175–88, 352–62.

―――. "The Colored Mission of Our Lady of the Blessed Sacrament, Philadelphia, PA." *The Woodstock Letters: A Record* 43 (1914): 10–23, 181–94.

Engh, Michael E. "Peter Paul Prando, S.J., 'Apostle of the Crows.'" *Montana: The Magazine of Western History* 34 (Autumn 1984): 24–31.

Enochs, Ross. "The Franciscan Mission to the Navajos: Mission Method and Indigenous Religion, 1898–1940." *U.S. Catholic Historian* 92 (January 2006): 46–73.

Fairclough, Adam. *Race & Democracy: The Civil Rights Struggle in Louisiana, 1915–1992.* Athens: University of Georgia Press, 1995.

Flanagan, Maureen. *America Reformed: Progressives and Progressivism, 1890s–1920s.* New York: Oxford University Press, 2007.

Fogarty, Gerald P., SJ. *Commonwealth Catholicism: A History of the Catholic Church in Virginia.* Notre Dame, IN: University of Notre Dame Press, 2001.

Foley, Thomas W., ed. *At Standing Rock and Wounded Knee: The Journals and Papers of Father Francis M. Craft, 1888–1890.* Norman, OK: Arthur H. Clark, 2009.

———. *Father Francis Craft: Missionary to the Sioux.* Lincoln: University of Nebraska Press, 2002.

———. "Francis M. Craft and the Indian Sisters." *U.S. Catholic Historian* 16 (Spring 1998): 41–55.

Foner, Philip S. "The Battle to End Discrimination against Negroes in Philadelphia Streetcars: (Part 1) Background and Beginning of the Battle." *Pennsylvania History: A Journal of Mid-Atlantic Studies* 40 (July 1973): 260–90.

———. "The Battle to End Discrimination against Negroes in Philadelphia Streetcars: (Part II) The Victory." *Pennsylvania History: A Journal of Mid-Atlantic Studies* 40 (October 1973): 354–79.

"Former Church Parishioner Reflects on the Legacy of Philadelphia's First Black Catholic Church." *Temple News* 7 (February 2000), https://temple-news.com/former-church-parishioner-reflects-on -the-legacy-of-philadelphias-first-black-catholic-church-2/.

Fossey, Richard, and Nancy Austin. "'Every Day Is a New Beginning:' Lela Gordon Mouton and St. Katharine Drexel's Rural School in Prairie Basse, Louisiana." *Catholic Southwest: A Journal of History and Culture* 24 (2013): 48–59.

Fossey, Richard and Stephanie Morris. "Courage under Fire: Saint Katharine Drexel and the Sisters of the Blessed Sacrament Confront the Ku Klux Klan." *Catholic Southwest: A Journal of History and Culture* 21 (2010): 7–22.

———. "St. Katharine Drexel and St. Patrick's Mission to the Indians of the Southern Plains: A Study in Saintly Administration." *Catholic Southwest: A Journal of History and Culture* 18 (2007): 61–84.

Franklin, Vincent P. *The Education of Black Philadelphia: The Social and Educational History of a Minority Community, 1900–1950.* Philadelphia: University of Pennsylvania Press, 1979.

Friedman, Emmanuel. "Louise Drexel Morrell: A Reminiscence." *Records of the American Catholic Historical Society of Philadelphia* 76 (March 1965): 63–66.

Gammage, Jeff. "Finally, Going Home." *Philadelphia Inquirer*, June 27, 2021.

Garneau, James F. "Saint Katharine Drexel in Light of the New Evangelization." *Josephinum Journal of Theology* 10 (2003): 131.

Garnett, Diana. "National Register Nomination for St. James the Greater Catholic Mission." MA thesis, University of South Carolina, 2015.

Gasman, Marybeth. "Swept Under the Rug? A Historiography of Gender and Black Colleges," *American Educational Research Journal* 44, no. 4 (December 2007): 760–805.

Gerdes, M. Reginald. "To Educate and Evangelize: Black Catholic Schools of the Oblate Sisters of Providence, 1828–1880." *U.S. Catholic Historian* 7 (Spring–Summer 1988): 183–199.

Gerlach, Dominic B. "St. Joseph's Indian Normal School, 1888–1896." *Indiana Magazine of History* 69 (March 1973): 1–42.

Golden Jubilee 1891–1941. Cornwalls Heights, PA: Sisters of the Blessed Sacrament for Indians and Colored People, 1941.

Gortner, Collin. "Reconciliation and Cultural Empowerment of American Catholic Indian Schools." *Journal of the West* 59 (Summer 2020): 25–37.

Gould, Donna Marie. "Sharing the Culture of the Pueblos People," *Global Sisters Report*, November 12, 2018. https://www.globalsistersreport.org/column/ministry/sharing-culture-pueblos-people-55602.

Gram, John R. "An Unintended Alliance: Catholic and Indigenous Resistance to the Federal Indian Boarding Schools." *Journal of the West* 59 (Summer 2020): 38–54.

Greene, Nicole Pepinster. "Flushing Out the Basements: The Status of Contingent Composition Faculty in Post-Katrina New Orleans—and What We Can Learn from It." *South Central Review* 24 (Fall 2007): 76–81.

Guidry, Sister Mary Gabriella, S.S.F. *The Southern Negro Nun*. New York: Exposition Press, 1974.

Haavik, Benjamin Knute. "Eden Hall: A Cultural Historic Landscape." MS thesis, University of Pennsylvania, 1998.

Haberman, Clyde. "Pope Beatifies Philadelphia Nun Who Educated Blacks and Indians." *New York Times*, November 21, 1988. https://

www.nytimes.com/1988/11/21/us/pope-beatifies-philadelphia-nun-who-educated-blacks-and-indians.html.

Hamilton, Martha McNeil, and Warren Brown. *Black and White and Red All Over: The Story of a Friendship*. New York: Public Affairs, 2002.

Hanley, Boniface, OFM. *A Philadelphia Story*. [Philadelphia]: Mother Katharine Drexel Guild, 1991.

Hannah-Jones, Nikole. "A Prescription for More Black Doctors." *New York Times Magazine*, September 9, 2015. https://www.nytimes.com/2015/09/13/magazine/a-prescription-for-more-black-doctors.html.

Harley, R. Bruce. "The Founding of St. Boniface Indian School, 1888–1890." *Southern California Quarterly* 81 (Winter 1999): 449–66.

Heinz, Helen A. "'We Are All as One Fish in the Sea...' Catholicism in Protestant Pennsylvania: 1730–1790." PhD diss., Temple University, 2008.

Hemesath, Sister Caroline. *From Slave to Priest: A Biography of the Rev. Augustus Tolton (1854–1897), First Afro-American Priest of the United States*. Chicago: Franciscan Herald Press, 1973.

Herbes, Sister Emily Ann, OSFS. "Histories of the Sisters of St. Francis of Philadelphia in Wyoming since 1892." Accessed September 7, 2020. https://dcwy.org/documents/2020/6/SistersofStFrancis.pdf.

Hodes, Martha. *Mourning Lincoln*. New Haven, CT: Yale University Press, 2015.

Holmes, Kristen E. "Moved from Bensalem, St. Katharine's Drexel Tomb Unveiled at Cathedral." *Philadelphia Inquirer*, October 30, 2018. https://www.inquirer.com/philly/news/saint-katharine-drexel-tomb-moved-bensalem-philadelphia-archdiocese-cathedral-peter-paul-sisters-blessed-sacrament-20181030.html.

Holscher, Kathleen. "Children's Graves in Canada Reflect Catholic Logic of Indigenous Vanishment." *National Catholic Reporter*, June 22, 2021. https://www.ncronline.org/news/accountability/canadian-native-childrens-graves-reflect-history-indigenous-vanishment.

Horne, Jed. *Breach of Faith: Hurricane Katrina and the Near Death of a Great American City*. New York: Random House, 2006.

Hoy, Suellen. *Good Hearts: Catholic Sisters in Chicago's Past*. Urbana: University of Illinois Press, 2006.

————. "Lives on the Color Line: Catholic Sisters and African Americans in Chicago, 1890s–1960s." *U.S. Catholic Historian* 22 (Winter 2004): 67–91.

————. "Ministering Hope to Chicago." *Chicago History* 31 (Fall 2002): 4–23.

Huey, Annie. "'Be Interesting but Tell the Truth at All Times': Katherine Burton's Fictional-Narrative Approach to Biographical Writing." *American Catholic Studies* 131 (Spring 2020): 57–78.

Hughes, Cheryl C.D. *Katharine Drexel: The Riches-to-Rags Story of an American Catholic Saint.* Grand Rapids: Eerdmans, 2014.

Hurd, Nicole Farmer. "The Master Art of a Saint: Katharine Drexel and Her Theology of Education." PhD diss., University of Virginia, 2002.

"Hurricane Katrina's Devastating Effect on African-American Higher Education." *Journal of Blacks in Higher Education* 49 (Autumn 2005): 56–63.

Jackson, Helen Hunt. *A Century of Dishonor: The Early Crusade for Indian Reform.* Edited by Andrew F. Rolle. 1881; reprint, New York: Harper & Row, 1965.

Jacobs, Margaret D. *White Mother to a Dark Race: Settler Colonialism, Maternalism, and the Removal of Indigenous Children in the American West and Australia, 1880–1949.* Lincoln: University of Nebraska Press, 2009.

Johnson, Karen Joy. "Another Long Civil Rights Movement: How Catholic Interracialists Used the Resources of Their Faith to Tear Down Racial Hierarchy." *American Catholic Studies* 126 (Winter 2015): 1–27.

Johnson, Nessa Theresa Baskerville. *A Special Pilgrimage: A History of Black Catholics in Richmond.* Richmond, VA: Diocese of Richmond, 1978.

Jones, Elsa Loacker. "Francis Martin Drexel's Years in America." *Records of the American Catholic Historical Society of Philadelphia* 85 (September, December 1974): 129–40.

Katharine, Mother M. "Sisters Visit Indian Homes." *Indian Sentinel* 4 (April 1924): 66.

"Katharine Drexel Canonized." *Temple News* 6, October 2000. Temple-news.com/Katharine-drexel-canonized/.

"Katharine Drexel Elementary School, History." Accessed February 17, 2021. https://www.lpssonline.com/schools/drexel/history.

Kendi, Ibram X. *How to Be an Antiracist.* New York: One World, 2019.

Kennedy, Susan Alice. "'You Have Made No Mistake in Seeking to Save Souls among Us': Catholic Evangelization among Black Nashvillians, 1898–1908." PhD diss., University of Tennessee, Knoxville, 2019.

Koenig, Harry. *A History of the Parishes of the Archdiocese of Chicago.* Chicago: Catholic Bishops of Chicago, 1980, vol. 1.

Labbé Dolores Egger. *Jim Crow Comes to Church.* New York: Arno Press, 1978.

Laborde, Katheryn Krotzer. "Hazel Motes Is Not Black." *Flannery O'Connor Review* 14 (2016): 63–69.

———. "Show and Tell." *South Central Review* 24 (Fall 2007): 67–75.

Lagarde, Roland, SBS. "A Contemporary Pilgrimage: Personal Testimony of Blessed Katharine Drexel's Charism." *U.S. Catholic Historian* 8 (Spring 1989): 47–50.

Lajimodiere, Denise K. *Stringing Rosaries: The History, the Unforgivable, and the Healing of Northern Plains American Indian Boarding School Survivors.* Fargo: North Dakota State University Press, 2019.

Landry, Christopher. "The Diocese of Lafayette's Crusade to Save Catholicism: Nationalizing Creole Communities in Southwest Louisiana in the Interwar Period." *Catholic Historical Review* 104 (Autumn 2019): 686–706.

Lannie, Vincent P., and Bernard C. Dicthorn. "For the Honor and Glory of God: The Philadelphia Bible Riots of 1840." *History of Education Quarterly* 8 (Spring 1968): 44–106.

Leab, Katharine Kyes. "Collecting, Auctions, and the Book Trade." *RBM: A Journal of Rare Books, Manuscripts, and Cultural Heritage* 11 (2010): 47–60.

Leonard, William C. "A Parish for the Black Catholics of Boston." *Catholic Historical Review* 83 (January 1997): 44–68.

[Letterhouse], Sister M. Dolores. *The Francis A. Drexel Family.* Cornwells Heights, PA: Sisters of the Blessed Sacrament, 1939.

"Letters." *TIME*, November 7, 1932. https://content.time.com/time/subscriber/article/0,33009,744659,00.html.

Lipinski, Jed. "On His Last Day at Xavier, Norman Francis Is Remembered for Providing Refuge to Freedom Fighters." *Times Picayune*, June 30, 2015. https://www.nola.com/news/education/article_373b537b-cac7-5094-b6b4-0caf77694840.html.

Lipperini, Patricia. "Privileged to Educate: Katharine Drexel and Catholic Social Teaching: An Engaged Pedagogy." *Religious Education* 108 (213): 392–402.

Lord, Daniel A., SJ. *Our Nuns: Their Varied and Vital Service for God and Country*. New York: Benziger Brothers, 1934.

Lovett, Bobby L. *America's Historically Black Colleges & Universities: A Narrative History from the Nineteenth Century into the Twenty-first Century*. Macon, GA: Mercer University Press, 2011.

Lucas, Lawrence. *Black Priest/White Church: Catholics and Racism*. New York: Random House, 1970.

Lynch, Patricia. "Collective Biography: Founding Women of the Sisters of the Blessed Sacrament." *U.S. Catholic Historian* 10 (1991/1992): 101–6.

―――. "Mother Katharine Drexel's Rural Schools: Education and Evangelization through Lay Leadership." In *Cross Crozier and Crucible: A Volume Celebrating the Bicentennial of a Catholic Diocese in Louisiana*, edited by Glenn R. Conrad, 262–74. New Orleans: Archdiocese of New Orleans, 1993.

―――. *Sharing the Bread in Service: Sisters of the Blessed Sacrament, 1891–1991*. Bensalem, PA: Sisters of the Blessed Sacrament, 1998.

Macaria, Sister, OSF. "Dream and Vision: St. Mary's Chippewa School." *Indian Sentinel* 3 (Summer 1933): 105, 124, 139.

MacCash, Doug. "Xavier University's New St. Katharine Chapel Designed with Mystery in Mind." *Times-Picayune*, October 1, 2012.

Magray, Mary Peckham. *The Transforming Power of the Nuns: Women, Religion and Cultural Change in Ireland, 1750–1900*. New York: Oxford University Press, 1998.

Mahoney, Irene, OSU. *Lady Blackrobes: Missionaries in the Heart of Indian Country*. Golden, CO: Fulcrum Publishing, 2006.

Mangan, Katharine. "America's Longest-Serving College President Has More to Do." *Chronicle of Higher Education*, January 14, 2013. https://www.chronicle.com/article/After-More-Than-44-Years/136623.

Markmann, Margaret Mary. "Katharine Drexel of Philadelphia: Educational Reformer and Institution Builder." PhD diss., Temple University, 2012.

Marshall, Patricia, SBS. "Sister Mary Frances Buttell (1884–1977): Visionary for Xavier University." In *Religious Pioneers: Building the*

Faith in the Archdiocese of New Orleans, edited by Dorothy Dawes and Charles Nolan, 287–98. New Orleans: Archdiocese of New Orleans, 2004.

Mattick, Barbara A. "Ministers in Black and White: The Catholic Sisters of St. Augustine, Florida, 1859–1920." PhD diss., Florida State University, 2008.

McCue, Michele Peseux. "Tapping a Treasure: The Impact of the Institute for Black Catholic Studies on Black Catholicism and the American Catholic Church." ThD diss., La Salle University, 2017. https://digitalcommons.lasalle.edu/religion_thd/3.

McGeer, Michael. *A Fierce Discontent: The Rise and Fall of the Progressive Movement in America, 1870–1920.* New York: Free Press, 2003.

McGreevy, John T. *Parish Boundaries: The Catholic Encounter with Race in the Urban North.* Chicago: University of Chicago Press, 1996.

McGreevy, Nora. "Calling Home," *Notre Dame Magazine*, Spring 2020. https://magazine.nd.edu/stories/calling-home-2/.

McGuinness, Margaret M. *Called to Serve: A History of Nuns in America.* New York: New York University Press, 2013.

———. "Why Relationships Matter: Sisters, Bishops, and the History of Catholicism in the United States." *Catholic Historical Review* 100 (Spring 2014): 219–42.

McNeely, Stanton Francis III. "A Qualitative Study of Hurricane Katrina and University Presidential Leadership." EdD diss., Northcentral University, 2013.

McQuade, Greg. "Former Cadets Push to Save Old African-American Military Academy." WTVR-TV, June 19, 2020. https://www.wtvr.com/i-have-a-story/former-cadets-push-to-save-old-african-american-military-academy.

McShea, Joseph. "Funeral Oration for Reverend Mother Katharine Drexel." *Records of the American Catholic Historical Society of Philadelphia* 66 (June 1955): 95–100.

McSheffery, Daniel F. *St. Katharine Drexel: Pioneer for Human Rights.* Totowa, NJ: Resurrection Press, 2002.

Medlin, Christine Lyons. "Catholic Sister Educators in Germantown's Parochial, Academy and Mission Schools." *Germantown Crier* 65 (Spring 2015): 4–18.

A Member of the Sisterhood. "Sisters of the Third Order of St. Francis, 1855–1928." *Records of the American Catholic Historical Society of Philadelphia* 40 (December 1929): 347–81.

Moloshok, Rachel. "Memories of St. Peter Claver Church." *Pennsylvania Legacies* 15 (Fall 2015): 3–5.

Moore, Andrew S. "Black and Catholic in Atlanta: Challenge and Hope." In *Catholics in the Vatican II Era: Local Histories of a Global Event*, edited by Kathleen Sprows Cummings, Timothy Matovina, and Robert Orsi, 135–56. Cambridge: Cambridge University Press, 2018.

Moore, Cecilia A. "Conversion Narratives: The Dual Experiences and Voices of African American Catholic Converts." *U.S. Catholic Historian* 28 (Winter 2010): 27–40.

———. "Keeping Harlem Catholic: African-American Catholics and Harlem, 1920–1960." *American Catholic Studies* 114 (Fall 2003): 3–21.

Moran, Katherine D. "Catholicism and the Making of the U.S. Pacific." *Journal of the Gilded Age and Progressive Era* 12 (October 2013): 434–74.

Morris, Stephanie. "The Drexel Women: Educators and Philanthropists." In *Sisterly Love: Women of Note in Pennsylvania History*, edited by Marie Conn and Thérèse Maguire, 59–68. New York: Rowman and Littlefield, 2014.

———. "St. Peter Claver Church and School, Philadelphia, PA: A Collaborative Effort." *American Catholic Studies* 128 (Spring 2017): 101–13.

Morton, Belisha. "History as Death and Living Ghosts: The Mislaid Memories of Saint Katharine Drexel." *Journal of Curriculum Theorizing (Online) Rochester* 29 (2013): 117–33.

———. "With Xavier, However, There Will Be This Distinction: Mapping the Educational Philosophy of Saint Katharine Drexel in the Intellectual Tradition of Black Higher Education in New Orleans, Louisiana." PhD diss., Louisiana State University, 2014.

Mosby, Ian, and Erin Millions, "Canada's Residential Schools Were a Horror." *Scientific American*, August 1, 2021. https://www.scientificamerican.com/article/canadas-residential-schools-were-a-horror/.

Mullenneaux, Lisa. "Doing Good and Making Trouble: A Look At Helen Hunt Jackson." *Ploughshares* 45 (Spring 2019): 188–96.

Muncy, Robyn. *Creating a Female Dominion in American Reform, 1890–1935*. New York: Oxford University Press, 1991.

Mundelein, George W. *Two Crowded Years: Being Selected Addresses, Pastorals, and Letters Issued During the First Twenty-four Months of the Episcopate of the Most Rev. George William Mundelein, DD as Archbishop of Chicago*. Chicago: Exposition Press, 1918.

Murphy, Edward F. *Yankee Priest: An Autobiographical Journey, with Certain Detours, from Salem to New Orleans*. Garden City, NY: Doubleday, 1952.

Murray, Cecilia. "Katharine Drexel: Learning to Love the Poor." *Catholic Education: A Journal of Inquiry and Practice; Los Angeles* 9 (March 2006): 307–19. http://digitalcommons.lmu.edu/ce/vol9/iss3/9.

Nash, Gary B. *First City: Philadelphia and the Forging of Historical Memory*. Philadelphia: University of Pennsylvania Press, 2002.

Neary, Timothy B. "Black-Belt Catholic Space: African-American Parishes in Interwar Chicago." *U.S. Catholic Historian* 18 (Fall 2000): 76–91.

———. *Crossing Parish Boundaries: Race, Sports, and Catholic Youth in Chicago, 1914–1954*. Chicago: University of Chicago Press, 2016.

Newman, Mark. *Desegregating Dixie: The Catholic Church in the South and Desegregation, 1945–1992*. Jackson: University Press of Mississippi, 2019.

Nolan, Charles E. *A History of the Archdiocese of New Orleans*. Strasbourg, France: Editions du Signe, 2000.

Noonan, Bonnie. "When Life Gives Your Lemons." *South Central Review* 24 (Fall 2007): 61–66.

Norwood, Wayne. *The Day Time Stood Still: The Hurricane of 1915*. Ponchatoula: Louisiana Treasures Museum, 2015.

Nuesse, C. Joseph. "Segregation and Desegregation at the Catholic University of America." *Washington History* 9 (Spring/Summer 1997): 54–70.

Oates, Mary J. *The Catholic Philanthropic Tradition in America*. Bloomington: Indiana University Press, 1995.

———. "The Role of Laywomen in American Catholic Philanthropy, 1820–1920." *U.S. Catholic Historian* 9 (Summer 1990): 249–60.

Ochs, Stephen J. *Desegregating the Altar: The Josephites and the Struggle for Black Priests, 1871–1960*. Baton Rouge: Louisiana State University Press, 1990.

O'Connell, Maureen H. *Compassion: Loving Our Neighbor in an Age of Globalization*. Maryknoll, NY: Orbis Books, 2009.

————. *Undoing the Knots: Five Generations of American Catholic Anti-Blackness.* Boston: Beacon Press, 2021.

O'Reilly, David. "Decreed a Saint Phila's Katharine Drexel Canonized." *Philadelphia Inquirer,* October 1, 2000.

Osborne, Catherine R. "Introduction: Writing Catholic History after the Sex Abuse Crisis." *American Catholic Studies* 127 (Summer 2016): 1–4.

Osborne, William A. *The Segregated Covenant: Race Relations and American Catholics.* New York: Herder and Herder, 1967.

Oubre, Claude. *A History of the Diocese of Lafayette.* Strasbourg, France: Editions du Signe, 2001.

Pak, Susie J. *Gentlemen Bankers: The World of J. P. Morgan.* Cambridge, MA: Harvard University Press, 2013.

Peiss, Kathy. "Going Public: Women in Nineteenth-Century Cultural History." *American Literary History* 3 (Winter 1991): 817–28.

Pember, Mary Annette. "Death by Civilization." *The Atlantic,* March 8, 2019. https://www.theatlantic.com/education/archive/2019/03/traumatic-legacy-indian-boarding-schools/584293/.

————. "'We Won't Forget about the Children: Additional Unmarked Graves Likely at US Indian Boarding Schools." *Indian Country Today,* June 2021. https://indiancountrytoday.com/news/we-wont-forget-the-children.

Penrose, Boise. "The Early Life of F. M. Drexel, 1792–1837: The Peregrinations of a Philadelphia Painter-Banker." *Pennsylvania Magazine of History and Biography* 60 (October 1936): 329–57.

Peterson, Donna Patricia. "Conflict, Tension, Strength: The History of St. Paul's Mission, St. Labre Indian School, and St. Stephen's Indian School, 1884–Present." PhD diss., University of New Mexico, 2015.

Philip Neri, Sister M. "The Medicine Dance." *Indian Sentinel* 5 (October 1925): 157–58.

A Pima Missionary. "Pima Missions: History in the Making." *Indian Sentinel* 2 (April 1922): 446–48.

Pitman, Bambra. "Culture, Caste, and Conflict in New Orleans Catholicism: Archbishop Francis Janssens and the Color Line." *Louisiana History: The Journal of the Louisiana Historical Association* 49 (Fall 2008): 423–62.

Poché, Justin D. "Crescent City Catholicism: Catholic Education in New Orleans." In *Urban Catholic Education: Tales of Twelve American*

Cities, edited by Thomas C. Hunt and Timothy Walch, 227–44. Notre Dame, IN: Alliance for Catholic Education, 2010.

———. "Religion, Race, and Rights in Catholic Louisiana, 1938–1970." PhD diss., University of Notre Dame, 2007.

———. "Stemming the Tide: Catholic Education in New Orleans." In *Urban Catholic Education: The Best of Times, The Worst of Times*, edited by Thomas C. Hunt, David J. O'Brien, and Timothy Walch, 129–46. New York: Peter Lang, 2013.

Portier, William L. "John R. Slattery's Vision for the Evangelization of American Blacks." *U.S. Catholic Historian* 5 (1986): 19–44.

"President Lincoln's Body," *Philadelphia Inquirer*, April 20, 1865, 7.

Prucha, Francis Paul. *The Churches and the Indian Schools, 1888–1912*. Lincoln: University of Nebraska Press, 1979.

Puleo, Gus. "A Holy Encounter." *American Catholic Studies* 129 (Spring 2018); 91–101.

"The Red and the Black." *TIME*, August 30, 1948. http://content.time .com/time/subscriber/article/0,33009,799109,00.html.

Riggs, Sister Mary Frances, SBS. "Attitudes of Missionary Sisters toward American Indian Acculturation." PhD diss., Catholic University of America, 1967.

Robertson, Clyde C. "Hurricane Katrina through the Eyes of African American College Students: The Making of a Documentary." *Journal of African American History* 93 (Summer 2008): 392–401.

Rogers, Kim Lacy. *Righteous Lives: Narratives of the New Orleans Civil Rights Movement*. New York: New York University Press, 1993.

Rottenberg, Dan. *The Man Who Made Wall Street: Anthony J. Drexel and the Rise of Modern Finance*. Philadelphia: University of Pennsylvania Press, 2001.

———. "The Shared Vision of Saint Katharine Drexel and Anthony J. Drexel." Philadelphia: Drexel University, 2000 (pamphlet).

Rouse, Michael Francis (Bede, Brother, CFX). "A Study of the Development of Negro Education under Catholic Auspices in Maryland and the District of Columbia." PhD diss., Johns Hopkins University, 1933.

Rzeznik, Thomas. *Church and Estate: Religion and Wealth in Industrial-Era Philadelphia*. University Park: Pennsylvania State University Press, 2013.

————. "The Church in the Changing City: Parochial Restructuring in the Archdiocese of Philadelphia in Historical Perspective." *U.S. Catholic Historian* 27 (Fall 2009): 73–90.

Sander, Kathleen Waters. *The Business of Charity: The Women's Exchange Movement, 1832–1900.* Urbana: University of Illinois Press, 1998.

Schmandt, Raymond H., ed. "Unpublished Letters of Blessed Katharine Drexel to Reverend Herman J. Heuser." *Records of the American Catholic Historical Society of Philadelphia* 102 (Fall 1991): 55–68.

Scott, Ann Firor. "The Ever-Widening Circle: The Diffusion of Feminist Values for the Troy Female Seminary 1822–1872." *History of Education Quarterly* 19 (Spring 1979): 3–25.

Sibbel, Megan Stout. "Reaping the 'Colored Harvest': The Catholic Mission in the American South." PhD diss., Loyola University Chicago, 2013.

Silcox, Harry. "Delay and Neglect: Negro Public Education in Antebellum Philadelphia, 1800–1860." *Pennsylvania Magazine of History and Biography* 97 (October 1973): 444–64.

"The Sisters of the Blessed Sacrament for Indians and Colored People." *Indian Sentinel* 6 (1907): 4–19.

Slawson, Douglas, CM. "Segregated Catholicism: The Origins of St. Katharine's Parish, New Orleans." *Vincentian Heritage Journal* 13 (Fall 1996): 141–84.

Slonecker, Blake. "A Church Apart: Catholic Desegregation in Newton Grove, North Carolina." *North Carolina Historical Review* 63 (July 2006): 322–54.

Smith, Helen Grace. "Sketch of the Life of Mother Katharine Drexel." *Records of the American Catholic Historical Society of Philadelphia* 67 (March 1956): 51–60.

Smith, Sister Marie Barat, SBS. "A History of St. Emma's Military Academy and St. Francis de Sales High School." MA thesis, Catholic University of America, 1949.

Southwick Sally J. "Educating the Mind, Enlightening the Soul: Mission Schools as a Means of Transforming the Navajo, 1898–1928." *Journal of Arizona History* 37 (Spring 1996): 47–66.

Stanislaus, Sister M. "Visiting the Indian Pueblos." *Indian Sentinel* 4 (October 1924): 71–72.

"St. Francis Celebrates Jubilee." *St. La Salle Auxiliary Bulletin* (1938), 72–75.

Bibliography

St. Francis in Eddington: A History of the Transition of an Institution, 1888–1988.

St. Francis Mission. *The Blackrobe in the Land of the Wigwam, St. Francis Mission, St. Francis, South Dakota.* South Dakota: St. Francis Mission, [1917].

"St. Katharine's Journey to Canonization." Accessed June 1, 2021. http://www.katharinedrexel.org/wp-content/uploads/2014/09/Journey-to-Canonization.pdf.

Sze, Corinne P. "Gone but Not Forgotten: St. Catherine's Industrial Indian School." *Bulletin of the Historic Santa Fe Foundation* 30 (Summer 2003): 1–21.

———. "'Roots That Are Very Deep': Excerpts from an Interview with Patrick Toya." *Bulletin of the Historic Santa Fe Foundation* 30 (Summer 2003): 25–31.

Tarry, Ellen. *The Third Door: The Autobiography of a Negro Woman.* Reprint; Tuscaloosa: University of Alabama Press, 1991.

Tentler, Leslie Woodcock. *American Catholics: A History.* New Haven, CT: Yale University Press, 2020.

Terruso, Julia. "Remains of Saint Katharine Drexel to Be Moved to the Cathedral This Summer." *Philadelphia Inquirer*, July 18, 2018. https://www.inquirer.com/philly/news/st-katharine-drexel-remains-basilica-sisters-blessed-sacrament-20180724.html.

Thiel, Mark. G. "Genealogical Treasures: From the Catholic School Legacy of Pioneers Msgr. William Ketcham and St. Katharine Drexel." *The Sentinel* 4 (Spring 2014): 14–15.

Titley, Brian. *Into Silence and Servitude: How American Girls Became Nuns, 1945–1965.* Montreal: McGill-Queens University Press, 2017.

Trennert, Robert A. "From Carlisle to Phoenix: The Rise and Fall of the Indian Outing System, 1878–1930." *Pacific Historical Review* 52 (August 1983): 267–91.

Tsinnajinnie-Paquin, Leola. "Decolonization for Educational Sovereignty: Considerations for Native Catholic Education in the Southwest." *Journal of the West* 59 (Summer 2020): 16–24.

"Up for Sainthood." *UNCF Journal* 6 (May 1987): 10.

Vecsey, Christopher. *On the Padres' Trail.* Notre Dame, IN: University of Notre Dame Press, 1996.

Wagener, Ursula, and Michel T. Nettles. "It Takes a Community to Educate Students." *Change* 30 (March–April 1998): 18–25.

Walker, Vanessa Siddle. *Their Highest Potential: An African American School Community in the Segregated South*. Chapel Hill: University of North Carolina Press, 1996.

Whitaker, Rosemary. "Helen Hunt Jackson 1830–1885." *Legacy* 3 (Spring 1986): 56–62.

White, Richard. *The Republic for Which It Stands: The United States during Reconstruction and the Gilded Age, 1865–1896*. New York: Oxford University Press, 2017.

Wilken, Robert. L. *Anselm Weber, O.F.M.: Missionary to the Navajo 1898–1926*. Milwaukee: Bruce Publishing, 1955.

William, Jessica. "Rudy Lombard, New Orleans Civil Rights Activist and Author, Dies At 75." *Times Picayune*, December 14, 2014. https://www.nola.com/news/politics/article_170962e1-a073-5f52-8918-337f2ff9e3b8.html.

Williams, Shannen Dee. "Black Nuns and the Struggle to Desegregate Catholic America after World War I." PhD diss., Rutgers University, 2013.

————. "Forgotten Habits, Lost Vocations: Black Nuns, Contested Memories, and the 19th Century Struggle to Desegregate U.S. Catholic Religious Life." *Journal of African American History* 101 (Summer 2016): 231–60.

Woodward, Kenneth L. *Making Saints: How the Catholic Church Determines Who Becomes a Saint, Who Doesn't, and Why*. New York: Touchstone, 1996.

"Xavier University: The Nesting Place for Black Doctors." *Journal of Blacks in Higher Education* 13 (Autumn 1996): 48–49.

INDEX

Numbers in *italics* refer to images

Aaron, Mary, 172
Abeyto, Joseph, Sr., 184
Academy of the Sacred Heart, 24
Adrian, William, 63, 188
Alexander, Raymond Pace, 9
Allen, Caritas, 85
Alma, Sister, 140
American Board of Catholic
    Missions (ABCM), 159
Americans, canonized, 1–2
American Scottsboro
    Committee, 124
Angelica, Sister, 70–71
Archdiocese of Philadelphia, 195

Bahr, Howard M., 111
Baldwin, Lou, 6, 22–23, 43
Banking, 19–20
Beasley, Mathilda, 54–55, 56
Becker, Thomas, 54
Benedicta, Sister, 119
Benevolent societies, 25–26
Bennett, James, 125–26
Bevilacqua, Anthony, 5
Biddle, Cordelia, 1, 18, 30
Biographies of Drexel, 3, 6, 11, 30

Birth of Drexel, 21, 23
Black Lives Matter, 168–69
Black Nun Looks at Black Power,
    A (Thibodeaux), 172–73
Black People: Black Power,
    172; Carlisle school, 93–94;
    Catholic Church, 120–21,
    125–26, 129–30, 151–52;
    Chicago, 138–40; Diocese of
    Lafayette, 130–31; education
    (general), 59–61, 67–69, 70,
    120, 126, 150, 153–54, 156,
    187; funding, 65; Harlem,
    142; Holy Providence, 70–71;
    Holy Savior Mission, 76–77;
    home visitations, SBS, 81–82;
    Immaculate Mother Academy,
    59–61; Louisiana, 130–
    31; Morrell, 124; and New
    Orleans, 51–52; Our Lady of
    the Blessed Sacrament,
    72–75; Northern US, 137–44,
    153–54; Philadelphia,
    67–69, 72–86; prohibited
    from joining SBS, 53–57,
    85–86, 120; St. Katharine's

Church, 52; St. Vincent de Paul's parish, 75–76; SBS, 13–14, 119–47, 156; school closings, 188; vocations, 57; women religious, 53–57, 161; Xavier curriculum, 166. *See also* Indigenous People; race

Blenk, James, 151

Bloom, Colette Madeleine, 126

Boniface, Mary, 161

Bonner, John J., 82

Boston, 143–44, 197–98

Bourgade, Peter, 99

Bouvier, Mary Louise, 34

Bouvier Drexel, Emma, 2, 12–13, 23, 24–28, 33, 127

Boyd, Mary, 129

Brady, Benjamin R., 111

Bresie, Amanda, 52–53, 131

Breslin, Donna, 194

Brown, H. Rap, 187

Brown v. Board of Education, 63, 119–20, 187

Brunner, Edward, 155

Bureau of Catholic Indian Missions (BCIM), 50, 88, 90, 95, 97, 98, 109

Bureau of Indian Affairs (BIA), 90

Burgmer, Adolph, 138

Burton, Georgiana, 54

Burton, Katherine, 3

Butler, Anne, 32, 35, 40, 68

Byers, David, 177

Byrne, Edwin V., 112

Byrne, Mary, 71

Byrne, Thomas S., 58–60, 61, 63

Cabrini, Frances, 31, 46–47

Canonization of Drexel, 1–2, 3–5, 9–10, 11, 23

Carlisle Indian School (Pennsylvania), 91–94

Catherine of Bologna, 28

Catherine of Siena, 4, 28

Catholic Interracial Council, 124

Century of Dishonor, A (Jackson), 94–95, 113

Chapelle, Placide, 99

Chaput, Charles, 196

Charity, 25–26, 29, 50

Chicago, 138–40

Chicago Defender, 138

Christmas, 78–79

Church Point (Louisiana), 189

Civil Rights Movement, 147, 164–65, 172, 185–93

Civil War, 20–21, 153

Cleophas, Sister, 189

Coburn, Carol, 96–97

Coffey, Ida Mae, 44

Collier, Brian S., 99, 103, 184

Confirmation of Drexel, 25

Congregation of American Sisters, 105

Connelly Foundation, 196

Consolata, Sister, 199

Constable, Ann, 184

Cooke, Jay, 20–31

Cooper, James Fenimore, 115

Corrigan, Joseph, 66

Costigan-Wagner Anti-Lynching Bill, 124, 160

Coulombe, Joseph, 122

Craft, Francis, 105

Cressler, Matthew J., 198

Cummings, Kathleen Sprows, 4, 9–10, 31
Currency trading, 19–20

Daily, Thomas V., 177
Davis, Marie, 141
Davis, Oscerean, 94
DAWN Community, 178–79
Death of Emma Bouvier Drexel, 28
Death of Francis Drexel, 29
Death of Katharine Drexel, 14, 165, 173–74
Delgado, Hattie Toppins, 144
Dever, Vincent, 76, 82
DiGirolamo, Joseph, 196
Diocese of Lafayette, 130–31, 133–35, 190–91
Divinus Perfectionis Magister, 4
Dolores, Sister, 70–71
Donnellan, Thomas, 181–82
Dougherty, Dennis, 21, 23, 76, 82–83, 125, 158–59
Downs, Patricia, 193–94
Drexel, Anthony, 1, 20–21, 23, 27, 71
Drexel, Ellen, 23
Drexel, Francis A., 2, 17–18, 20, 21, 23, 25, 26–27, 28–29, 31, 40, 158, 175, 176
Drexel, Francis M., 12, 18–20, 21, 23, 27
Drexel, Morgan & Co., 27–29
Drexel and Smith, 20
Drexel Institute/University, 71, 193
Drexel Langstroth, Hannah, 2, 12, 21
Drexel Morrell, Louise. *See* Morrell, Louise

Drexel Smith, Elizabeth, 2, 21, *22*, 23, 32, 39–40
Driscoll, Francis, 57
Du Bois, W. E. B., 68–69
Duffy, Consuela, 24, 30, 38, 42–43, 56, 175–76, 186

Education: abuse, 115–16, 197; arts, 159; bishops, 189–90; Black People, 14, 59–61, 67–69, 70, 120, 126, 150, 153–54, 156, 187; Carlisle Indian School, 91–93; catechism, 101, 102; Catholic Church and Indigenous, 90–91; Catholic high schools, 77–78; character, development of, 153; coeducational, 154–55; death of students, 93, 111, 116, 197; Diocese of Lafayette, 133–34; Drexel, 28; Emerick, 74; Emma Bouvier Drexel, 27; funding, 65, 88–89, 91, 95–99, 103, 136–37, 147; Holy Providence, 70–71, 83; hunger, 136; Immaculate Mother Academy, 59–63; Indigenous schools, 89–94, 116–17; New Orleans, 130; Philadelphia, 67–78; and philanthropy, 27; poverty, 79, 157; and race, 79–80; religious, 78; residential schools, 92–93, 98–99, 103–4, 115–16, 197; sacramental, 101–2; St. Catherine's Indian School, 87–88, 99–104; SBS, 7, 9, 11, 69, 76–79, 81, 89–94, 125,

156; school closings, 83–84.
See also segregation; Xavier
University; *specific names and
organizations*
Eisenman, Sylvester, 104,
106, 113
Elizabeth, Mary, 179
Elliott, Walter, 97
Emerick, Abraham, 72–74,
84, 129
Emmanuel, Maureen, 86
Episcopalian Church, 23, 24
Eucharia, Sister, 135
Eucharist, 40
Evangelist, Sister M., 87, 88, 111
Everett, Marjorie, 108

Financial Panic of 1837, 19–20
First communion of Drexel, 25
Fitzpatrick, Mary Elizabeth,
84–85, 145, 181–82
Frances, Mary, 44, 152–53
Francis, Miriam, 163
Francis, Norman, 150, 165, 166
Francis A. Drexel Chair of Moral
Theology (CUA), 31
Franciscans, 109–12
Freedom Riders, 165
Fumasoni-Biondi, Pietro, 155

Gabriella, Sister, 136
Gallagher, Bernard, 19
Ganss, Henry, 91–92
Garneau, James, 5–6
Gavin, Ken, 195
Gehlen, E. G., 181
George, Francis, 146
Gesu school, 74, 84
Gibbons, Edmund F., 48

Gillen, Agnes, 44
Gould, Donna, 199–200
Grace, Mary, 64
Grant, Ulysses S., 90
Grant's Peace Policy, 90
Great Depression, 64, 78, 136,
157, 175
Grey, Martin de Porres,
Sister, 191
Gutherman, Robert, 4–5

Haiti, 194
Hallinan, Paul, 187–88
Harlem, 141–42
Harr, Lois, 1
Hayes, Patrick, 142
Haynes, Juliana, 10, 56, 177, 179,
192–93
Health issues of Drexel, 30,
65–66, 173
Hearing, 5–6
Hill, Khalillah, 168
Historically Black Colleges and
Universities (HBCU), 150,
154
Hodges, Elsie, 138
Holland, Clifton, 168
Holscher, Kathleen, 115–16
Holy Providence School
(Pennsylvania), 70–71, 83
Holy Savior Mission
(Pennsylvania), 76–77
Hookey Drexel, Catherine, 19,
21–23, 24
House of Prayer (Georgia), 194
Hughes, Cheryl, 30
Hughes, William, 98
Hurd, Nicole Farmer, 121
Hurricane, 1915, 152

Hurricane Katrina, 149–50, 167–68
Hyland, James, 135
Hylebos, Peter, 29

Immaculate Mother Academy (Tennessee), 58–63, *62*, 188
Income tax, 63–64
Indian Girls' Boarding School (Wisconsin), 64
Indian Sentinel, 113, 114
Indigenous People: assimilation, 93, 99, 104; "bleached Indians," 96; Carlisle Indian School, 91–93; Catholic Church, 90–91; culture, 114–15; Drexel's 1883–84 trip, 29, 88; Drexel's 1887 trip, 32; evangelization, 29; funding, 65, 88–89, 91, 95–99, 103; home visitations, 113, 115; missions, 32–33, 35, 65; O'Connor, 33, 34–35; residential schools, 92–93, 98–99, 103–4, 197; St. Catherine's Indian School, 87–88, 99–104; St. Stephen's, 42–43; and SBS, 88–94, 112–15; schools, SBS, 89–94, 116–17; sexual abuse, 99; Sisters of Providence, 35; transfer to tribes, missionary congregations, 107; wealth of Drexel, 35, 38–39
Inez, Mary, 40, 44
Influenza epidemic, 80–81, 111–12
Institute of Black Catholic Studies (IBCS), 168

Jackson, Helen Hunt, 94, 115
Janssens, Francis, 51, 125–26, 130
Jeanmard, Jules, 76, 131, 132, 133, 134–35, 136
Jesuits, 73
John, Mary, 72
John Paul II, Pope, 1, 4, 5
Johnson, Lyndon B., 186
John XXIII, Pope, 178
Josephina, Sister, 164–65
Josephine, Mary, 111
Justin, Sister, 94
Jutz, John, 41

Katharine Drexel Chapel, 169
Keith, Samuel J., 60–62
Kendi, Ibram X., 10
Kenny, Josephina, 163
Ketcham, William, 50, 95, 97
King, Martin Luther, Jr., 186
King, Sheila, 195
Kiniry, Katy, 49
Klein, Charles, 176
Krol, John, 3, 4, 83, 84–85
Kuppens, F. X., 41

La Farge, John, 123, 124
Lagarde, Agnes G., 134
Lagarde, Sister Roland, 134
Laguna Pueblo, 199
Lake Pontchartrain, 149–50
Lankenau, John, 24
Lankenau Drexel, Mary Johanna, 24
Lasance, F. X., 129
Leandro, Mary, 177
LeBeau, Peter, 130
LeDoux, Jerome, 166

Leo XIII, Pope, 30–31, 46
Letterhouse, Mary Dolores, 39
Lewis, Emma, 73
Liberation theology, 102,
    166, 172
Lichtenberger, Francis, 132
Liguori, Sister, 105
Lilly, Thomas, 69
Lincoln, Abraham, 17–18
Lombard, Rudy, 165
Louisiana, 14, 120, 129–37, 181.
    See also New Orleans
Loyola University of New
    Orleans, 160–61
Lucas, Lawrence, 142–43
Lynch, Patricia, 56, 132, 138,
    191, 193

Macaria, Sister, 98
Magnini, Sandra, 180
Mark, Sister Louis, *183*
Marshall, Patricia, 123, 124
Martino, Joseph, 4, 9–10
Marty, Martin, 88
Marty (South Dakota), 104–9
Mary of Grace, Mother, 134
Mary of Lourdes, Sister, 105–6
Mary of the Sacred Heart,
    Mother, 62–63
Mary of the Visitation, Mother,
    107, 112, 158
McCann, Mary Anselm, 3, 163,
    173–74, 176–77
McCarthy, Loretta, 194
McCormick, J. Carroll, 78
McShea, Joseph, 175
Meyer, Albert, 145
Michel, Marie, 77
Miracles of Drexel, 4–5

Mission Helpers of the Sacred
    Heart, 51
Moore, Cecilia, 143
Morgan, Thomas Jefferson, 91
Morrell, Edward, 36, 39, 95, 127
Morrell, Louise, 2 3, 6–8, *22*, 24,
    27, 32, 36, 39–40, 50, 124–25,
    127, 157, 158, 177
Morris, John, 138
Mortification, 174
Mundelein, George, 138–40, 159
Murphy, Edward F., 155, 156
Murphy, Gerard, 65
Murphy, John, 48
Murphy, Mary Healy, 12

Nace, Arthur J., 83
Nash, Diane, 143
Navajo, 109, 110, 112, 114, 115
Neary, Timothy B., 139, 140
Neri, Sister Philip, 114
Neumann, John, 1–2
Newman, Mark, 188, 190
New Orleans, 14, 51–52, 130,
    151–53, 164
Northern Liberties section,
    Philadelphia, 2
Notre Dame School (Louisiana),
    135–36
Novitiate, Drexel's, 38–39
Nunlitz, Ursus, 41
Nutt, Maurice, 169

Oates, Mary, 25–26
Obedience of the judgment, 43
Oblate Sisters of Providence,
    57, 69
Oblate Sisters of the Blessed
    Sacrament (OSBS), 105–9, *108*

O'Connell, William, 143–44
O'Connor, James, 3–4, 33–37, 38, 39, 88, 89
O'Connor, Katherine (Mother Mercedes), 44, 47, 48, 66, 72, 101, 143, 151–52, 158, 174
O'Connor, Michael, 33, 38
Odin, Jean-Marie, 120–21
O'Donnell, Mary Jane, 146, 181, 193
O'Hara, John, 3, 176
O'Reilly, David, 1
Orphans, 54, 71
Osborne, Catherine R., 198
Our Lady of Lourdes (Georgia), 181–82, 187–88
Our Lady of Mercy School (Louisiana), 145, 185–86
Our Lady of the Blessed Sacrament (OLBS), 72–75, *75*, 83–84
Outing System, 93

Painting (Drexel), 18–19
Patricia, Sister, 96
Paul of the Cross, Sister Mary, 152
Peacemaker, 3–4
Pelli, Cesar, 169
Pepper, George Wharton, 64
Philadelphia, 1–2, 13, 17, 20, 35, 38, 39, 67–87, 195
Philadelphia Nun Loophole, 64
Philanthropy, 26–27, 31–33, 43, 50–53, 58, 174
Photos of Drexel, *22*
Pius XII, Pope, 176
Plunkett, Thomas, 58
Point à la Hache (Louisiana), 133

Poverty, vow of, 49, 50
Pratt, Richard Henry, 92–93
"Program for On-Going Education on Black and Indian Concerns," 191–92
Propaganda Fide, 46
Pueblos, 199

Race: anti-racism, 10, 122; and canonization of Drexel, 9–10; and Catholic Church, 7–8, 121–22; "Directional Paper on Racism," 123; and Drexel, 2–3, 6–12, 120, 121–26; and education, 79–80; and integration, 145; "Katharine Drexel on Racial Justice" statement, 123; La Farge, 123; money, Drexel, 123; and Morrell, 6–8; Nashville, 61–62; questions, 8–9; St. Joseph's Hospital, 6–7; and SBS, 8–9, 53–57, 79–80, 122–23; Xavier, 150, 160–61
Rainach, William, 164–65
Ready, W. P., 60
Reservations, Native American, 13, 32. *See also* Indigenous People
Riggs, Francis Mary, 114–15
Rogan, Patricia, 179–80
Roosevelt, Franklin D., 124, 160
Rosebud Reservation, 32
Rosita, Sister, 199
Rottenberg, Dan, 19–20, 29–30
Roux, Vincent, 165
Ruth, Mary, 96, 188
Ryan, Agatha, 136, 156–59, *158*, 160–61, 162–63

Ryan, Johanna, 23, 41
Ryan, Patrick, 35, 39, 42–43, 46, 52, 73–76, 80, 88

Sacred Heart Schools (Lousiana), 131, 171
St. Ann's School (Louisiana), 134
St. Anselm's (Illinois), 141, 143
St. Augustine's Indian Mission (Nebraska), 89
St. Catherine of Siena parish and school (Pennsylvania), 65, 84–85
St. Catherine's Indian School (Santa Fe), 87–88, 98–104, 110, 183–85
St. Dominic's parish (Louisiana), 130
St. Edward's School (Louisiana), 119, 132, 136
St. Elizabeth Indian School (Oklahoma), 96
St. Elizabeth's (Illinois), 139–41, 145–46
St. Elizabeth's (Louisiana), 135
St. Emma's (Virginia), 127–28, 144
St. Francis de Sales Church (Louisiana), 187
St. Francis de Sales School (Virginia), 127, 129, 144
St. Ignatius School (Pennsylvania), 85–86
St. Joseph's Hospital (Philadelphia), 6–8
St. Jude's School (Louisiana), *131*
St. Mark's (New York), 141–43
St. Mary's Indian School (Wisconsin), 98

St. Michael's (Arizona), 109–12, 116, 180
St. Michael's Shrine (Philadelphia), 25
St. Michel (Pennsylvania), 27, 45
St. Monica's (Illinois), 137–38
St. Paul Indian School (South Dakota), 104–9
St. Peter Claver (Philadelphia), 13, 67, 69, 72, 77, 85
St. Stephen's Mission and School (Wyoming), 41–43
St. Vincent de Paul's parish (Philadelphia), 75–76
Schexnayder, Maurice, 190–91
Schuyler, George, 123–24
Sebastian, Mother, 42
Second Vatican Council, 114, 178
Segregation, 7, 10, 51, 68, 83, 125–26, 132, 138, 144–45, 151, 163–64, 186, 187–90
Sexual abuse crisis, 197–98
Sioux, 104
Sisson, Elise, 159
Sisters of Mercy, 13, 37, 38–39, 45
Sisters of Notre Dame de Namur, 69
Sisters of Providence, 35
Sisters of St. Francis, 36–37, 53, 176–77
Sisters of the Blessed Sacrament (SBS): abuse, 197–99; and Black and Indigenous People, 2–3, 7–9, 12, 40, 47–48, 81–82, 85–86, 87–115, 119–47, 139–40, 146, 156, 181–82, 197, 198, 200; and Black women,

8, 53–57, 191–92; centennial, 193–94; Chicago, 139–40; Civil Rights Movement, 186–87, 191; death of Drexel, 14, 173–77; decline, 15, 84, 141, 144–47, 180–85; *decretum laudis*, 45–46; "Directional Paper on Racism," 123; education, 7, 9, 11, 69, 76–79, 81, 89–94, 125, 156; first members, 44–45; founding by Drexel, 13, 37, 43; and Franciscans, 109–12; and Hannah Drexel's remains, 21–22; Haynes, 10, 192–93; home visitations, 81–82; Immaculate Mother Academy, 59–60; Indigenous schools, 89–94; influenza epidemic, 80–81; international missions, 193–94; Irish members, 47, 48–49; motherhouse, 45, 100, 195, 196; mother superior, Drexel as, 44–45, 101; and Native culture, 114–15; New York, 141–42; Outing System, 93; Philadelphia, 13, 39, 67–68, 76–77, 85–87; prohibition of Black women from joining, 53–57, 85–86, 120; and race, 8–9, 53–57, 79–80, 122–23; recruitment, 47–48; Rule, 45–47; Ryan, Agatha, 162; and St. Catherine of Siena school, 84–85; and St. Catherine's Indian School, 87–88, 99–104; St. Michael's, 116; and St. Paul's, 104–9; and St. Stephen's, 41–42; and

segregation, 164, 186, 190; social work, 82; superior general, Drexel as, 47; uniqueness, 12; vicar general, Drexel as, 66; vows, Drexel, 40, 47; Xavier Prep, 167, 179; and Xavier University, 150, 154–56, 163, 165–66, 182–83, 200

Sisters of the Holy Family, 161
Slattery, John, 56–57, 58, 65
Slavery, 20
Smith, Martha, 96–97
Smith, Walter George, 95
Society of the Divine Word, 138–39, 140
Society of the Sacred Heart, 34
Spalding, Martin, 120
Spendthrift clause, 29
Stachow, Mary Anne, 150
Stanislaus, Sister, 113
Staton, Mabel Landry, 143
Stephan, Joseph, 53, 87, 88, 95
Suchalski, Patricia, 146
Summerville, James, 61

Tarry, Ellen, 129
Teacher Training Institute, 132
Tennelly, J. B., 177
Thibodeaux, Mary Roger, 171–73
Tolton, Augustus, 137–38
Tomb of Drexel, 195–96
Toolen, Thomas J., 187
Torresdale section, Philadelphia, 25, 26–27
Toya, Patrick, 103
Tyler, Eleanor, 75
Tyne, John, 188
Tyne, Thomas, 60

United Negro College Fund
(UNCF), 163

Veronica, Mary, 165
Vianney, Sister John, 140, 186
Vincentians, 51–52
Vocation, religious, 33–40
Vow, Drexel, 40, 47

Wackerman, Albertine, 67, 77
Wall, Amy, 5
Wealth of Drexel, 2–3, 7, 10,
    11–12, 13, 28, 29–30, 32, 35,
    37, 38–40, 43, 173–77
Weber, Anselm, 110, 111–12
Wilkins, Roy, 123–24

Williams, Mariam, 172
Williams, Shannen Dee, 55
Women religious and clerical
    authority, 95–97
Wood, James, 69
Wyoming, 41–42

Xavier, Francis, 48–49, 152
Xavier Prep, 167, 179
Xavier University, 6, 9, 14,
    57, 133–34, 149–69,
    182–83, 200

Young, Mother David, 83, 141,
    145, 177, 184, 186–87,
    189, 191